Making Marriage a Success

Pearls of Wisdom from Experts Across the Nation

Making Marriage a Success

Pearls of Wisdom from Experts Across the Nation

By Jaleh Donaldson

ACKNOWLEDGEMENT

I would like to thank everyone that has contributed their efforts and wisdom on what makes marriage a success. The publication of this book could not have been possible without you. Know that you are making a positive difference in relationships and marriages across the United States.

I would also like to thank my dear husband, Klint, and my beautiful children, Ryan and Matthew. To Klint, who always provides me with the support and encouragement that I need to accomplish any goal. And to my children, whose sweet spirits and smiles give me the inspiration to be a better person.

DISCLAIMER

This book details the author's personal experiences with and opinions about making marriage a success. The author is not a healthcare provider.

The author and publisher are providing this book and its contents on an "as is" basis and make no representations or warranties of any kind with respect to this book or its contents. The author and publisher disclaim all such representations and warranties, including for example warranties of merchantability and healthcare for a particular purpose. In addition, the author and publisher do not represent or warrant that the information accessible via this book is accurate, complete or current.

The statements made about products and services have not been evaluated by the U.S. Food and Drug Administration. They are not intended to diagnose, treat, cure, or prevent any condition or disease. Please consult with your own physician or mental healthcare specialist regarding the suggestions and recommendations made in this book.

Except as specifically stated in this book, neither the author or publisher, nor any authors, contributors, or other representatives will be liable for damages arising out of or in connection with the use of this book. This is a comprehensive limitation of liability that applies to all damages of any kind, including (without limitation) compensatory; direct, indirect or consequential damages; loss of data, income or profit; loss of or damage to property and claims of third parties.

You understand that this book is not intended as a substitute for consultation with a licensed healthcare practitioner, such as your physician. Before you begin any healthcare program, or change your lifestyle in any way, you will consult your physician or other licensed healthcare practitioner to ensure that you are in good health and that the examples contained in this book will not harm you.

This book provides content related to topics physical and/or mental health issues. As such, use of this book implies your acceptance of this disclaimer.

INTRODUCTION

"That will never happen to us."

How often I've heard these words spoken by well-intentioned but misguided couples! Convinced that marriage will *always* be romantic, fun and in perfect harmony, they think that they're some how immune to the problems that plague other marriages. They're so high on life and love that they don't even have to work on marital success, at least not in the beginning – success happens automatically, just part of the territory. These couples mistakenly believe that conflict will never happen in *their* marriage, and if by some strange reason it does, it will resolve quickly and smoothly.

But what happens when, marriage does become work, and there's no more coasting down Easy Street? When wedded bliss suddenly evaporates and marital success is neither automatic nor guaranteed, the uninformed, unprepared couple will struggle, wondering what happened and why they "failed." Insinuations and accusations will start to fly, and stress levels will rise. What used to be fun suddenly is no fun anymore, and the relationship is in peril.

No Marriage Is Immune

Despite the best of intentions, every married couple, without exception, will encounter situations that will test their marriage. Difficulties and disagreements can arise in the area of finances. Or sex. Maybe friction will develop over household chores, children, religion, past history, careers, politics, or those annoying little habits that only get bigger and more annoying with time.

Life happens. An unexpected storm can appear from nowhere and throw a bevy of lightning bolts into what once seemed a "perfect" relationship. Will you and your loved one survive such an attack? I believe that you can, but only if you are prepared, you're willing to communicate, you don't play the "blame game," and you're not afraid to roll up your sleeves and work together to make things right.

1

Success Is a Learned Trait

How do you prepare yourself to face conflict in marriage? You begin by acknowledging and accepting that occasionally, and inevitably, conflict is part of being in a relationship; it's unrealistic to expect perfect harmony all the time. You cannot avoid conflict. But what you can do is develop the skills to weather those storms and come through with a marriage that's stronger and better than ever. Success can be learned, but if you haven't been taught how to make your marriage successful, challenges will keep testing it.

Where do you go for help? If you decide to turn to friends or family members, proceed with caution. Even though you may glean some genuine nuggets of wisdom from them, it's just as likely that they're too close to you, your spouse, or the situation to offer unbiased counsel. A better approach is to turn to a professional in the field who knows how to deal with issues and is equipped to dispense sound advice.

Dozens of Qualified Experts At Hand

Imagine having a marriage expert give you tips on making marriage a success. It would make your road a little smoother, wouldn't it? Now imagine two experts sharing with you the best tips they have to offer. Even better, right? So how about *dozens* of experts ready and willing to share their words of wisdom with you and your spouse? Now you're talking!

That's exactly what you'll find inside *Making Marriage a Success*, my groundbreaking book that brings advice from dozens of qualified experts directly to you. Within these pages you'll find a wealth of knowledge from licensed counselors, therapists and other professionals with expertise in the issues couples face. These qualified psychotherapists and other relationship professionals candidly share with you pearls of wisdom, making this book a real-world, accessible resource one just as valuable as talking to a number of therapists and cheaper!

I've compiled the very best advice from experts in each state. Their advice stems from one or more sources: the excellent education they've received, their own personal experiences or the relationship therapy they've provided to clients.

Keep Informed To Stay Strong

Whether you have been married one month or fifty years, there's something in this book for you. By incorporating into your marriage the words of wisdom offered by many different experts from across the nation, you can make your marriage a happy and successful one. The tips shared within these pages can give you valuable insights regardless of where you are right now in your marriage. If you already have a great relationship, the experts' advice can help you keep going strong. If your marriage has seen better days, their advice can help you and your spouse restore those better days.

Making Marriage a Success doubles as a resource directory. Along with the professional experts' marital pearls of wisdom, their websites are included, multiplying the valuable material available to you. On these sites you will find information about their background, areas of expertise, philosophies, and in some cases relevant articles for extra advice and inspiration. If you'd like to utilize the services of a professional face-to-face, check out the section located at the end of the book. There you can look up psychotherapists and other specialist within your own state.

As you prepare to dive into this treasure trove of advice for married couples, allow me to share with you my own advice: You now have pearls of wisdom at your fingertips. Know that these pearls don't have any value unless you have the desire to use them. If you do, your marriage will be a success.

Sandra Reishus, Clinical Sexologist, Sacramento, California
sandrareishus.com
"A great way to make marriage a success is to find new things as a couple to do together. Skinny dipping in the nearest body of water, building a personal retreat for both of you in your backyard, learning to kiss five different ways, washing each others hair, taking a drive somewhere close by that you've never been, cooking dinner in the nude, are some examples."

Santhi Periasamy, Ph.D., Licensed Psychologist, Houston, Texas
www.drsanthi.com License# TX-33429
"It is often a sign of being enmeshed when you cannot consider yourself without your spouse. Try not to become enmeshed with your spouse because suffocation usually leads to rebellion and the potential death of a marriage."

Keith A. Kaufman, Ph.D., Washington, D.C.
www.KeithKaufmanPhD.com License# PSY1000626
"Constantly striving to blend powerful ingredients like love, passion, boredom, fear, acceptance, patience, doubt, certainty, frustration, attraction, temptation, trust, and so many others associated with spending life with another into a mix that works. Then, having the courage and awareness to realize when the mix is awry, and learning what it will take to get it back into harmony."

Dr. Debra Laino, DHS, M.ED, MS, ACS, ABS, Wilmington, DE
www.delawaresexdoc.com
"When two people want the same things and if there is a divide, then a couple needs to find things that they want to grow and do together."

Amy Serin, PhD., Psychologist, Peoria, Arizona
www.TheSerinCenter.com License# 3859
"If you feel upset about some aspect of your relationship, make a list of the reasons you fell in love and focus on how you can create those feelings again by taking simple action like expressing what you love about your spouse when he or she does not expect it."

Rev. Daniel Gowan, LCDC, LPC-S, Dallas, Texas
www.DanielGowan.com License# TX LPC-S 20319
"I could never begin to love my wife for who she is until I got past
who I needed her to be. We are the limiting factors in our own
relationships until we do our work."

Michael Keller, Ph.D., Licensed Psychologist, St. Paul, Minnesota
www.psychologicalserviceassociates.com License# MN LP 4821
"On July 21st 2003 my fiancée Suzanne and I were supposed to get
married. We went on a motorcycle ride on July 12th, 2003. At about
4:20 pm, on 7/13/2003, westbound Hwy 97 about 1.5 miles east of
Hwy 15, in Scandia, MN, my rear tire began to flatten due to a road
hazard. As the tire deflated, I said, 'Hang on Suz, we'll make it.' Right
at that point, she hugged me close, leaned over my shoulder, and said,
'I can't wait to be your wife.' At that exact moment, we flipped over,
and smashed on to the roadway. She died in my lap...

My pearl of wisdom; Never take anything for granted, tomorrow is not
assured, do all you can to let your significant other know that you love
them, and don't wait to do so until it is too late."

Kwai Kendall-Grove, Ph.D., Centennial, Colorado
www.drkendallgrove.com License# 2321
"To help increase the success of your marriage be aware of how your
family of origin impacts your own marriage. It is very common for
many couples to fall into the trap of communicating and fighting the
same way that they observed their parents fighting and
communicating."

Steven Smith, Psychologist, Lexington, Kentucky
Wisdomoftheheartinc.com License# 0559
"In your marital relationship, strive to be the person that you desire
your spouse to be. It's very easy to focus on a spouse's shortcomings
and to focus on what's not working in the relationship. By focusing on
what is working and making your best effort to be at your best, your
loving actions open the door to that which you are seeking."

Maria Mellano, LICSW (License# 111055), Boston, Massachusetts
WWW.MariaMellanoTherapy.com WWW.LivePassionatelyNow.com
"Great sex does not just happen! It takes skills, which can be learned, experimented and practiced. Most importantly, know that more often than not, women need more than intercourse alone to achieve orgasm. Things that can help: Get over the stereotype that 'men should know' about sex. This serves few and harms most. Get a clean shave. Sure a scruffy beard can be sexy and mysterious but it can feel like sand paper during the most sensitive moments, which can be an instant turn off. The same is true for legs and bikini lines ladies so if you want to be saying 'ooohhh' instead of 'ouch' keep it smooth and reap the benefits. Try a vibrating toy for either the clitoris and / or G spot that you experiment with together. There are even toys you can wear during intercourse ~ yes, it's true… and they really do work. Apply that lubrication because dry sex is painful! Remember, great sex is good for you and the success of your marriage!"

Julie Dubovoy, LCSW-R, Babylon, New York
http://www.juliedubovoy.com/
"The Silent Signals: Sometimes, working on *how* we communicate can be as important as *what* we communicate. Most couples can relate to those awkward moments when you just wish your spouse could read your mind. For example, you may not want to socialize with a particular person or your spouse may be about to say something you'll both regret.

We like to think our spouses are attuned to our every need, but that is not a realistic expectation, nor is it fair. To avoid the fallout of a *faux pas,* I recommend to the couples I counsel to develop 'Silent Signals' beforehand. A 'Silent Signal' is a simple gesture, known only to you and your spouse, such as the squeezing of your spouses' hand in a particular way."

This way you can subtly alert your spouse to extricate you both from impending disaster. As an added bonus, sharing secret codes always draws co-conspirators closer together."

Lisa Hartwell, PsyD, RN, Honolulu, Hawaii
www.hidrlisa.com License# Psy800
"As you are pointing your finger at your spouse and blaming them for an issue, be sure and check out your hand and see how many fingers you have pointing back at yourself."

Elaine St. Marie, M.Ed., LPC, Austin, Texas
www.hiketointegrity.com License# 64391
"Issues you have with your spouse should be handled with your spouse-- not with friends, family or neighbors. Often we are frustrated about something our spouse has said or done but try to fix the problem by sharing it with others. Unless you are sharing your issues with a trusted therapist, this is useless and frustrating and leads to what I call 'growing an enemy garden.' Instead of planting and nurturing seeds of love, trust and kindness, we find ourselves growing a garden of anger, doubt and resentment and wanting our friends to help us water it! Going directly to our spouse to work out the problem (issues of abuse notwithstanding) is a much cleaner, simpler way to air your differences and to find your way back to each other. The relationship 'garden' grows when we learn to work on our issues within the confines of the relationship."

Steve Orma, Psy.D., San Francisco, California
http://www.drorma.com License# PSY 23785
"Encourage your partner to pursue his or her values, whether it's a career, education, hobby, or something else. Support them in any way you can—financially (if you can afford it), emotionally (as their cheerleader), and logically (as an objective voice). When they succeed, celebrate their achievement. If they fail, congratulate them for their effort and root them on to new challenges. Pursuing and enjoying values leads to happiness, and when you're both personally happy, you'll have a more fulfilling marriage."

Perri Shaw Borish, MSS, LCSW, BCD, Philadelphia, PA
www.perrishawborish.com License# CW016052
"Keep laughing through it and keep trying to make each other laugh."

Joyce Thompson, MS, LCMFT, Wichita, Kansas
www.emotionaljourney.org License# 734
"If you want to make your marriage work, you'll find a way. If you don't, you'll find an excuse."

Wendy Dickinson, Ph.D., Psychologist, Atlanta, Georgia
www.growcounseling.com License# PSYCH 3256
"Let the loudest thing that your spouse hears from you be praise. It's easy to let the things that we love about our partners go unsaid or assumed. We have a tendency to voice concerns or criticism and forget to sing praise. So make a conscious effort, every time you can find the opportunity, to praise their strengths…loudly, in public, to friends, in the bedroom, in front of the kids, on Facebook, and everywhere in between."

Bridget Engel, PsyD, Erie, Colorado
FrontRangePsychology.com License# 2909
"One of the most important things to do in a marriage, and perhaps one of the most difficult, is letting go of stubbornness. When we become hurt or annoyed by our spouse, it is easy to dig in your heals and perpetuate conflict because you want to be right, or to be vindicated in some way. It's crucial to accept an apology and move on. Furthermore, many couples can become stuck because they stubbornly refuse to let go of anger or refuse to forgive. While it's easier to hold onto that hurt, it is destructive and unhealthy for your marriage. Practice forgiveness!"

Brent O'Bannon, LPC, Certified Life Coach, Sherman, Texas
www.brentobannon.com License# 13223
"10 Second Hugs and Kisses: Remember how you lingered hugging and kissing when you were first in love? Sadly most couples over time get disconnected because of hugging and kissing less. Instead of giving that 2 second pat on the back or peck on the cheek, make a commitment to linger for a full 10 seconds when you hug and kiss your spouse. This quick effortless blink of the eye habit will create more intimacy, passion, and love momentum."

Steve Orma, Psy.D., San Francisco, California
http://www.drorma.com License# PSY 23785
"If you want Chinese and your spouse wants Italian, then alternate each week so you both get what you want. If you hate Chinese or Italian, then pick up both and each have what you like, or have something you both like. Apply this same principle to any difference in preferences (vacations, TV shows, where to spend the holidays, etc.) and you will have one essential ingredient to a successful marriage!"

Kenneth Joe Heard, LPC, LCMHC, Bryant, Arkansas
www.kjoeheard.com License# P8012118
"Develop strategies to cope with your conflict at an agreed time when you are both calm and have a mindset of problem solving. The worst time to problem solve is when you are emotional."

Dr. Sarah Villarreal, Psy.D, Palo Alto, California
www.entelechywellness.com
"When you are upset with your spouse, before you try and communicate your feelings, ask yourself, 'What is my intention?' If you are able to do this, it will often times change the outcome of the conversation for the better."

Anna Valenti, LCSW (License# 11769), Phoenix, Arizona
www.annavalenti.com or www.SANEresources.org
"Everyday write down at least one thing you like, love, appreciate or respect about your spouse. Then during a 20-minute face-to-face 'connecting time' share what you wrote down."

Florence Soares-Dabalos, LMFT, Chico, California
www.florencemft.com License# MFC40331
"Post-Partum Depression can impact a marriage. In order for a marriage to be successful it's important for both partners to understand this is a real illness and to research all available options such as therapy and medication. Husbands can support their wives by doing chores, taking care of the kids, offering reassurance and allowing her to get plenty of rest so she can begin to feel like herself again."

Chrisanna Harrington, M.A., R.D., L.M.H.C., Port Charlotte, FL
www.nutegra.com
"Before the words come out of your mouth, think if they will draw your beloved closer to you or will your words push them away. Words can crush or nourish a heart, so be mindful of your words."

Merrill Powers, MSW, LCSW, Auburn, California
www.powerstherapist.com License# LCS 19451
"Know that the characteristics of your partner that concern you at the beginning will only bother you more later, so be sure you can accept and not try to change them."

Michelle L. Delevante, LCSW, Sex Therapist, West Babylon, NY
www.babyloncounseling.com
"My professional experience has indicated that couples want to be happy and love as well as listen to one another. They often get stuck in patterns that don't meet either of their needs. Couples tend to take one another's 'inventory' rather than focus on what they can do to improve communication, intimacy, and conflict resolution. I have seen tremendous improvement when couples take their own 'inventory', REALLY listen to one another, and make a genuine effort to date and improve intimacy. What worked when you were dating STILL works years later! Personally I can say that like most things in life, the effort you put in yields the satisfaction you feel (or don't feel). It is well worth the effort-TRUST ME!!!!!"

Victoria Zurkan, Licensed Marriage Family Therapist, California
http://www.zurkan-therapy.com/ License# 43872
"Love, intimacy and compassion in a relationship can be therapeutic and reduce stress. One of the greatest gifts a relationship can provide for you is insight on what you can work on about yourself.

Relationships can trigger emotions in unexpected ways that might be unresolved wounds. Acknowledging these areas and working on them alone as well as together as a committed couple can be a huge source of healing, growth and change. "

Louise Mastromarino, Certified Counselor, Staten Island, NY
www.distantholistic.com
"Marriage is the universal symbol for unity. Unity is wholeness at the core level. Unity creates a marriage sacred, unionized to God's will, and boundless beyond measure."

Dr. Debra Laino, DHS, M.ED, MS, ACS, ABS, Wilmington, DE
www.delawaresexdoc.com
"Search for novelty within the relationship, not outside the relationship."

Teresa L. Oglesbee, Ed.S, NBCC, NBCCH, LPC, Rincon, Georgia
http://www.sccforu.com/ License# LPC004615
"Stop Making Excuses: Making excuses about your actions in a marriage don't serve any purpose. In fact, it simply tends to tear down your spouse's trust in you."

Michael G Quirke, L.M.F.T., San Francisco & San Mateo, CA
www.michaelgquirke.com License# MFC39030
"Criticism does tremendous damage in relationships. Voicing complaints or frustration is a very different thing than implying that there is something wrong or inferior with a person. Any implication that there is something wrong with him or her can be very damaging to the emotional bond that exists between the two of you."

Donna Pollard-Burton, MA, LMHC, NCC, BCC, Indianapolis, IN
www.cairncottagecounseling.com License# 39002176A
"Each of us has our own path to walk, but we are all connected to each other, to this planet, to life and we walk our paths together. In marriage, we make a conscious choice to walk with one another on these unique paths."

Lori Carpenos, LMFT, Hartford, Connecticut
www.3Principlestherapy.com License# LMFT000551
"Judgment is toxic; it will drive a wedge between you and your spouse and it won't improve anything about your marriage."

Dr. Jeffrey Bernstein, Exton, Pennsylvania
www.drjeffonline.com
"Even more important than what you say to your spouse is what you say to yourself about your spouse."

Ella Hutchinson, MA, LPC, Houston, Texas
www.comfortchristiancounseling.com License# 63012
"For couples struggling with the sex addiction of a spouse, there is hope, even when it seems there is none. The partner of a sex addict must realize it is not her fault and she is not a co-sex addict, no matter what she is told. The sex addict must be willing to immediately stop the behavior and get into recovery. Recovery is multi-faceted and not only includes counseling and meetings, but a change in how he relates to his spouse. He may have to work hard to develop empathy and patience, as he allows her to grieve however she needs to, for as long as she needs. The spouse should seek support through counseling and support groups as well and also set clear boundaries that the behavior will not be tolerated. By taking these steps a couple struggling with the issue of a sex addiction can begin to heal and work towards having a successful marriage."

Daniela Roher, PhD., Scottsdale & Carefree, Arizona
www.droherpsychotherapy.com
"The most important part of any intimate relationship is the feeling of emotional safety between partners (You have my back; I have yours.). Check if safety is present and if not, ask yourself what you need to do to bring it back.."

Leyla Mahbod Kenny, PhD, LICSW, Washington, D.C.
www.washingtondcpsychotherapy.com License# LC3000857
"Don't displace your feelings towards your parents onto your spouse. Journal your feelings towards your parents and be honest about who your feelings are directed towards. For example, if you resent your dad for constantly picking on you, then don't explode at your spouse if s/he requests for you to close the cabinet doors. Monitor your reactions to make sure your response fits the current situation."

Dr. Carol Doss, LPC, Fort Worth, Texas
www.family-counseling.org License# 08962
"You can fill the glasses with champagne and surround the bedroom with red rose petals but if you and your partner have unresolved issues, you probably won't have much naked fun."

Alisa Lewis, PhD, LICSW, Washington D.C.
www.alisamlewis.com License# LC303495
"I believe that one of the most important things in marriage is to show compassion for your spouse. Having compassion for your spouse can guide you even in the most troubling times. Compassion is a term used often in Buddhist philosophy, and it is believed that compassion, the ability to care for someone else's feelings as much as your own, is the way towards openness and acceptance of others. When we feel our partner's pain and suffering during moments of tension, we will be open to meeting these experiences with the acceptance and the openness, which are vital to marriage."

Scott Keller, LCSW, Tampa, Florida
www.scottkeller4u.com License# SW 9501
"As a therapist practicing from a Christian foundation, I believe it is essential for a marriage to be firmly rooted in Biblical principles. Christ is love. He offers unconditional compassion and understanding for anyone who seeks him. Christ is selfless and he asks the same of us. A marriage should not be about what you can get from your spouse, but what you can give to your spouse. A marriage will be successful when husband and wife give themselves completely to each other and this beautiful union."

Keith Magnus, Ph.D., Indianapolis, Indiana
www.woodviewgroup.com License# 20041351A
"Put energy into deeply understanding your spouse's perspectives and experiences. This is a simple idea but frequently challenging to practice in relationships. Being heard and fully understood, however, nurtures your spouse, softens disagreements, and engenders a willingness to reciprocate this understanding."

Dr. Poppy Moon, Ph.D., LPC, NCC, Tuscaloosa, Alabama
www.poppymoon.com
"If he didn't put his clothes in the hamper while you were dating, he is not going to put them in the hamper when you get married – so don't get frustrated when he doesn't change."

Cynthia Swan, M.A., C.M.F.T., L.P.C., Niwot, Colorado
www.cynthiaswan.com
"It takes 10 positive appreciations to right one negative and angry word directed at your partner spouse."

Janet Holt, LPC, Hot Springs, Arkansas
www.janetholt.com License# P1007048
"Money is not a romantic topic and no one likes to talk about it-yet it is a subject that arises frequently between couples in my counseling office. One spouse expresses bitterness because of unmet expectations or dreams that haven't materialized. Or the resentment between a frugal 'save for the future' person and an impulsive 'you only go around once' spouse bubbles to the surface. The stories I hear vary but the root cause for the impasse is the same: the couple failed to negotiate this important aspect of their lives together. They did not address questions such as, 'How are we going to make decisions about spending?' 'Who will pay the bills?' 'Will we have separate accounts or joint?' 'How will I feel if you earn substantially more than me?' 'What if I want to drop out of the workforce to parent or follow a passion-will you be willing to support me?'"

Romantic or not, money can be a major source of marital conflict. Investing some time in frank discussion that leads to a clear understanding of each other's money personalities can save a lot of heartache."

Jay P. Granat, Ph.D., LMFT, River Edge, New Jersey
www.StayInTheZone.com and www.DrJayGranat.com
"Try to get on the same page or a compatible page as often as you can."

Thomas L. Volker, Ed.D., LMFT, Florence, Kentucky
www.thomaslvolkeredd.com License# 0406
"Keys to a Successful Marriage!
Stay away from the BARS:
B Blame
A Anger
R Resentment
S Shame

Don't whack your partner over the head with these hard sticks.
Keep them under the couch for marital Bliss!"

Octavia Carlos, LCSW-C, Largo, Maryland
www.octaviacarlos.com License# 05995
"Discuss fully your thoughts and ideas of what you think your roles
(husband/ wife, mother/ father) are in the marriage. If you find you
have different expectations than your partner then 'A' you have found
the possible source of many issues/conflicts and 'B' you now have a
starting point for how to negotiate and compromise."

Denise Humphrey, Ph.D. in Clinical Psychology, Dallas, Texas
www.denisehumphrey.com License# 32345
"Creating harmony in personal relationships is vital, although many
things in life that are worthy and valuable don't happen easily if
pursuing harmony isn't mutually active. Life is a journey that takes
unexpected dips and turns in various phases of life, which can weaken
the symmetry of physical, emotional, spiritual, and sexual connections
in a relationship. Acceptance, forgiveness, respect, and reciprocity is
required by each individual for the other in order to create ongoing
love, because no two people are ever the same."

Daniela Roher, PhD., Scottsdale & Carefree, Arizona
www.droherpsychotherapy.com
"Remember what President Kennedy said in his Inaugural Address:
'Don't ask what your country can do for you. Ask what you can do for
your country.' Apply it to your marital relationship."

Haylee Heyn, AMFT, Salt Lake City, Utah
wasatchfamilytherapy.com License# 7976237-3904
"When Cortez came to settle and colonize the new world in America, he burned all of the ships in the harbor once they arrived. He knew that it was going to get really hard for them and that they would get on the ships and leave if they had the choice. In marriage, times are going to get really tough too, but it is important to burn the ships so that you stay and work through the tough stuff, rather than escaping from it. Marriage is worth the hard work and pain."

Mary B. Mattis, LCSW, Austin, Texas
http://www.marymattis.com License # 53118
"Being in a marriage of blended race or religion usually means being in a marriage of mixed culture. Consider yourself a special honored guest of your partner's culture, and honor your partner as a guest of your own. Communication is key, as each of you will become teacher and learner, host and guest. It is up to each of you as a partner in the marriage to protect and defend your spouse's culture as well as your own. You will find yourselves best off as a joined force against any outside forces that want to push you apart. Respect your spouse's right to cultural differences as much as you do your own, and above all, remember that marriage is a partnership. As a united force you can get through anything."

Dr. Heather M. Browne, LMFT, Garden Grove, California
www.TheHealingHeart.net License# 34523
"Honesty is vital to a healthy marriage. You can be kind in how you use it, but it needs to be truthful. Your spouse can never love nor care for you well, if they are uncertain of who you really are or what you really need. Hiding is not making you feel safe nor loved, just alone."

Joe Lowrance, Psy.D., Clinical Psychologist, Atlanta, Georgia
www.FinancialPsychologyCeus.com
"Marriage is an experience of two individual financial psychologies interacting together over time. The compatibility and workability of those 2 financial psychologies is essential for marital success."

Kim Illig, Certified Intuitive Counselor, Snoqualmie, Washington
www.kimillig.com
"Before you marry, remember that the idea is that you will grow old together. After you marry, remember the child's grin that is always behind your partner's wrinkles."

Michael Kuiper, PhD., Licensed Psychologist, Redding California
www.buildingjoy.net License# 14346
"If you've ever tried to sit on a two-legged stool, you know that a three-legged one tends to give a good bit more stability! That marvelous time of excitement and infatuation during courtship inevitably gives way to the demands and disappointments of post-wedding adjustment. Each partner, stressed out to some degree or another, looks to the other to lean on. Money problems, in-laws, children and job strain all tend to activate unconscious dependency needs, regressive longings not to have to be the strong one, always giving and taking care of others. When your partner is feeling the same thing at the same time, chaos can ensue. But this is also a great time to turn to the One who designed marriage in the first place. Three is better than two!"

Amy Meyers, PhD, LCSW, New York, New York
http://www.psychotherapynyc-healing.com/
"Silence is golden. There is a big difference between lack of communication and shared silence. Sharing quiet times and being able to enjoy each other in silent company defines closeness. Being able to 'just be' with your spouse may just be the deepest aspect of your relationship. Enjoy the company of your mate on various levels."

Taryn Bostwick, LPC, Denver, Colorado
www.TheButterflyWithin.com License# 6214
"When you're married it is vital to remember who you are, and not lose yourself in who 'we' are. The whole is nothing without the individuals who contribute to it. When you are true to yourself you are true to the relationship. When you make choices that are right for you, you are doing what is right for the relationship."

Matt Borer, Ph.D., Licensed Marriage Family Therapist, Florida
www.mattborer.com and www.breakupplan.com
"The term Bro's before Hoes is not only irrelevant but also false. Your partner should always come first because when your Bro's get married, their partner will be the most important part in their life, leaving you without a bro or a wife."

Sharman Colosetti, LCSW, PhD., Decatur, Georgia
www.drsharman.com License# GA 2559
"Married to an addict and want to improve the success of your marriage with your spouse? Learn to detach lovingly. Get into a support group like Al-Anon that will support you in growing as an individual and help you stop trying to solve problems that aren't yours to solve."

Nikki Lively, MA, LCSW, Chicago, Illinois
www.nikkilively.com License# 149.010124
"Expect that you will feel the full range of human emotions both with and about your spouse. You will feel attracted, not attracted, loving, resentful, nurturing, annoyed, admiring, etc. There is no way you can emotionally invest in a relationship like marriage, and not have intense reactions to the person you marry. However, if you can learn to tolerate all of these feelings, and still stay connected to your spouse, then a marriage can be one of the most enriching and healing relationships of your life."

Robinson Arteaga, MA, LPC, Houston, Texas
www.InnovationsCounseling.com License# 66207
"Anger can get in the way of a happy marriage. I often see clients whom have made it a habit resulting in separation or even divorce. One way to combat anger, using a preventative technique, is to keep a mental scrapbook of the positive memories you create with a spouse. It is also beneficial to share those memories since most people tend to talk about the negative occurrences that happen to them. The idea is to not only manage the negative emotions but also cultivate the positive ones."

Sharon Sanborn, MA, LMHC, CHT, ATR-BC, Seattle, WA
www.SeattleArtTherapy.com License# LH00009318
C apture a positive vision and keep it handy
H ave fun
E mphasize each other's talents and strengths
M ystery remains-always
I magine things better than you can possibly imagine
S elf care
T rust deeply-and then some
R espect each other greatly
Y es, Yes, Yes!!!
P.S. He says, always put both seats down!"

Jill Pomerantz, Licensed Clinical Social Worker, California
www.jillpomerantzlcsw.com License# 24287
"A successful marriage is one in which the couple will embrace one another's differences."

Marlo J. Archer, Ph.D., Psychologist, Tempe, Arizona
www.DrMarlo.com License# 3300
"When your spouse's behavior is driving you nuts, that is the exact time when they most need your compassion and the exact time when you probably feel they least deserve it. However, if you can force yourself to be compassionate to your spouse who is behaving badly, it can help them come to their senses and deal with whatever is bothering them in a more productive manner. So, if you find yourself wanting to wring your partner's neck, convince yourself to give them a hug instead."

David Behar, MA, LMFT, Pelham New York, New York
http://www.westchester-therapist.com/
"You can't have a good marriage unless you have a good business relationship. A good business relationship consists of two things: honoring contracts and curtailing abuse. If the partners do what they say they will do when they say they will do it and resist hostile communications, you have a good business relationship."

Robert A. Moylan, LCPC, Naperville, Illinois
www.robertmoylan.com License# 180005037
"Relationships are all work. Some partners only want to work part time when the job is a full time job."

Alison Gamez, MA, NCC, LPC #13402, Surprise, Arizona
"You can control your words and thoughts, and if you can't, seek medical help."

Julie Weiner-Dabda MC, NCC, LPC (License# LPC-13264), AZ
http://julieweinerdabdacounseling.community.officelive.com
"'Rules for making marriage a success'
1. Never be angry at the same time.
2. Never yell at each other unless the house is on fire.
3. If one of you has to win an argument, let it be your mate.
4. If you have to criticize, do it lovingly.
5. Never bring up mistakes of the past.
6. Neglect the whole world rather than each other.
7. Never go to sleep with an argument unsettled.
8. At least once everyday try to say one kind or complimentary thing to your life's partner.
9. When you have done something wrong, be ready to admit it and ask for forgiveness.
10. It takes 2 to make a quarrel, and the one in the wrong is the one who does the most talking."

Laurel A. Fay, M.S., LCMFT, Silver Spring, Maryland
www.laurelfay.com License# LCM167
"This is a tip I occasionally share with my clients: when you feel really angry or misunderstood by something your spouse has said or done, picture yourself at their funeral. See your future self looking back on your life together, and now facing life without them, and see how your mood/thoughts/perspective changes. When I myself do this, oftentimes whatever ridiculousness I have been clinging to no longer looks so appealing. While it may sound macabre, this little exercise never fails to give some perspective on what really matters."

Jan Talen, LMFT, Grand Rapids, Michigan
www.funlifellc.com License# 4101006087
"Becoming bilingual is crucial to having a successful marriage. Each of you has a unique way of communicating. So, just as if you were going to be good friends with someone who spoke Chinese, you would learn to speak Chinese so that you could talk with your friend and you would learn Chinese customs and habits that would honor your friend. By learning your spouse's communication style and language you honor and enhance the friendship and enjoyment between the two of you. Although it is hard work and a bit clumsy at times, it is also very rewarding when you are successful in speaking "Chinese" to your spouse."

Gal Szekely, LMFT, San Francisco, California
MindfulLifeCenter.com License# 50301
"Hidden inside of every criticism is a desire for a better connection. Whatever your spouse is complaining about they are actually telling you, indirectly, something about their deepest wishes and desires. If you listen carefully, and not be fooled by their words, you'll hear their needs for love, closeness, partnership and recognition. These are the real keys to their heart."

Joyce Marter, LCPC, Co-Owner of Urban Balance, Chicago, IL
www.urbanbalance.org License# 180-002902
"Finding a healthy balance between emotional and physical intimacy is the key to relationship success. A healthy relationship is one that is interdependent (not dependent or disconnected.). It is one where each spouse is a complete and defined 'circle' and the relationship is where the circles overlap. Good relationships involve separate healthy people who are connected in a balanced way."

Teresa L. Oglesbee, Ed.S, NBCC, NBCCH, LPC, Rincon, Georgia
http://www.sccforu.com/ License# LPC004615
"Keep Your Oath of Fidelity: The entire concept of marriage is founded on the idea that you are taking an oath of fidelity to another person."

Ginna Beal, LCSW, Austin, Texas
www.ginnabeallcsw.com License# 32880
"The Quickest Way to A Man (Or Woman's) Heart Is Through Your
Ears: Yep! The quickest way to your spouse's heart (and bedroom!) is
through your ears. We all have a need to be heard and understood. Fill
that need for your spouse and watch the fire being rekindled."

Jay Jameson, LMFT, Laguna Hills, California
jayjameson.com License# MFC 34802
"The old adage in marital therapy is that 'If we could just treat our
spouse as well as we treat our friends, there would be a lot less divorce
in the world.' If you could do just one thing to improve your marriage,
this would be it."

Anna Valenti, LCSW (License# 11769), Phoenix, Arizona
www.annavalenti.com or www.SANEresources.org
"Keeping "your own side of the street clean" which means paying
attention to your own judgmentalism, projections, entitlement,
resentment and victim-thinking, instead of focusing on your spouse's
'faults'."

Leslie Rouder, LCSW, CHT, Boca Raton, Florida
www.addadults.net License# SW5937
"No one person can give you 100% of what you need 100% of the
time. Seek to build and develop nurturing friendships, passionate
interests and talents, and make meaningful contributions to the world
around you."

Claudia Sinay-Mosias, MFT, San Francisco, California
www.sanfranciscocounseling.com License# MFC27519
"When you fight, and you inevitably will, make bridges and not 'cases'.
If a couple can argue well, the argument serves to clear the air, release
tension, and bring them closer. This can only happen if partners get off
their defensive stances. If you're making your case, you are not
listening. If you are building a bridge, chances are your ears are wide
open."

Lynn Hoyland, Licensed Marriage & Family Therapist, Arizona
www.lynnhoyland.com License# 0346
"Love is an action step. If you want love in your marriage, behave in loving ways."

Laurel Steinberg, LMHC, Licensed Psychotherapist, NY, NY
www.LaurelSteinberg.com
"'Get over it.' There are some people who just can't seem to get over things and who repeatedly bring up issues from 100 years ago. How can your spouse improve if s/he is always being punished for ancient transgressions? And why would s/he want to? Once you've discussed something and come to a resolution, move on and approach the future with a positive and carefree outlook, expecting the best from yourself and your spouse. When we damn each other by harping on the ways our spouses have wronged us time and time again, we are robbing ourselves of the opportunity to enjoy our here and now and to move forward to happier times."

Susan L. Pocasangre, MA, LPC, LSOTP, Houston, Texas
www.pocasangrescounseling.com License# 17855
"It's easy to let pride get in the way of compromise. As difficult as it may be, try to remember that both people need to do what is best for the marital relationship, not for the individual. That is the only way a marriage can work. When the goal of each person is to help the other be successful, the marriage prospers. This can prevent resentment, anger and feeling shortchanged in the relationship. "

Guy D. Burstein, LCSW, Portland, Oregon
www.guyburstein.com License# 2931
"At our core, we carry a deep wound of being unlovable, unworthy, guilty and powerless. Marriage is an amazingly efficient cauldron in which these wounds can either fester or heal. When we live within our wound, expecting or coercing our beloved to make us well, we disown our own curative power. In the process, we constellate our spouse as either a hero or a villain but never an object of our compassion. There is no wounder like the wounded."

Dawn Gilner, LPC, Lenexa, Kansas
www.DawnGilner.com License# LPC 2076
"The moment you wake up and are not completely excited about the person laying next to you, you should run - not walk - to a trained therapist. Do NOT wait until you are to the point of walking away to seek out help."

Marcel Schwantes, Life Design Coach, Chattanooga, Tennessee
www.marcelcoaching.com
"Want to eliminate drama from your marriage? Here's a simple and ancient truth: 'seek first to understand.' Essentially, this means owning the idea that if you want fulfilling communication with your spouse, understanding him/her must come first. When you try to be understood before you understand, the effort is felt by both sides, and communication often breaks down. You may end up with two strong egos knocking heads. However, seeking first to understand is a theology of effective communication. When practiced, your spouse will feel listened to and understood, translating to a more loving relationship."

Dr. Heather M. Browne, LMFT, Garden Grove, California
www.TheHealingHeart.net License# 34523
"A healthy marriage is one where the gift of invitation is not lost or forgotten. When you were dating, you spent extensive energy on being aware of your partner's desires, needs, and joys. You asked to be together and wanted this time, valued this time. It is equally important after your vows to keep invitation alive and to acknowledge your commitment to each other: How can I love you right now or show you how much I care this very moment? I choose you...today, yesterday and tomorrow...you are the only one I want, and I am so grateful that I get to be with you and only you."

Frieda Ling, Licensed Marriage & Family Therapist, Arizona
www.psychologytoday.com License# LMFT-10199
"To regard the other as inferior to oneself is fatal. Such a relationship, even if maintained, is doomed to misery."

Lynn Hoyland, Licensed Marriage & Family Therapist, Arizona
www.lynnhoyland.com License# 0346
"Don't avoid the conflict; avoid the bad behavior that often comes with it."

Diane DuBois, LMFT, San Francisco & East Bay, California
www.duboistherapy.com License# MFC30808
"You will both feel better if you keep your conflicts, for the most part, to yourselves. This helps you to have good, strong boundaries both with each other and with your children. Your children feeling secure and safe will lessen the chance of their acting out, which in turn puts less stress on the marital relationship. Grown-up conflict is too much stress for children, in general, and you will feel more in tune with your spouse if you have not let your adult issues bleed into the parent-child relationship. If an argument seems to be starting in front of your child, you might consider saying, 'This seems like something we should talk about when we have private, grown-up time. Let's set it aside for now.'"

Kimberley L. Benton, Psy.D., Roswell, Georgia
www.peachtreepsychology.com License# PSY003416
"No matter how long you have known your spouse, no matter how much you think you know about him or her, you never know it all. Never stop being curious about your spouse. Ask about their dreams, their hopes, their work life, even their favorite foods or colors. Curiosity is what keeps marriages alive and can save a marriage in danger of ending. The desire to know your spouse is the basis for a happy, long-lasting life together."

Hillary Glick, Ph.D., Clinical Psychology, New York, New York
hillaryglickphd.com License# 011217-1
"Learn to fight fair, an essential skill in marriage. To weather the storms of serious disagreements, stay with a difficult topic until each spouse feels a sense of resolution. This does not mean that one-person gives in due to fear or exhaustion, but that both people feel heard and that a genuine compromise has been reached."

Dr. Heather M. Browne, LMFT, Garden Grove, California
www.TheHealingHeart.net License# 34523
"Before you say or do something, ask yourself two questions. Is this honoring to God? Is this honoring to my spouse? If you can't say yes to both, STOP!"

Vanessa B Tate, LMFT, San Francisco, California
www.VanessaBTate.com License# MFC 48163
"Marriage is a scenic marathon with satisfying stretches of peaks and valleys. In order to maintain endurance throughout, spouses need to be invested in the relationship and reciprocally transparent, honest, mindful, non-judgmental and willing to be vulnerable for marriage to last the tests of time."

Linda Nusbaum, Licensed Marriage & Family Therapist, CA
www.lindanusbaum.com License# 45519
"Many of us grow up with a dream of a perfect marriage; where everyone is happy and no one cheats. Unfortunately people do have affairs and this causes great distress. Many marriages end in divorce because the betrayal feels too painful. I know as a relationship counselor there **is** a way for two people who love each other to find their way back and make their marriage a success. It takes real desire and the willingness to be honest from the one who had the affair. The one who was betrayed must also be willing to work through the anger and resentment. Both have to want to go to a deeper place with their spouse. This includes dealing with the pain and the guilt and putting them to rest. It's a long process but it's one that can improve and strengthen the connection between the couple, and that's something that was lacking before the affair took place."

Lauren Crawford Taylor, LCSW, Atlanta, Georgia
www.laurencrawfordlcsw.com License# 02831
"Instead of engaging in the power struggle when it comes up, try to take 15 minutes to 'cool down.' When you return to the conversation, share your needs with each other, and practice responding by giving your spouse validation, understanding and respect."

Daisy S. Vergara, LPC, Round Rock, Texas
www.daisyvergara.com
"Ingredients: 1 cup of respect, 1 cup of trust, 1 cup of honesty, 1 cup of acceptance, 1 cup of support, 1 cup of quality time and 1 cup of privacy. Serves 2.
Method for a making a marriage a success:

1. Divide the ingredients into two. In a home for two, mix all the ingredients together. Stir well until blended, and each create feelings of content and happiness.
2. Keep the communication open and clear. When heated, take time-out, then return to talk about issues. Be specific of needs and wants.
3. Add affections, and surprises as needed.
4. Enjoy!"

Risa Hobson, MA, LPC, Portland, Oregon
www.wtlcounseling.com License# C2656
"If you are a military couple with one spouse who has been deployed overseas, it is important to recognize that, as one of you has had to adjust and adapt to life on active duty, the other has had to adjust and adapt to life without their spouse being physically present. For many this includes functioning as a single parent during the separation. During deployment, each of you will have developed and taken on new roles in life and with each other that do not just disappear the moment you are reunited. Each of you may have new strengths, new challenges, and new ways of looking at yourselves and the world. When you return you will need to not only re-discover who you are in your home environment, but you will also need to re-discover who your spouse has grown into while you were apart. A way to do this with the success of your marriage in mind, is to approach this discovery process as the exciting adventure it has the potential to be."

Hadassah Ramsay, PsyD, Durham, New Hampshire
www.drhramsay.com
"Talk about your issues, not around them. Focused and clear communication goes a long way."

Cristina Castagnini, Ph.D., Psychologist, Livermore, California
www.pathtohealtherapy.com License# PSY20435
"People spend more time and effort maintaining their vehicles than they do their marriages. Then they wonder, after years and years of neglect, why they are no longer having sex or enjoying spending time with one another. If people spent years and years not getting oil changes, tune ups, or new tires on their cars, nobody would wonder why after years of this much neglect, that their car broke down on the side of the road. Yet people wonder why, after years of putting off date nights, saying words of appreciation to their spouse, and not taking the time of talk they end up not being happy together. MAINTAIN YOUR RELATIONSHIP OR IT WILL FALL APART!"

Sylvia Pritchett, MFT Intern BBS #63454, Sacramento, California
"Before I was an MFT Intern, I worked as a gemologist for over 20 years. Whenever I designed or helped select a piece of jewelry for couples, admittedly mostly heterosexual ones, celebrating a 30th, 40th, or even 50th anniversary, I would ask them what the secret for the longevity of their marriage is. Almost 90% of the time the wife would say something like 'Lots of patience and compromise. You really have to work through the tough times. Never stop talking to each other' and on and on. The men invariably said, 'Quickly learn the phrase Yes, Dear. My 20 years of 'research' seem to show that gender differences are alive and well, and that understanding, accepting and appreciating them goes a long way in making the amazing partnership called marriage work."

Dr. William I. Perry, Psychologist, San Francisco, California
www.drbillperry.com License# PSY10384
"My grandparents were married for over 65 years. But here's the thing - they were *happily* married for over 65 years! So many people just become each other's habit but the relationship ceases to be a source of happiness. So I asked Grandma Fanny one day what was the secret of their happy marriage. Her response was: 'You don't *always* have to *love* each other, but you *always* have to *respect* one another!' Then, as an afterthought, she added, 'Separate bedrooms didn't hurt either.' "

Barbara J Peters, LPC (License# LPC002758), RN, Cumming, GA
www.bjpcounseling.com and www.thegiftofalifetime.net
"'Sneak an affair with your spouse'. Being the 'other' woman just might be the thing to add excitement to your marriage. In counseling it's become apparent that many have lost 'that loving feeling' and were more of less just treading water in their relationship. I suggest having an affair with each other. Doing the things to make it exciting: sending love notes, meeting in secret places, sending provocative text messages, leaving a date card with special details of where to go and when (of course, having already made arrangements for the kids in advance)."

Elayne Savage, PhD., Licensed Marriage Family Therapist, CA
http://www.QueenofRejection.com License# MFC 17077
"Give each other a long, warm hug when you first come together after work. Talking can come later it's the hug connection that sets the tone for the rest of the evening. A hug in the morning before starting your day works great too."

Kenneth Joe Heard, LPC, LCMHC, Bryant Arkansas
www.kjoeheard.com License# P8012118
"In blended families, conflict arising out of issues regarding treatment of the stepchildren is one of the main reasons second marriages fail and at a much higher rate than first marriages. The key to making a blended marriage successful is to understand that stepchildren will often be resistant. Understand that you have a responsibility to help them develop into well-rounded adults. Do the right thing regardless of what anyone else in the family is doing. Love is a verb, not a noun. The action is more important than the feeling. If you don't feel loving toward your stepchild, be the adult in the formula and act as if you do."

Anna Valenti, LCSW (License# 11769), Phoenix, Arizona
www.annavalenti.com or www.SANEresources.org
"Learn to appreciate routine and familiarity instead of needing drama to feel alive. Serenity doesn't necessarily mean boredom."

Karen Stewart, Psy. D., Clinical Psychologist, Santa Monica, CA
www.drkrarenstewart.com
"Male erectile dysfunction can really be a challenge for couples, not just the male spouse. To make a marriage a success I would always recommend that the couple attend couples therapy sessions to discuss this issue. The dysfunction is affecting BOTH partners, not just the male! Patience, respect and love are keys to dealing with this issue."

Kevin Rhinehart, LMFT, LCSW, CSAT, Meridian, Idaho
www.kevinrhinehart.com License# LCSW 612 & LMFT 2705
"A strong foundation is key. As part of that foundation, it is important for both parties to value growth in awareness and acceptance, both in themselves and each other. Valuing growth means that we understand change will happen. Who I am today will be different in ten years. Who you are today will change as well, and we are okay with that. Growth means change. Awareness means I am in touch with my emotions, thoughts, and values, and I am in touch with yours. Acceptance means I accept both myself and you. For the 'formula' to work, both parties must be engaged in the journey to embrace these principles. If only one person of the coupleship embraces these ideals, the relationship will lack balance and relational disintegration is a likely outcome. When a couple is able to grow in these principles, the likelihood of marital success climbs dramatically. Evidence of the opposite is clear. At the core of most failed marriages is the lack of growth, awareness, and acceptance in either one or both parties."

Jodi Blackley, LMFT, Orange County, California
http://www.jodiblackley.com
"Don't forget to appreciate how important the little things are in a relationship. Whether your spouse offers to go to the store and pick up some medicine, to bring you breakfast in bed, or to even get you a glass of juice, these little things can go a long way. Make these simple gestures part of your relationship everyday. If you're on the receiving end of these gifts, make sure you appreciate what your partner is doing for you. It's the give and take in a relationship that helps it flourish and be successful."

Tracy G. Epstein, MS NCC, LPC, Tucson, Arizona
www.arizonafamilycounseling.com
1. "Carpenter Rule: think twice speak once. While you're *measuring* your words decide; on the scale of 1-10, how important is this (topic/subject) to you?

2. Are you putting the same emotional LEVEL (scale 1-10) into it or GREATER?

3. If the **importance of topic** and the **emotional scale** don't equal out, stop and don't continue otherwise one of you or both are headed for a blow up.

4. Recognize power situations, certain situations pull at us and it is not unusual for one partner to feel powerless or "need more control". But as partners, the goal is to encourage each other."

Hadassah Ramsay, PsyD, Durham, New Hampshire
www.drhramsay.com
"Enjoy... the highs and lows, the bitter times and the sweet... the challenges and the successes. It is worth it."

Leah Schoen, LPC Intern, Portland, Oregon
www.schoencounsel.com
"I like what Buddhist philosopher Daisaku Ikeda said, 'A marital relationship should be a source of inspiration, invigoration and hope. If you genuinely love someone, then through your relationship with him or her, you can develop into a person whose love extends to all humanity. Such a relationship serves to strengthen, elevate and enrich the inner realm of your life.'"

Tabi R.Upton, MA, LPC, Chattanooga, Tennessee
www.tabiupton.com and www.chattanoogacounselor.com
"What I've observed is that a joint commitment to remain married no matter what issues arise and the decision to love unconditionally once the romance has faded is what keeps couples in it for the long haul."

Israel Helfand MS, Ph.D., CST, LMFT, Cabot, Vermont
Cathie Helfand, MS, Cabot, Vermont
www.sexploration.org and www.marriagequest.com
"Lets put the FU back in FUN. Erotic pleasure is a major source of
fun, pleasure and a useful bonding technique for married couples.
Create a role-play drawing upon any fantasy that feels naughty. Being
that sexual fantasies are rooted in our early memories of childhood,
fantasy could be a great, cathartic and fun exercise. Play dress up,
adult hide and seek, teacher student, play doctor, the ideas are endless
and the idea is to have fun."

Amanda S. Davison, LMFT, Albuquerque, New Mexico
nmfamilyconnection.com License# NM 0099731
"Depression is something that affects both people in a marriage.
However depression doesn't have to be something that takes you both
down. Trying to support your spouse with depression means realizing
a few key things:
1. It's not your fault.
2. Don't try to "fix" your partner or expect that they can 'snap out of it.'
3. You can't change depression, only your partner can but you can love
them through it.
4. Get help for yourself."

Scott Lloyd Sherman, LMFT, PCE, Eureka, California
shamanicvisionpsychotherapy.blogspot.com License# MFT14936
"YOUR SPOUSE: YOUR MOST WORTHY OPPONENT!
Sad as it may seem, what marriages are really about is not 'living
happily ever-after.' They are more about provoking us to go into our
depths and heal our wounded or corrupted selves. Those who do not
rise to the challenge will be doomed to continue to experience PTSD:
Unresolved Grieving, which I see as the illness of our culture. We,
most all of us, are stuck in one phase or another of the grieving
process, about loosing our innocence. The phases are Shock, Denial,
Anger, Bargaining, Depression and finally, Resolution. Embrace the
challenge and move through the pain and into Living Happily Ever-
after!"

Lori Carpenos, LMFT, Hartford, Connecticut
www.3Principlestherapy.com License# LMFT000551
"It's a bad idea to take what we think seriously when we're in a bad mood; in fact it's a good idea to always question what we think. You may see it differently tomorrow!"

Christopher Old, MFT, LPC, NCC, Truckee, California
www.mountainmentalhealth.com License# MFC 44697
"Like a house, a marriage needs to be built on a solid foundation and that foundation is commitment. You can learn many great communication skills, ways of cooperating, and other important relationship enhancing techniques but none of that will matter if it is not built on a solid foundation of commitment. What you are both committed to in the relationship should be discussed often to keep it alive and fresh. Too often couples state their commitment to each other at their wedding and then never again."

Etan Ben-Ami, LCSW, Brooklyn, New York
http://www.effective-therapy-ny.com/
"If you want to have a happy marriage, remember to be kind. When all is well: be kind. When you're quarreling: be kind. When you're stressed out, hurt, and angry: be kind. Be assertive, be wise, set boundaries, don't give up fulfillment of your individual wants and needs, but remember to also be kind. You're not perfect, and you can't possibly be a perfect mate. Your kindness won't be perfect either. But whenever you have the ability: be kind."

Nicole Eaton, LCSW, CCHT, Boise, Idaho
www.nicoleeaton.com
"Living with someone experiencing a mental health issue is and can be exhausting. Resentment can build up due to anger and hurt, often with a lack of understanding. Researching ways to gain insight into your loved one's world, whether through books, support group, and/or a genuine curious discussion with your partner can relieve layers of stress. Be willing to ask how you can approach them and assist them in their struggle areas."

Dr. Jeffrey Bernstein, Exton, Pennsylvania
www.drjeffonline.com
"Empathy is the emotional glue that holds intimate relationships together."

Crystal Anzalone, MS, PLMHP, NCC, Omaha, Nebraska
http://www.thereflectioncenter.com http://arborfamilycounseling.com
"In regard to lasting love it takes development. The contemporary yet ancient words, 'When I was a child, I spoke and thought and reasoned as a child. But when I grew up, I put away childish things' (1 Corinthians 13:11). As we enter into longevity of the marriage commitment we learn about the limitation of our spouse's ability to meet our deepest longings. We carry these longings subconsciously with us from long ago in attempt to find the perfect soul mate. When we begin to accept the fact that our partners are also seeking, 'What's in it for me,' too, the more mature love will say I need you because I love you, not I love you because I need you. Perhaps it is time to put away childish things."

Angela Tatum Fairfax, LPC, BC-DMT, NCC, Wilmington, DE
www.goodfruitexpressivearts.com License# PC0000438
"The art of seduction and mutual attraction that serves as the catalyst of most budding relationships often gets forgotten in the busyness of life. As the relationship blossoms and the honeymoon phase wears off, we are faced with the reality of who our spouse really is. Just as financial stability or emotional support is important for many married couples, sexual fulfillment is a high priority for others. When you think about seduction, things like flirting, teasing, tempting, enticing, or persuading for the purpose of sexual engagement probably comes to mind. In marriage it is important to maintain the art of seduction as a means to make one's partner feel desired, vivacious, and alluring. A key point to remember is that sexual intimacy first begins with a mental image (paint a vivid picture for your mate) that elicits an emotional response (create a sense of elation and excitement) followed by physical sensation and release (know your spouse's hot spots). Find what works and do it more often."

Beth Honey, LMFT, Somers, Connecticut
www.therapeuticconnections.vpweb.com License# 000996
"Good communication is like a good pitch in baseball. It's all in the delivery."

Dr. Brian S. Canfield, LMFT, LPC, Bossier City, Louisiana
www.canfieldcounseling.com License LMFT #19 & LPC #120
"The happiest people I know are married and the most miserable people I know are also married. The difference may be attributed to expectations, personal commitment and a willingness to make things work."

Aimee Vadnais, Psy.D, LMFT, San Diego, California
www.cvpsych.com License# PSY 21368 & MFC 39973
"Navigating the waters of infertility can be an emotionally and physically draining process on a couple. However, there are several steps that couples can take to contribute to marital success through the process. These include the following 5 L's. The first is LOVE one another--this may seem like a simple step, but remember to focus on the love you have for your spouse and the reasons why the two of you fell in love in the first place. The second step is LAUGH--laughter is good medicine through this trying time and can boost morale, help you reconnect, and improve mood. The third step is LEARN--while learning about your various fertility options, make it a joint effort to also learn new things about your spouse in the process. The fourth step is LET GO of the outcome--this can be a very difficult step for couples who often have a narrow focus on the end result of having a baby, but the process of letting go can be freeing, can help you focus on the present and each other, and can help you think outside the box. The fifth step is LOTS OF POSITIVE THINKING--keeping focused and positive will help to reduce stress, improve mood, and improve your chances of success. These five steps can help couples to stay connected to one another in their quest to have a baby and it can bring them closer together rather than apart through this difficult time. Taking steps at maintaining marital success before bringing baby home will help in the next adventure of parenthood."

Rick Deitchman, Ph.D., Charlotte, North Carolina
www.charlottepsychotherapy.com License# 892
"Often situations occur in marriage where you get to be right, or you get to be happy, but not both at the same time. Choose being happy."

Heather Hanlon, MS, LMFT, Bethel, Connecticut
http://www.heatherhanlon.com
"If you are a spouse who is married to a partner that has been diagnosed with Bipolar Disorder, it is important to not lose your individuality or your relationship to the diagnosis. Do not use the diagnosis to make excuses for your own behavior, your spouse's behavior or any detrimental issues within the marriage. It is crucial to acknowledge the impact that Bipolar Disorder has on each of you, yet it is not favorable to use it as an excuse to individual or marital impasses. The goal is to nurture your marriage and challenge your own self growth and support your spouse in doing the same. It is beneficial for both of you to become educated in regards to Bipolar Disorder as well as to receive your own support, whether in a group or one on one setting. If you are the spouse of someone who is coping with Bipolar Disorder, you must fight against any tendencies that you have towards denial and also be an advocate for your spouse as needed. An example would be if you are in tune to the signs of your spouse entering a manic period, it is best to address it one on one along with any professionals who are involved in their treatment. There can be no secrets when you are addressing each other's mental, physical, spiritual health and the prosperity of your marriage."

Dr. Rosalind S. Dorlen, Psy.D., Psychologist, Summit, New Jersey
www.drdorlen.com License# 1369
"Unhappily married couples tend to attribute their unhappiness to failings and disappointments in their partner. However, I believe that the most important question that can improve any marriage is not 'what is it like to be married to your spouse' but 'What is it like to be married to me.' Willingness for both parties to reflect and change their behavior in response to a rigorous self-inventory can have tremendous power to improve one's marriage."

Ellie Zarrabian, Ph.D., Spiritual Director, Los Angeles, California
www.centeronpeace.com
"Sometimes we are too quick to jump into divorce. Learning to sit still and observe as to how we are contributing to the problem should come before contemplating divorce."

Cyndie Westrich, M.A., A.T.R.-BC, LPC, Marietta, Georgia
www.easel-arttherapy.com
"Figure out what works for you both as a couple…forget what others say!"

Deborah A. Bruno, MSW, LCSW, Miami, Florida
www.mindbuild.net License# 6832
"A successful marriage is one that has love. Love has boundaries. Love allows one to grow and encourages time apart as well as together. Love is respecting your partner. Love is trusting. Love means sharing common values. Love is communicating freely without agreeing. Love is compromise and meeting half way. Love is making decisions without judgment. Love believes in faith. Love forgives. Love understands. Love is safe and secure. Love is caring not controlling. Love is playful and fun. Love is open and honest. Love is romantic with a partner."

Karen Hoving, Ph.D., Aurora, Colorado
www.drkahoving.com License# 10245
"If you haven't done so already it is very important that you do a 'Financial Disclosure.' Who is the saver? Who is the spender? How much debt and savings do you have? What are your long-term financial goals (a house, finishing school, etc). Make sure you are on the same financial page - it will save a LOT of fights in the future (remember, most couples fight about money and sex - this will take ONE off the plate!)."

Donna Botinelly, DMin, LCMFT, Wichita, Kansas
www.actscounselingcenter.com License# 147
"Pray together as a couple every day."

Brock A. Bauer, LISW-S, Columbus, Ohio
www.bauercounseling.com License# I.0700102-supv
"If we were to exert as much focus on listening to the words and
feelings of our loved one, as we do with formulating our verbal
emotional expression, the efficiency of communication would unfold
more naturally."

Dianne Greyerbiehl, Ph.D., LPC, PCC, Greenville, South Carolina
www.lifecoachinginstitute.net License# 4805
"When couples have disagreements with each other, or are simply
irritated with something their spouse did, it often means a personality
difference is involved. For example, if one person is mainly task
oriented, very analytical and outcome driven, they may think their
spouse, who is a feeling based and concerned about people, is unable
to be objective and think clearly when they respond emotionally. In
turn the feeling based spouse thinks their task based spouse is
unfeeling and doesn't care about them. Another example is an
extrovert who has to talk about their problem in order to think it out
and their introverted spouse doesn't say anything. The extrovert thinks
the introvert doesn't care while the introvert feels cornered because
they are still thinking about what to say since they need to time to
think! So find out what your personality type is by taking a test like the
Myers-Briggs Type Indicator…it will increase your appreciation of
your spouse's skills and cure many misunderstandings that develop
into hurt feelings and arguments."

Jan Talen, LMFT, Grand Rapids, Michigan
www.funlifellc.com License# 4101006087
"Successful marriages come with successful parenting. Successful
parenting comes with successful marriages. To have success in both
areas requires that parents learn to lead. Knowing how to love and
forgive, be patient and kind, change and adapt to new challenges with
positive attitudes is essential to success in both arenas. So, continue to
develop your parenting skills and you will develop your relationship
skills. Continue to develop your relationship with your spouse and
watch your kids thrive! So FUN!"

Leyla Mahbod Kenny, PhD, LICSW, Washington, D.C.
www.washingtondcpsychotherapy.com License# LC3000857
"Make love, not sex. Don't just physically screw each other but invest
in the sacred act of making love with one another. Look into each
other's eyes and make love with every cell in your body."

Jenny Grace Shaw, LMHC, M.ED., Maui, Hawaii
www.jennyshawtherapy.com License# 256964
"As far as 'perfection' goes; it's not whether he or she is perfect, it's
whether or not the two parties are perfect for each other."

Sally Broder, Psy.D., San Francisco, California
www.drsallybroder.com License# PSY 22229
"Making marriage successful with a football player. Keep in mind that
this is his dream. If you find yourself losing patience with parts of his
NFL lifestyle, check in with yourself before coming down on him. If
your spouse feels you are raining on his parade, he will resent you for
it. Imagine if it was your once-in-a-life-time dream.

Instead create your own life. Reach for *your* dreams, *your* goals, and
interests that are big enough to grab and hold your passion. Get a
degree, start a business for real, not just as a hobby. Have an identity
that stands alone. You will already be thought of as so-and-so's wife,
but you will know you are much more than that; Your own person."

Peggy Halyard, BBA, MA, LPC (License# 14706), Houston Texas
http://www.couples-help.com and http://www.imagorelationships.org
"What comes to my mind with my husband, Doug, is that we keep the
romance alive by doing a check in every night on how we want our
evening to look. For example, we may decide to take ballroom dancing
and enjoy the closeness and connection that dancing brings us."

Cheryl Gerson, LCSW, BCD, New York, New York
www.cherylgerson.com
"Don't be afraid of pain. The spouse in the most pain is the one most
likely to grow and change."

Anita Gadhia-Smith, PsyD, Washington, D.C.
practicaltherapy.net License# 11151
"A healthy marriage grows over time if both people continue to work on their own side of the issues."

Eleanor Laser, Ph.D, Chicago, Illinois
www.laserhypnosis.com
"Usually when children are born and the mother gets overly involved with the babies and all the work involved. She sometimes looses sight of the husband. She thinks he is a grown man who can help, understand, and cope. But, in many instances, the husband becomes dethroned and put aside; basically jealous of the attention the children get and not him anymore. This is a situation that smolders and becomes a disaster, sometimes in divorce. Men are just taller, older, and fatter, but basically overgrown babies. So, keep this in mind and keep giving your husband attention."

Shelly Clubb, M.S., M.A., NCC, Denver, Colorado
www.transformativecounselingservices.com License# 12176
"Marriage is one of the ultimate paradoxes. As a lived-experience, it requires devotion, commitment, and lasting loyalty. However, it also asks us to have good personal boundaries. When my spouse is having a bad day, I do not need to take that personally. It takes a great deal of humility to 'make room' for the other person's life, holding them with care and support, while at the same time remembering that we each have our own lives to live, our own growth and personal path, apart from the other but ultimately lived in relationship with them."

Ilene A. Serlin, Ph.D, BC-DMT, San Francisco, California
www.union-street-health-associates.com License# PSY 11092
"Second marriages be very clear about defining values and priorities before marriage; importance of money, security, families and step-families, expectations about work/retirement/mixing friends. Building a new life together has many challenges, but can benefit from conscious choices made from reflection on past patterns and behaviors."

Dr. Jennifer A. Bennice, Licensed Clinical Psychologist, SC
www.wecharleston.com
"Looking for ways to help make your partner's day a bit easier, and expressing appreciation each day for something your partner has done to help ease your stress."

Christy Sorden, LPC, Colorado Springs, Colorado
www.SordenCounseling.com
"Going back to the basics of respect encompasses the healthy foundation of making a relationship successful. The simple feat of asking oneself, 'Is what I'm about to say or do going to bring me closer to my spouse?' This is a quick evaluation tool anyone can employ. Many times people react out of emotional defense to protect themselves from hurting as opposed to doing what is best for the relationship. By taking on a strong stance to provide respect towards your spouse will enable your marriage to grow to healthy levels of success."

Cliff Crain, Licensed Marriage Family Therapist, Danville, CA
www.4creativeliving.com License# LMFC 30798
"I have found that most people expect the other spouse to bring them happiness. This is, in the long run, not really possible. One of the main tasks we have in life is to realize our own personal power, and practice finding joy and peacefulness within each day... even when there are detours and unexpected situations. Only when we can do this, can we co-create a truly successful marriage."

Melinda Yachnin, LCPC, Lagrange, Illinois
http://www.melindayachnin.com License# 180-005280
"After years of counseling couples through crisis, and preparing engaged couples for marriage, I find myself saying one thing over and over to each spouse. Women: be gentle and affectionate with your husband, because a little tenderness will go a long way with him. And men: listen to your wife and take her wants and needs seriously even if you don't agree with them. You will reap much more than you sow if you do."

Amy Jones, LPC, DCC, Westminster, Colorado
www.growthworks.net License# CO 2693
"Hold a family meeting with your spouse once a week. Discuss important topics of interest, such as dynamics, household chores, parenting, money and future plans. Giving yourself the time and space on a consistent basis to air any concerns will facilitate open communication and intimacy and will help minimize conflicts. Make these meetings an integral part of your life."

Ken Siegmann, Roseville, LMFT, Roseville, California
http://www.insight-counseling.org License# MFC41274
"It's easy to get lost in the day-to-day pressures of life and forget that even something simple can remind your spouse how much you cherish them. So grab your spouse and kiss her in the middle of the supermarket. Call him in the middle of a busy day to say, 'I love you.' Keep the romance going."

Susanne Slay-Westbrook, LPC-S, LMFT-S, Austin, Texas
www.aworldofrespect.com License# LPC-S #1175 & LMFT-S #1013
"Marriage isn't just about two people. If it was it might be relatively simple. But the truth is we each bring with us our families and generations of traditions, good and bad.

The hard part is in the challenge of bringing together all of the subtle and not so subtle differences in cultural and familial values and traditions. Even if you have the same skin tone, are from the same country and the same faith, there are bound to be multiple nuances in perspective, from how to celebrate holidays to food choices and ways to accomplish daily tasks.

No matter the size or scope of your cultural value differences, you're much farther ahead in having a good, solid marriage if you can specifically name and talk about those differences in a non-judgmental way, preserving and honoring the unique qualities you each bring into the union, yet blending and negotiating the areas of your lives that can complement and enrich who you both can become together."

Frieda Ling, Licensed Marriage & Family Therapist, Arizona
www.psychologytoday.com License# LMFT-10199
"A good marriage is a safe haven from the storm of life. A bad marriage is the very scene of disaster."

Gary Lange, Ph.D., Marriage & Family Therapist, California
www.GaryLangePhD.com License# 25633
"Usually when our spouse tells us something, our first instinct is to do the opposite. Such as interrupt, get defensive, give our suggestions, but a great alternative is to breathe, and invite them to 'tell me more'. Often this allows them to unload the pent up problem, which is often a solution in itself. A second suggestion is to 'look at the big picture' and don't get caught up in the minutia. Life is too short to get upset with the little details, which will mean nothing an hour or month from now."

Jodi Blackley, LMFT, Orange County, California
http://www.jodiblackley.com
"Ever wonder why relationships don't work when you invest 50/50? It's because you're only investing 1/2 of yourself. Look at your efforts as needing to be 100/100. If each of you is consistently putting a 100% into the relationship, then your efforts won't rely upon your partner to become whole. At 100%, you're already whole and you don't need to depend on your partner to make the changes. You can put 100% of the effort in knowing you're giving it your all. If your partner wants to make this marriage work, then hopefully they are committed 100% as well. It's about giving the relationship your all, not just 1/2 of you."

Joan Levy, LCSW, LCS, ACSW, Kapaa, Hawaii
www.joanlevy.com License LCSW #3046
"How do you view mistakes or problems? From a JUDGMENT MODEL: As evidence of wrong-doing where someone is guilty and must be blamed and punished? Or from a LEARNING MODEL: As evidence that something is in need of attention. A needed resource is missing. Gather and apply the missing resource and the problem is solved and the mistake is remedied."

Alison Howard, Psy.D., Washington, D.C.
www.AlisonHoward.com License# PSY1000439
"Sex is an important ingredient in marriage. It allows us to be selfish and generous at the same time."

Barbara Winter PhD, Boca Raton, Florida
www.drbarbarawinter.com License# PY4034
"Being present is key. We believe that because we are connected (phone, computer) we are truly connected. True connection requires 'face time'-being in each other's presence AND with each other's heart."

Dr. Sara Denman, Psy.D, Psychologist, Danville, California
drsaradenman.com License# Psy19808
"If you would like your spouse to just listen and not solve your problem for you, tell him/her that. There are generally two types of people, problem solvers and processors. Processors do not want to tell their spouse a challenge they are having and hear about the ways to solve it. They truly want to just talk it through. Problem solvers are always going to hear about a difficulty their spouse is having and will try to figure out solutions. Be clear with your spouse before you start those conversations about whether you would like to process or get suggestions for solutions."

Rene Lewellyn, LMFT, Brentwood, Northern California
www.renelewellynmft.com License# MFC42173
"Many married couples make the mistake of getting caught up in 'score keeping'. In other words, keeping an internal list of either perceived wrongs the other has done, or an internal list of all of the things they want but the other spouse has not provided. Sometimes 'score-keeping' involves comparison and 'keeping up with the 'Jones' - looking at other relationships, comparing, and a feeling of coming up short. Over time, this practice results in resentment and tends to get in the way of spouses being more able to live with gratitude and their awareness of the things that are going well in the relationship as well as ways in which their spouse does provide care and love."

Dr. Don Gilbert, LMHC, Ankeny and West Des Moines, Iowa
www.newlife-counseling.com License# 00178
"When my second daughter had a wedding shower, her future mother-in-law gave her this pearl of wisdom 'Always Fight Naked'."

Margie Slaughter, ALMFT(# A115), Birmingham, Alabama
http://therapists.psychologytoday.com
"Don't stop getting to know one another. Of course you want to have a good sense of who you are marrying, but even after marriage, perhaps especially after marriage, assume that you still have things to learn about each other, and about yourselves. You will learn a lot about each other informally through conversation and observation, but you can also be intentional in your efforts by taking personality assessments such as the Myers-Briggs Type Indicator and studying the Enneagram. Assessment tools such as the Myers-Briggs can help you understand your own personality as well as your spouse's. More importantly, you will learn how those personalities fit together in ways that both balance each other out and serve as a source of irritation to one another. Understanding that your partner's irritating habit may be a classic, objectifiable personality trait common to a large percentage of the population rather than a mortal character defect takes the sting out, enabling you to empathize with your spouse without taking his or her ways so personally."

Lynda K. Tyson, PhD, Pensacola, Florida
www.mmtmentalhealth.org License# LMHC 9018 & CMHP 50608
"My husband of 23 years and I both spent 20 years in the army. During emotionally elevated discussions, we learned to incorporate a military tactic. The military will frequently retreat, rethink and re-approach to prevent making rash decisions. In civilian terms, that means when things become too emotionally elevated it is OK to walk away as long as you come back and finish talking about it.

Similar to how unfinished military conflicts continue to rise, the unfinished disagreement will do the same. Sometimes you may have to retreat more than once!"

Trudy M. Johnson, LMFT, Buena Vista, Colorado
www.missingpieces.org License# 755
"REMEMBER WHY YOU GOT MARRIED. Why did you get married? Usual answer besides sex is...*because we enjoy each other's company, we have fun together.* Today's marriages are faced with so many stressors, the fun times get lost in the shuffle. When you feel your relationship sliding away it is time to re-group and spend some conflict-free time of fun together. Make a pact between the two of you that you will NOT discuss stressful topics during these times of fun!"

Dr. Debra Laino, DHS, M.ED, MS, ACS, ABS, Wilmington, DE
www.delawaresexdoc.com
"It's okay if a couple sees things differently. It just means they are their own unique individuals. It is that uniqueness that needs to be celebrated."

Karen Schwarz, LMHC, CASAC, Syracuse, New York
"A successful marriage is one that avoids the temptation to have an affair. Affairs can be very appealing when one's relationship is struggling, and/or the other person seems so perfect in so many ways. I guarantee you; the other person is not as perfect as you think. Anyone can be attractive and passionate when you only have short time periods with each other. Instead seek counseling and, only when you and your current spouse agree to a divorce, if you still want, feel free to call that 'affair' up and try it again!"

Alison Howard, Psy.D., Washington, D.C.
www.AlisonHoward.com License# PSY1000439
"Intimacy is not the result of merging our two selves into one person. It is what emerges through the acceptance of imperfection."

Raelene S. Weaver, Licensed Marriage Family Therapist, CA
www.raeleneweaver.com License# 46608
"If possible, allow each person to have their 'own space.' I think a separate bathroom for him, and a separate bathroom for her is great. And if he folds his towels differently than hers, that's okay too!"

M. L. Grabill, M.Ed., L.P.C., L.A.C., Colorado Springs, Colorado
mlgbehavhlth.com License# LPC 5825 & LAC 170
"For a successful marriage keep God in the center."

Kevin M Hallinan, LCSW, CAP, SAP, ICADC, Melborne, Florida
www.Kmhpsychotherapist.com License# SW6611
"A successful marriage is one where the couple seeks help when they
need it and finds a therapist that can be helpful. As with any
counseling situation, the therapist must address and utilize the unique
personalities, circumstances, experiences, beliefs and emotionality of
each individual; applying and adapting general principles to unique
situations."

Laurel Steinberg, LMHC, Licensed Psychotherapist, New York
www.LaurelSteinberg.com
 "'Get a life!' When both spouses have independently fulfilling lives,
their happiness does not depend on their spouse's mood or how they
interact with him/her on a particular day. When each has meaningful
interests in which to invest time and energy such as friends, jobs,
volunteer projects, athletic activities, hobbies, pets, etc., it enriches
that person's quality of life and makes him/her more autonomous and
resilient. Furthermore, these interests relieve one spouse of the burden
of being the family's only source of entertainment and also give
couples time away from each other, allowing them to miss each other.
Later, they can connect while sharing rich conversations about the
interesting things going on in each of their lives."

Kenneth J. Wade, Ph.D., LPC, Birmingham, Alabama
License# LMFT 119 & LPC 461
"Look beyond conventional wisdom. In popular parlance love often
refers to infatuation, dependency, or possession. Love that nurtures a
relationship is not giving in order to get. Rather love is more like
putting the best possible interpretation on the other's behavior. Loving
yourself and your spouse is a practice rather than a feeling. To
whatever degree you can know and love yourself, you will increase
your capacity to love your spouse."

Dorian Mintzer, Ph.D.(LICD Psychologist, #2812), Boston, MA
www.dorianmintzer.com and www.couplesretirementpuzzle.com
"Life can throw you 'curve balls' throughout your marriage. One curve
ball may be when a spouse becomes ill or declines in health. No matter
how much you love your spouse and want to help, being a care-giver
can be very stressful. It's important that you find things that give you
strength. You need support and opportunities for time apart so you
don't 'burn out.' Check what resources may be available for you and/or
your spouse. Ask for and accept help from relatives and friends. Find a
support group in your community or via the Internet. Take care of
yourself as you help care for your spouse."

Donna Pollard-Burton, MA, LMHC, NCC, BCC, Indianapolis, IN
www.cairncottagecounseling.com License# 39002176A
"Sexual abuse is a hurt that is dragged with a person from place to
place through life much like a padlocked trunk. Not only does the hurt
get locked in that trunk, but so too our ability to trust and feel safe. Are
you married to this person? Are you this person? Is this affecting your
sex life? Know that your spouse is not doing this to you; it was done to
your spouse. Do what you can to let down your hurt and defensiveness
and remember that in marriage we are allies in life, sharing in each
other's unique journey. Listen, learn, seek help, try to understand,
compromise, seek help, be patient, be trustworthy and gentle with each
other. Oh, and did I say seek help? Sharing in the healing together as
partners and allies can be a profoundly deep experience of love."

Anna Valenti, LCSW (License# 11769), Phoenix, Arizona
www.annavalenti.com or www.SANEresources.org
"Remain calm, centered and within your own boundaries even when
your spouse is losing control."

Julia White, LCSW, Denver, Colorado
www.juliamwhite.com License# 992173
"So many women do more than their fair share in marriages, especially
when there are kids involved. Set expectations early on that you are
not solely responsible for household chores and childcare."

Ellie Zarrabian, Ph.D., Spiritual Director, Los Angeles, California
www.centeronpeace.com
"There is no manual on how to have a good marriage, because a good marriage between two individuals is an art form. It has to be shaped with care and a great deal of patience."

Cyndie Westrich, M.A., A.T.R.-BC, LPC, Marietta, Georgia
www.easel-arttherapy.com
"Be a united front especially with in-laws and with your children."

Michael G Quirke, L.M.F.T., San Francisco & San Mateo, CA
www.michaelgquirke.com License# MFC39030
"When you have an argument, try to look beyond what happened and see if you can discern what it meant to your spouse. Couples don't fight because someone left the cap off the toothpaste tube. They fight because it meant something about someone's power, value or safety."

Joyce Thompson, MS, LCMFT, Wichita, Kansas
www.emotionaljourney.org License# 734
"When you find yourself or your spouse spending too much time on the computer and not with each other, don't ignore the problem. Try sitting down together, face-to-face and heart-to-heart. Attempt to figure out what might be missing in your marriage and look for ways to fill those needs with each other, instead of separately. Explore various ways in which you could spend more quality time together as a couple."

Natalie A. Cherrix, LCSW, DVS, Seaford, Delaware
www.nataliecherrix.com
"Sexual abuse is a widespread issue, so it is not uncommon for marriages to be impacted by the effects of surviving past abuse, such as difficulty with trust and sexual intimacy. For the survivor, it is important that you know the abuse was never your fault. For the spouse, being supportive, patient, and understanding is key. You each must honor your own feelings and needs, while also joining together as allies to heal and grow stronger."

Yvonne Wilson, Clinical Psychologist, LMFT, Corona, California
yvonnewilsonphd.com License# MFT26092 & Psy17078
"Marriage is like a 'Merry-go-round', put in the effort to stay for the ride or fall off."

Angela R. Stern, LCPC, Crofton, Maryland
http://therapist.psychologytoday.com/44031
"Modern technology has brought us social networking sites, individual cell phones and text messaging, and the proliferation of pornography via the internet, which have been the Pandora's Box for extramarital connections and sexual addictions. Old fashioned barriers, such as one phone per household, once kept honest people honest in their marriages, but the privacy, anonymity, and opportunity afforded by the internet and individual cell phones seems to have made a impact on the fidelity of marriages, as I have observed in my work with couples in my practice. Couples who avoid or overcome these challenges of the modern world are those who forgo this new level of privacy by either not participating in social networking sites and / or by freely sharing their passwords or lock combinations to their cell phones with their spouse."

Dr. Eileen R. Borris, Licensed Psychologist, Paradise Valley, AZ
www.dreileenborris.com and www.globalpeaceinitiatives.com
"The transformational power of forgiveness moves us from being helpless victims of our circumstances to becoming powerful co-creators of our reality."

Stephen Clarke, M.S., LGPC, Baltimore, Maryland
www.presenceproject.net License# LC4084
"Essentially marriage is about giving up any personal territory, any way that we close down our hearts and minds. Marriage is a binding agreement to put the other person's happiness before one's own. This requires us to practice the essence of the world's spiritual paths, thinking about others before ourselves. As Sakyong Mipham states: 'If you want to be happy, think of others. If you want to be miserable, think of yourself.'"

Patricia Brawley, PhD, LPC, McComb, Mississippi
http://www.PatriciaBrawley.com License# 0608
"Don't forget that a woman's ear is a sex organ. What she hears has a lot to do with what happens in a relationship."

Gloria Saltzman, MA, MFA, Psychotherapist, San Francisco, CA
www.GloriaSaltzman.com
"What ever the recipe is for you and your spouse to find what will increase safety and closeness for both of you has to be discovered by taking the time to understand each other's needs."

Susan Reuling Furness, M.Ed., LCPC, LMFT, PTR, Boise, Idaho
jeffersonstreetcounseling.com License# LMFT 39 & LCPC 70
"Carl Whitaker, the renowned family therapist, once said, 'Marriage is the major leagues in the relationship game.' As a marriage and family therapist *and* as a married woman, I know that successful marriage requires more than a hope or a wish to win. To play the game means we must also take responsibility for our performance, accept coaching and corrections to our game, and remain open to hours, months, years of hard work. We must be patient when our spouse is off their game, realizing no one ever bats a thousand. Staying in the game means rebounding from personal slumps, taking turns at bat, and sometimes sitting in the bullpen while your teammate shines at home plate. Finally if we play fair and square, we are rewarded knowing we are loved and respected in return."

Dr. Gary Chapman, Winston-Salem, North Carolina
fivelovelanguages.com
"We discovered that what one person considers to be an apology is not what another person considers to be an apology. Learning the apology language of your spouse communicates your sincerity."

Michael T. Halyard, LMFT, MBA, San Francisco, California
www.SFtherapy.com License# MFC42122
"The quality of your life and marriage will be based on your capacity for forgiveness."

Kate Feldman, MSW, LCSW, Hesperus, Colorado
www.consciousrelationships.com
"LIFE IS FOREPLAY. Joel and I have realized how much the little
things count to help keep our connection strong, sexy *and* soulful: Lots
of touch in and outside the bedroom, tenderness, laughter, making play
out of every day events and the old favorite: compromise! Keep your
marriage juicy, fun, alive and satisfying. Turn everyday interactions
into FOREPLAY."

Angie Ridings, MHR, M.Ed., LPC, LADC, Oklahoma City, OK
http://www.angelaridingscounseling.com/ LPC #4177 & LADC #736
"When dealing with alcohol and other drug addiction, if a marriage is
going to succeed, getting the family involved in the healing process is
essential. When a spouse is suffering from addiction, the other half
often expects the addict to get help and everything will be fine. If the
co-addict is willing to participate in the treatment then restoration of
the relationship and sobriety is more likely. Having the co-addict
participate means taking a look at the family dynamics and being
willing to change any behaviors that are contributing to the problem.
In addition to ongoing family or marital counseling, I also believe that
regular individual therapy, group therapy, and support groups are
highly important for the addict. This will enable them to get the
professional help they need, peer interaction, accountability, and
understanding."

Merrill Powers, MSW, LCSW, Auburn, California
www.powerstherapist.com License# LCS 19451
"Once you're married, have independent lives that are connected
emotionally. Because being together constantly can take the
excitement out of a relationship quickly."

Brock A. Bauer, LISW-S, Columbus, Ohio
www.bauercounseling.com License# I.0700102-supv
"We are responsible for practicing our own good self care, not other's
sole responsibility to care for us. The less we export our happiness
onto another's hand, the more diplomatic the marriage."

Dawn Gilner, LPC, Lenexa, Kansas

www.DawnGilner.com License# LPC 2076

"People don't seem to think twice about going to spend 8 hours of training for their career, but often hesitate to spend that same amount of time in counseling. Invest in your relationship - the rewards will be ten fold."

Nicole Eaton, LCSW, CCHT, Boise, Idaho

www.nicoleeaton.com

"In working with couples that have children with serious behavior issues, or even just general parenting, they forget the game plan. What game plan? The couple's intention is to raise responsible, loving children, but the path to get there is from two perspectives. Get a plan! It will definitely help keep the marriage successful."

Dr. Robert C. Allanach, LMFT, CGP, New Orleans, Louisiana

www.doctorallanach.com License# 697

"Being in a relationship is engaging another human being in a profoundly intimate way. This human being is different from all others in the life circle. (S)he is the object of your deepest affection. It can get messy and confusing at times. This is normal. Most lovers confuse this part of the human condition as aberrant. It isn't the mess we make out of our relationships. It's how well we clean it up."

Suzanne Mallouk, M.D., Physician Surgeon, New York, New York

www.drsuzannemallouk.com

"Most people get so fixated on what they are not getting from their spouse that they forget to LOVE their spouse. Instead focus more on loving and giving rather than receiving."

Kavita Acharya Hatten, MS, LPC, Phoenix, Arizona

www.phoenixcounseling.net License# LPC-0952

"I am no longer confused about how to have a loving relationship. I no longer have to guess what my spouse needs or wants. I've learned to look within, to honor and trust myself. Through this process, I see the truth unfold."

Brittany Smith, LCSW, Little Rock, Arkansas

www.EatHappy.org License# AR-1984C

"I once heard someone say, 'If the grass looks greener on the other side, water your own lawn'. I think if everyone followed this quote it can help make their marriage a success."

Dr. Sarah Villarreal, Psy.D, Mill Valley, California

www.entelechywellness.com

"Create 'rules' for arguments. Rules should be based on how each person is wired. An essential rule should be to never threaten divorce when arguing. It is not a concept you want to be desensitized to as a couple."

Raelene S. Weaver, Licensed Marriage Family Therapist, CA

www.raeleneweaver.com License# 46608

"Helping each other feel seen, heard, and understood is very important to long-term happiness. One way to ensure this is happening is by asking each other how their day went."

Maria Mellano, LICSW (License# 111055), Boston, Massachusetts

WWW.MariaMellanoTherapy.com WWW.LivePassionatelyNow.com

"Conflict is part of marriage. When handled well, it can bring deeper intimacy. Remember you and your spouse are not *just* the most extreme parts that emerge during conflict. Seeing beyond this illusion in the heat of the moment can cool flames. Reflecting back what you've heard your spouse say, using the exact key words, until you get it right according to your spouse's needs could do wonders for peace. If things really heat up, take space in a different room or by taking a walk. BEFORE leaving make sure to commit to resolution; otherwise intense fears of abandonment could ignite. Apologize when your partner has been hurt by your behavior. Even if you didn't mean to do or don't believe that you did whatever it was that hurt your partner, understand that your partner's experience of it was *hurt*- and that if your intention is deeper intimacy, healing the hurt will enable vulnerability, which is essential for intimacy. The power of sincere apology cannot be underestimated."

Dr. Poppy Moon, Ph.D., LPC, NCC, Tuscaloosa, Alabama
www.poppymoon.com
"My husband always loses everything – his phone, his wallet, his keys. This drives me crazy and it irks me when I have to help him find things! While we were searching, I thought about lecturing him about putting things in one place. I knew that this would hurt his feelings, so I kept my mouth shut, sighed, and instead took another look under the bed."

Jonathan Mahrer, Ph.D., San Francisco & Mill Valley, California
www.BlueMountainCounseling.com License# PSY 14351
"We have an incredible power to *amplify* what we focus on. Unfortunately, we can tend at times to have a laser beam focus on the negative in our partner; on what they *are* doing that we think they shouldn't, or what they *aren't* doing that we think they should. Reverse that: Shine the spotlight first on your own contribution to the problem, even though you might feel that you played the smaller role. Own your own role first!

Then, make it your job to focus on the reasonable and the good in your partner (even if at times the positive feels like the exception). Work to *find the kernel of truth* in your partner's perspective. Also, make sure that your partner knows the various ways you like, love, value, respect, admire, and appreciate them. See how powerful and positive it can be to focus on and amplify the good in your partner!"

Joyce Thompson, MS, LCMFT, Wichita, Kansas
www.emotionaljourney.org License# 734
"If your spouse is often away from home due to the demands of work, try to remember that they too are lonely and missing you. To keep things spiced up in your marriage and to keep them eager to return home to you, find unique, long-distance ways of flirting with them. For example, tuck a handwritten note, a card, or a photo of yourself into their briefcase or suitcase. If they stay busy flirting with you, or wondering what might be coming next, they will stay focused upon you and only you!"

Teresa Trower, M.A. LMHC, Jacksonville, Florida
www.stressbustercoach.com License# MH0002000
"Find out what makes your spouse feel loved and make sure the sun does not set without giving your spouse this gift."

Dr. Debra Laino, DHS, M.ED, MS, ACS, ABS, Wilmington, DE
www.delawaresexdoc.com
"All couples should spend time naked holding one another (not for the sake of sex) but for the sake of intimacy and connection."

Marne Wine, M.A. LPC, CST, Denver, Colorado
www.btid.com
"Humor, humor, humor, but never at the expense of the other. If you inadvertently say something you think is funny, but your spouse is hurt by your comment, be quick to apologize on the spot. And then later, come back to them again, take their hands in yours (or something similar), look them in the eye, and apologize again. They'll know you mean it and it will be easier for them to forgive, and for both of you to move on."

John Sovec, Psychotherapist, MA, LMFT, Pasadena, California
www.JohnSovec.com License# MFC 46376
"Couples need to be creative and willing to think outside the box to build their own model of how their relationship works. In building this model, it is important to set a strong foundation from the beginning so that there is open communication and healthy development of the path to realizing their dreams and goals."

Thomas L. Tobias, M.Ed., LMHC, NCC, Tavares, Florida
www.triadpsychologicalservices.com License# MH1516
"Marriage is a partnership in which each person gives their very best effort, during every minute of every day, to treat their spouse with perfect trust, respect and affection. Each makes the other the absolute, number one, top priority in life. Whatever else may be different about them, they must share the same core values or they will tend to grow apart."

Dr. Cynthia Chestnut, Couple, Family & Sex Therapist, Delaware
www.drcynthiachestnut.com
"It's a beautiful act to give gifts you want your spouse to have. It is also an amazing precious gesture to give gifts that you know your spouse wants."

Michelle Risser, LISW, Columbus, Ohio
www.michellerissercounseling.com License# I 0700128
"Breastfeeding can a wonderful bonding experience with many benefits for mom and baby. But it can also be frustrating, challenging or painful, and is often a topic that carries with it deep feelings of guilt or inadequacy for a mom whether she chooses to nurse her baby or not. She may think that her spouse or partner does not understand or empathize, which leaves her feeling anxious and isolated. She needs encouragement, support for her decisions and a cheerleader when things get tough. She may feel that her feelings are minimized or dismissed, and the most helpful thing her significant other can do is listen, acknowledge and validate those feelings with patience and kindness."

Raelene S. Weaver, Licensed Marriage Family Therapist, CA
www.raeleneweaver.com License# 46608
"Accept the 'whole package.' He might crack his knuckles, she might bite her nails, but in the big picture, who cares?"

Ce Eshelman, LMFT, Sacramento, California
www.attachmentandtraumatreatmentcenter.com License# MFC27146
"Romantic relationships are attachment relationships. Our deepest fears get activated by those we love the most. If you are attachment challenged from early childhood abuse or adoption, you are likely prone to pulling away and rejecting your partner during conflict. Here are three important steps to follow to keep yourself attached during conflict: 1) Go closer instead of further away when upset, 2) Hold hands through every difficult conversation, and 3) Say what you are afraid of before saying anything else (Yes, you are afraid. Admitting that to yourself is the first step.)."

Mary-Michael Levitt, LMFT, DRCC, Hackettstown, New Jersey
www.riverviewcc.com License# LMFT 37F100153100
"Compromising is not giving in but meeting your spouse halfway."

Haylee Heyn, AMFT, Salt Lake City, Utah
wasatchfamilytherapy.com License# 7976237-3904
"My husband seems to be a lot more helpful and considerate when I
praise him for things he should be doing."

Brittany Neece, LMFT-A, Austin, Texas
www.brittanyneece.com License# 201534
"Be careful not to 'hit 'em where it counts' regarding your spouse. In
any significant relationship or marriage, partners naturally become
more vulnerable with one another and learn about each others'
sensitive and delicate issues. With such vulnerability, they can begin to
learn exactly what to say or do that makes their spouse angry, hurt, or
feel guilty. When spouses begin to intentionally use this information to
hurt or manipulate one another mentally or emotionally, it is a sure-fire
strategy to deeply damage the relationship. In short, do not use this
information as ammunition towards your spouse or it will backfire!"

Daniel L DeGoede, Ph.D, Clinical Psychologist, Pioneertown, CA
www.drdanieldegoede.com License# PSY9479
"You never get it all and rarely get it now, so quit trying and figure out
what part you truly want."

Gal Szekely, LMFT, San Francisco, California
MindfulLifeCenter.com License# 50301
"The most difficult task in a marriage is realizing one basic truth:
when your spouse does or says something which makes you really
upset / angry / sad / stressed / disappointed, it's not really about him or
her... It's about you! Whatever they did just hit a very sensitive nerve
for you, meaning they were just pushing a button that was already
inside of you. So, before you go ahead and tell them how wrong they
are for making you feel this way, ask yourself – why is it that I got so
upset? Why is this issue so important to me?"

Robert A. Moylan, LCPC, Naperville, Illinois
www.robertmoylan.com License# 180005037
"The more a husband stays committed to his wife, the more feminine traits he learns and acquires. The more a wife stays committed to her husband, the more masculine traits she learns and acquires. Real growth and real maturity allows a man to be more feminine, and a woman to be more masculine."

Amanda S. Davison, LMFT, Albuquerque, New Mexico
nmfamilyconnection.com License# NM 0099731
"Ornery is love. Being able to laugh at ourselves and each other is the key to aging gracefully individually and within our marriage."

Fran Ryan Ph.D., Kansas City, Missouri
www.psychologytoday.com License# PY01723
"Without trust, a couple cannot achieve true intimacy. True intimacy can only be achieved through private interaction and confidentiality.

We humans often fear intimacy so much that we triangulate others into our relationship with our significant other to lessen our own discomfort. Or we allow others to insinuate themselves into our private world. This is called splitting. Both triangulation and splitting can lead to resentment and, ultimately, to mistrust, which destroys true intimacy."

Greg Febbraro, PhD, Licensed Psychologist, Windsor Heights, IA
www.counselingforgrowthandchange.com License# 00896
"A successful marriage is about more than just two people being passionate about one another. It involves companionship, compatibility and compromise over time. This is something I believe couples sometimes lose sight of over the course of their marriage."

Louise Mastromarino, Certified Counselor, Staten Island, NY
http://www.distantholistic.com/index.html
"A successful marriage takes guts, honesty, love, commitment and truth to survive."

Leslie Rouder, LCSW, CHT, Boca Raton, Florida
www.addadults.net
"Let go of your story when arguing, stick to the principle, not the content."

Michael Giordano, MSW, LICSW, Washington, D.C.
www.WhatIHearYouSaying.com License# LC3000893
"As a psychotherapist, I suggest that if you're feeling jealous, you take the opportunity to examine it. First, accept your jealousy. Then, try to see what is behind the jealousy. Hurt, anger or feelings of loneliness? There are many feelings that jealousy masks.

After you identify the feelings, you can then try to discuss it with your spouse. If you are able, try to do so in a non-blaming fashion. Claim your feelings. For example, 'When I think of your relationship with Kris, I feel lonely and forgotten.' You can then get reassurance. Your loved one will find it much easier to be there for you if you are not attacking her or him. If talking to your loved one is not possible, or if you find it too consuming, you may need other venues - like a support group, a best friend, or a therapist or counselor."

Stuart A. Kaplowitz, MFT, Chino, California
www.encouragingyourlife.com License# MFC 36347
"Intimacy is what we all yearn for. Connecting with our partner is one of the most important things we can do and unfortunately one of the easiest to overlook. In fact, I fear we screw this up all the time --but there is hope. Every single day, you have that power and ability to enhance that connection. It has to be you. No excuses; just get it done!"

Donna Pollard-Burton, MA, LMHC, NCC, BCC, Indianapolis, IN
www.cairncottagecounseling.com License# 39002176A
"Each of us has our own path to walk, but we are all connected to each other, to this planet, to life and we walk our paths together. In marriage, we make a conscious choice to walk with one another on these unique paths."

Dr. Sarah Villarreal, Psy.D, San Francisco, California
www.entelechywellness.com
"The research shows that women want to be treasured and men want to be respected."

Carmen Gloria Avendaño, LMFT, Wayzata, Minnesota
www.lifebalancetherapy.com License# 2104
"I have been married for 28 amazing, loving, passionate years. My secret is that I think of my husband as my 'boyfriend with benefits.' I flirt with him, send him sexy text messages, have lots of dates with him, and surprise him. I don't take him for granted. We always make our relationship a priority by spending intentional time together."

Larry Cappel, M.A., LMFT, Denver, Colorado
http://downtowndenvertherapy.com/ License# LMFT715
"Integrity, the Juice That Keeps Things Working
Integrity is one of the key ingredients that keep long-term relationships healthy. But many people don't realize that integrity is a two-way process. In order to have integrity with your spouse you first have to have integrity with yourself. As the saying goes, 'To thine own self be true.' This means being kindly honest with yourself and then with your spouse. If you agree just to get along, not considering your own needs and preferences, resentment builds over time. By the time you are empty-nesters that resentment becomes the poison that kills the relationship. Commit to keeping the space between the two of you clear of resentment so the poison can't build up."

Cindy Foster, LCSW, ACSW, NBCCH, Martinez, Georgia
mindbodystressreduction.com License# CSW002401
"Stay in the present moment. As we consciously pay attention in any given moment, we can choose to observe what is occurring within us and around us in a non-judgmental way. When the mind is focused in the present moment, it is not reacting to regrets, grievances or resentments of the past, nor speeding too far into the future with fears and anticipation. We can respond more thoughtfully and really enjoy our time with our spouse."

Dawn K. Kozarian, LMHC, NCC, Indianapolis, Indiana
www.KozarianCounseling.com License# 39001738A
"Keeping a bi-fold frame with a childhood picture of your spouse can help. This can be a reminder to view your partner with grace and know that nurturing the relationship will go a long way in creating an atmosphere where both can be human, make mistakes, learn from them, and ultimately thrive."

Marcel Schwantes, Life Design Coach, Chattanooga, Tennessee
www.marcelcoaching.com
"Wife: Understanding Your Husband

A man who is meeting his woman's needs from Part II will find that she will respond and meet four core needs that every man has: companionship, respect, support, and physical intimacy.

Companionship. A woman will respond with the kind of friendship that makes a man feel masculine—wanting to do things that he likes—golfing, watching Nascar, or taking you to your favorite action flick.

Respect. A woman will admire and respect her man and make him feel important, and that she values her husband. She will express the words 'I'm proud of you' often to affirm her husband's manhood.

Support. Every man needs to know his wife stands with him, encourages him, cheers for him, and has his back. She is a great encourager and supporter, motivating him to pursue his dreams and aspirations.

Physical Intimacy. Few things affirm a man in his masculinity, as does his wife's sexual responsiveness. If your sex life is fading, don't blame your wife. First look in the mirror and ask this question, 'Am I giving her what she needs?' Most likely if you are, and your wife is someone who takes care of her 'whole' being -- spiritually, mentally, and physically, you will get back one of your core needs: physical responsiveness, and an active and healthy sex life."

Jayne Raquepaw, PhD., Licensed Clinical Psychologist, Texas
www.myhoustonpsychologist.com
"Take pleasure in pleasuring your spouse. When your spouse is feeling good about you and the relationship because of how well you attend to your spouse, your spouse will give right back to you. Realize that what's good for your spouse is good for you. If both of you take this approach, you're in for a wonderful relationship."

William Hambleton Bishop, MA, Longmont, Colorado
www.thoughtsfromatherapist.com License# 6156
"Empathy is the key to creating a marriage filled with understanding, bonding, security, acceptance, resiliency, and compassion. Empathy is when a person opens up their emotional boundaries and allows another person's feeling to be cradled and nurtured within the loving hands of his/her understanding. Empathy is holding a narrative of another person and allowing yourself to feel the person's emotions related to his or her storyline while understanding that these are not your own emotions. Life has its fair share of difficulties… men and women both desire for their spouse to be present and to offer an empathetic ear with far greater frequency than they want their spouse to 'fix' their problem. In short, the key to happiness is to offer compassionate listening and to control your impulse to 'fix it.'"

Ellie Zarrabian, Ph.D., Spiritual Director, Los Angeles, California
www.centeronpeace.com
"Marriage is another path to self-enlightenment. Our partner mirrors for us what we need to look at within."

April Lok, Ph.D., Licensed Psychologist, Southlake, Texas
Doc-Lok.com
"Practice Grace. We all make mistakes. Knowing someone is going to hold each one against you generates fear, anger, stress, and defensiveness….which often leads to conflict—and more mistakes. Forgive your spouse the way you want to be forgiven, and you'll both experience a sense of freedom. Grace is the difference between walking on eggshells and walking on cloud nine."

Peter Gaffney, Psychiatrist, Sacramento, California
www.psychiatricadvice5cents.com
"A dear friend of mine, at his 80th birthday party, was asked by the
crowd how he had maintained such a successful and happy marriage
for all those years. He laughed and said, 'I found out the secret. Stop
disagreeing...!'"

Sharon Morgillo Freeman, PhD, PMHCNS-BC, Fort Wayne, IN
www.centerforbrieftherapy.com License# 70000153A
"Remember that each of us has those things we would like to change
in our partner and ourselves. However if your focus is on what you
would like to change in your partner, instead of what you are grateful
for, you will be unhappy, and most likely, single again."

Jody Eyre, MS LMFT, North Kingstown, Rhode Island
www.mfcounseling.com License# RI MFT000126
"Marriages are a unique paradox of balancing individual needs with
the needs of a spouse. This is oftentimes a very difficult thing to
accomplish successfully due to the barriers of communication.
Communicating effectively will require that both people in a marriage
manage their emotions, particularly when they don't want the same
things. Another important skill to develop is the ability to get back on
track after a disagreement has occurred, especially if the disagreement
has turned into an unpleasant argument. Couples who develop a
system to repair after an argument will be in a good position to have
positive interactions without either party feeling hostile about the
relationship. As married partners, it is vitally important to develop a
way to reset after a dispute."

Katherine Clausen, LCSW, Brooklyn, New York
katherineclausenlcsw.com License# 076379
"When two people get married, they become part of a larger whole.
The balancing act in marriage is for each person to maintain his/her
individual identity while also embracing an identity as husband or
wife. I think happy couples have figured out the balance of
togetherness and separateness that works for them."

Dee Desnoyers, M.Ed., LPC, Decatur, Georgia
www.atlantacounseling.org License# LPC005453
"Be aware of the stressors affecting your marriage. Long work hours, frequent business trips, and finances are not the only things that can wear on a relationship. Does your community--familial and societal-- affirm your relationship? It is important to find sources of support that respect and honor your spouse and family."

Tina Lepage, Psy.D., Psychologist, CEO/CFO, North Carolina
www.lepageassociates.com License# NC 2865
"Flexibility is extremely important when it comes to the success of marriage. People too often approach marriage with an agreed upon path without considering flexibility. For example, 'we will do a, b, and c over the years.' But that leaves no room for change and growth. The person agreeing to a, b, and c will not be the same exact person in 5, 10 or 20 years later, just by the happenstance of life providing new experiences and information. It can be hard when a spouse wants to change something that had been agreed upon, but the higher commitment is to the person and not the line item, which means being flexible and allowing for change."

Pam Snyder, LCSW, Arvada, Colorado
www.pamsnyderlcsw.com
"While life is always changing, there is a need for flexibility to adapt to changes and frequently evaluate your priorities. It is a juggling act to manage relationships, career, family, self-care, time with partner and whatever else may be a priority. A successful marriage is one, which is open to change, while maintaining the marital relationship as a priority. "

Jodi Milstein, LMFT, Los Angeles, California
www.JodiMilstein.com and www.RockStarTherapy.com
"A marriage requires similar attention as one would give to raising a child. The relationship grows and thrives through continual attention, nurturing, love, understanding, warmth, communication, trust and compassion."

Dr. Jill Zimmerman, LMFT, Hudson, Wisconsin
www.integracounselingservices.com License# LMFT 189-124
"There's nothing worse than being parented by your spouse. Respect each others' personal decisions knowing both of you are educated and responsible people."

Daniel Cowley, PsyD, Charleston, South Carolina
www.INGing.org License# 438
"A successful traditional marriage begins with two healthy individuals who are growing in self-awareness, growing in self-love, and growing in self-forgiveness, who value being truthful, who refuse to believe anything bad anyone says about them as a manipulative ploy, who ask others what they are thinking or feeling—or why they are doing or not doing something—rather than guessing and then acting as though their guesses were correct, and who value the core values of honor, respect, and devotion to duty.

Two such individuals as above, in union, strive to be sensitive to the other's needs, purposefully behave in loving ways to the other, and forgive the other's failed attempts at trying to live up to the credo above. In such a marriage, the two partners strive to be gracious to the other, hold the fewest demands and expectations of the other, work at learning how to listen and communicate with open heart and mind, and tell the other what they think they mean by what they say, and ask for feedback—and ask for it a different way if they don't get it."

David Earle, LPC, business coach, author, Baton Rouge, LA
LAhttp://Therapists.PsychologyToday.com/rms/34753 License# 1834
"Almost no other opportunity avails us to know ourselves better than participating in the mystery of marriage. In this unparalleled experience, we invest our hopes, dreams, and expectations in another person, anticipating them to protect us from our deepest fear, ourselves. Most happiness is not dependent on the relationship with a significant other but more dependent on our attitudes and our relationship with ourselves. The ability to love another is directly related to healthy self-love."

Elizabeth Sloan, L.P.C., L.C.P.C., McLean, Virgina
www.CaringCouples.com
"Take the long view: Before making a hasty decision, think forward to your 25th wedding anniversary party. If you were given a toast, what would you like people to say about you and your marriage?"

Lind Butler, LPC, LMFT, Houston, Texas
www.lindbutler.com License # LPC 11187 & License# LMFT 2856
"Couples in which one spouse has bipolar disorder can face specific challenges. In order for the marriage to be successful, both partners need to have a deep understanding of Bipolar Disorder, as well as how it specifically manifests in that individual and in the relationship. There are several key factors for this to occur:
1. Both individuals are willing to be educated and have a thorough understanding of the disorder.
2. Compassion, with an absence of 'blame' is vital when moods are intense.
3. Partners need to strive not to take episodes of depression or mania personally.
4. Before the onset of extreme mood fluctuations, often one spouse recognizes this before the other. It is helpful if there is openness to discuss and strategize together how to minimize excessive stimulus and stressors.

In a supportive relationship, where vulnerability and openness are valued, some of the difficulties of Bipolar Disorder can be greatly reduced. Couples can have an increased opportunity for intimacy by working together to create a calm, safe emotional environment within the marriage."

Frieda L. Ferrick, Licensed Marriage Family Therapist, CA
www.friedaferrick.com
"This might sound strange but in order to have a successful marriage it is important to acknowledge loss when you come together to get married. The loss is about making a choice that will change your life in one direction, which is to live a life of being married not single."

Elayne Savage, PhD, Licensed Marriage Family Therapist, CA
http://www.QueenofRejection.com License# MFC 17077
"Coming from a place of yearning goes a lot further than complaining. Know what you need from your spouse and ask for it clearly and respectfully. This will make all the difference in the world!"

Trudy M. Johnson, LMFT, Buena Vista, Colorado
www.missingpieces.org License# 755
"DITCH THE WORD PERFECT. I've heard so many times the angst of married couples after only a year of marriage. They are always 'so surprised' that their mate isn't the *perfect person* they were expecting them to be. You see, many people get married with the *expectation* that the person they married will take away alllllllllllll their pain! How disappointing when that person doesn't happen. A much better perspective would be for the two of you to be as healthy as possible when you get married. When couples have dealt with their painful past individually, they will be far less disappointed to find out their spouse is not after all perfect."

Lee Crespi, LCSW, New York, New York
www.LeeCrespiLCSW.com License# 020649
"All love contains elements of ambivalence. Don't think that just because there are things about your spouse that you dislike or days that you can't stand him/her that it means you don't love him/her. Indifference is the true opposite of love, not hate. So go ahead and hate sometimes. You'll love each other that much more as a result."

Rachel Moheban, LCSW, New York, New York
www.TheRelationshipSuite.com License# R053394-1
"It is very important to have a sense of self before you enter into a partnership, you must know who you are and what your triggers and sensitive points are. You have to discuss and process these with your partner in an effort to work on prevention because this can escalate and take on a life of it's own after many years of marriage. Kindness, generosity, teamwork and insight into each other can make a big difference."

Jay Jameson, LMFT, Laguna Hills, California
jayjameson.com License# MFC 34802
"'You can be right or you can be married.' This is an old adage in the
marital therapy world for a reason. Many married couples engage in
brutal and harmful arguing just so they can try to prove that they are
right. This is the quick road to an unhappy marriage or divorce. Letting
go of your ego and not needing to be right can make a marriage a
successful one. It also sends a clear message that you respect your
spouse's opinion, even if it differs from yours."

Frieda Ling, Licensed Marriage & Family Therapist, Arizona
www.psychologytoday.com License# LMFT-10199
"A wise man says, 'Don't sweat the small stuff.' In marriage, the small
stuff is often the overt manifestation of the covert big stuff. So use the
small stuff to locate and deal with the big stuff before the cyst turns
cancerous."

Ellen Farrell, MA, LPC, EEM-CP, Savannah, Georgia
www.ellenfarrell.com
"As we change in life, going through professional, family, and
personal challenges and transitions, we need to realize that life is a
roller coaster. What time is it in your life that your marriage inhabits?
When I had children, it felt like my body was part of a science
experiment. Now, we have children preparing to leave home, aging
parents, death, and our own mortality to process! Change is the ever-
present given. One's body and physical abilities will shift, as well as
our professional, personal and/or spiritual needs (if we are paying
attention). However, we can appreciate the vigor of youth, sexuality,
and energy – and honor each other as we go through the transitions of
aging, coping with financial and self-identity changes, and we can
have new needs and ways of expressing our truth, joy and love."

Michael T. Halyard, LMFT, MBA, San Francisco, California
www.SFtherapy.com License# MFC42122
"Quickly admit when you're wrong and apologize; apologies are
relatively painless but net huge rewards."

Juli Fraga, Psy.D., Licensed Psychologist, San Francisco, CA
www.drjulifraga.com License# PSY20718
"Celebratory events like having children are often stressful to
marriages. Some tips for taking care of your marriage during early
childhood years includes:
1. Don't forget the small things- voicemails, emails and
communication that lets your spouse know you are thinking of them.
2. During times of stress in the very early child-rearing days,
remember that everything is temporary and this will not be how it is
forever.
3. For at least 15 minutes a day spend time talking with your spouse.
4. Lean on neighbors and friends to start a baby-sitting cooperative so
you can go out on a date.
5. Realize that everything changes and being open to and accepting
change is part of making marriage work."

Jonathan Swinton, LMFT, Salt Lake City, Utah
www.swintoncounseling.com
"Selfishness is the poison of relationships. If you are experiencing
problems in your relationship, one of the best things you can do is
honestly ask yourself, 'What am I doing that I need to change to make
this relationship better?' The answer to that question will do more to
help your marriage than any amount of focus on your spouse's
limitations."

Janis R. Cohen, MSW, LCSW, Atlanta, Georgia
www.cohenfamilycounseling.com
"When you are each other's 'soft and safe place to land' and you can be
your most vulnerable; where all of your weaknesses, fears,
insecurities, and past mistakes are unconditionally accepted and you
heal from the love you give and receive from your spouse."

Anita Gadhia-Smith, PsyD, Washington, D.C.
practicaltherapy.net License# 11151
"A healthy marriage grows over time if both people continue to work
on their own side of the issues."

Dr. Andrew Mendonsa, Clinical Psychologist, Sacramento, CA
www.DrMendonsa.com License# PSY23208
"What makes a marriage a success? In my view it's waking up everyday and asking what new aspect of 'us' can we uncover and build on today. It avoids the stagnation that often floods relationships. Being willing to reflect when you've fallen down and not just want to get up, get a bandaid and move on."

Stacy Watkins, LPC, Austin, Texas
www.therapyinsession.net License# TX 62220
"When it comes to a spouse struggling with food and/or body image issues even the strongest couples falter. When a spouse is saying, 'I feel fat' or 'I'm struggling with food,' he/she is often dismissed, misunderstood, or given solutions to fix this 'problem.' It is most helpful to remember that the food and/or body image talk is a smoke screen, hiding an emotional experience that isn't being verbalized. Spouses can maintain success in their marriage when they can approach these comments with curiosity, warmth, and the intension to help the other keep talking about what he/she is feeling. This might sound like, 'What's going on?' or 'Tell me more about what you are struggling with.' These type of questions help partners go beyond the surface smoke screens and connect and know each other better on a deeper, more fulfilling level."

Nicole Eaton, LCSW, CCHT, Boise, Idaho
www.nicoleeaton.com
"You know how you have that friend you go shopping with, or that one who is like a built-in therapist? How about the one you can sit in silence with and have a drink? Rarely is that all-in-one, so acknowledge your spouse is not going to be all of those things, all the time."

Lisa Hartwell, PsyD, RN, Honolulu, Hawaii
www.hidrlisa.com License# Psy800
"You do not choose your family. You choose to be married every day."

Eleanor Laser, Ph.D, Chicago, Illinois
www.laserhypnosis.com
"How you greet your spouse and groom yourself leaves a lasting impression through out the day and evening. So my advice is to look good, smell good and sound good."

Miranda Palmer, LMFT, Modesto, California
http://counselingmodesto.com License# MFC 42393
"It is almost never about WHAT you fight about, it is always about HOW you fight. We get to see everyday the WRONG way to fight as we see people whose relationships end- that is the norm nowadays. Learn how to have a healthy process of conflict, and your conflicts can bring you closer together instead of pulling you apart."

Ken Waldman, Ph.D., Houston, Texas
counselinghouston.com License# Psychologist # 2-1460 TX
"One of the keys to reducing conflict in marriage has to do with issues related to criticism and defensiveness. No one likes to be criticized. I believe this to be universal, regardless of gender, race, religion, sexual orientation, socioeconomic status, ability, education, or culture. Everyone reacts to criticism the same way: they get defensive. This is the natural, automatic response to criticism. If there are exceptions, they are quite rare: Perhaps Mahatma Ghandi, Martin Luther King, the Dalai Lama or Mother Theresa didn't automatically respond defensively. For the rest of us, defensiveness is virtually automatic, and not responding defensively takes intentionality, thought, practice, skill and patience. Not responding defensively when you feel you are being attacked requires being able to ignore your natural reactions in order to be able to do something extraordinary."

Leslie Karen Sann, MA, LCPC, Chicago & Geneva, Illinois
http://www.lesliesann.com
"Be grateful for the opportunity to give and receive love. Nourish your connection by turning complaints into requests. Take responsibility for creating solutions rather than focusing on problems and watch your relationship flourish."

Diane DuBois, LMFT, San Francisco & East Bay, California
www.duboistherapy.com License# MFC30808
"Use humor if you think it won't irritate your partner, for example if your spouse is a bit cranky you might lighten things up by saying something like, 'Uh oh, did you let Mr. Cranky-Pants out again?'"

Ellen Farrell, MA, LPC, EEM-CP, Savannah, Georgia
www.ellenfarrell.com
"I remember what brought us together, and our shared dream of happiness. My husband and I met at a lecture given by a visiting healer from California, at a Channeler's loft in NYC (in the Village). When we sat next to each other, I had a cosmic shift that made me think I was going to fly through the roof. What was amazing is that when we turned to each other in those moments, and shared what we'd felt, it was the same. Later, we talked until dawn, and he proposed to me that night. I remember to value what my spirit knows that my mind alone could never know, as it relates to my life, and my marriage (we celebrate our 25th anniversary in the autumn of this year, 2011)."

Sari Fine Shepphird, Ph.D., Clinical Psychologist, California
DrShepp.com License #PSY20922
"Trust and friendship are even more important than chemistry between partners. When you feel safe and valued you are more likely to both ask for what you need AND think about how to please your spouse. Chemistry is fleeting but trust, security and friendship have long lasting benefits in every area of marriage, including sex! Friends will usually go the extra mile for each other to ensure they experience pleasure, and they feel safe enough to ask for what pleases themselves, so find friendship with your spouse for a better sex life - and a better overall partnership."

Lynn Hoyland, Licensed Marriage & Family Therapist, Arizona
www.lynnhoyland.com License# 0346
"Consider asking yourself this question every morning 'where do I want my marriage to be at the end of the day, and what do I need to do to get myself there?'"

Christopher Old, MFT, LPC, NCC, Truckee, California
www.mountainmentalhealth.com License# MFC 44697
"Like a house, a marriage needs to be built on a solid foundation and that foundation is commitment. You can learn many great communication skills, ways of cooperating, and other important relationship enhancing techniques but none of that will matter if it is not built on a solid foundation of commitment. What you are both committed to in the relationship should be discussed often to keep it alive and fresh. Too often couples state their commitment to each other at their wedding and then never again."

Jennifer Kogan, LICSW, Washington, D.C.
www.JenniferKogan.com License# LC 302938
"Try to learn your spouse's inner psychological terrain by asking them open-ended questions about their hopes and dreams. You will most certainly learn something new every time. This process will bring you closer and give you insight to hold on to and refer back to when times are good and bad."

Shelly Clubb, M.S., M.A., NCC, Denver, Colorado
www.transformativecounselingservices.com License# 12176
"The best marriages are like really interesting stories that need to be told. We need to imagine a bigger, richer narrative apart from just our own. Our marriages go through all sorts of trials, villains and muses are part of the plot lines, characters enter and leave, homes and places and ways of living are part of the tale that requires an imagination beyond each of us to become something larger than either of us could have lived without our beloved."

Jay White, LPC, Mount Pleasant, South Carolina
www.charlestontherapy.com License# 4619
"Kids are a wonderful addition to the family; however, they do not outrank your spouse. The moment you find yourself agreeing more with the children than your husband is the moment you start to lose both. Agree on a parenting plan as a team and stick to it, whether things seem a big deal or small."

Lori Carpenos, LMFT, Hartford, Connecticut
www.3Principlestherapy.com License# LMFT000551
"Whether we take something personally or see it from the other person's perspective is a choice we make in the moment."

Joyce Thompson, MS, LCMFT, Wichita, Kansas
www.emotionaljourney.org License# 734
"It's important to honor your spouse on special occasions. Gifts, even small ones, can send such a special message to the one you love. It can tell them they are loved, appreciated, and worth remembering on their special day."

Shoshana Kobrin, LMFT, Author, Walnut Creek, California
www.kobrinkreations.com License# MFT 23716
"The 'intimacy imprint' that we learned from our parents greatly affects our attachment style – how we bond or connect to our spouse. *Pleasers* give and give, then become resentful that they're not getting enough back. *Avoiders* are independent and self-sufficient, steering clear of feelings and intimacy. *Ambivalents* want intense connection but easily feel rejected. Then they withdraw. *Controllers'* slogan is 'I'm always right.' *Victims* feel helpless and try their utmost to keep the peace. A happy marriage consists of *Secure Connectors* – open, trusting, giving and receiving respect and caring, with a firm sense of self. Which one are you?"

Charlyne Gelt, Ph.D., Clinical Psychologist, Encino, California
www.drgelt.com License# PSY22909
"The 'magnetic draw' and hidden forces towards certain relationships may lead to suffering, yet it also offers the couple an opportunity to look into their own lives and begin to confront the true source of their pain. The couple learns how to identify, confront and heal the kind of wounds whose source remains a mystery. We were so well trained to listen and obey, and found it easy to go into self-protective, altered states. It's time to learn new tools! You cannot change the relationship without first knowing the self and changing the self."

Nadim S. Ali, MA, LPC, ICCDP, GCADC-III, Atlanta, Georgia
Nadimali.com License# LPC 03775
"Marriage has seasons and one must prepare for the marital seasonal changes as we do climatic changes. The hope of spring = The newness of marriage. The heat of summer = The intensity of intimacy. The reaping of fall = The benefits of marriage. The challenges of winter = The obstacles and choices that every couple face in marriage."

Katrina Kuzyszyn-Jones, Psy.D. Durham, North Carolina
www.lepageassociates.com License# NC 3728
"We all make mistakes and hurt one another at some point in our marriage. It's easy to decide not to forgive someone, it's harder to forgive and acknowledge the part we play in the dynamics of our relationships. Although there are certainly times when one person does something egregious against the other, most often, it takes two to create a problem, and usually two to fix it."

Melinda Yachnin, LCPC, Lagrange, Illinois
http://www.melindayachnin.com License# 180-005280
"My grandmother used to complain regularly about the bright red new barn that was built in her old garden, just outside her kitchen window. 'Why does it have to be red?' she'd say, 'It just sticks out like a sore thumb.' She missed her old view of green grass, trees and corn growing across the road. One day, after spending the day shopping in a neighboring town, she returned home, put her bags of groceries down on the table, and noticed that outside her kitchen window the barn was no longer red. Without saying a word, my grandfather had spent that day painting the side of the barn that faced her window green to match the surroundings. She was happier than if he'd bought her a diamond ring."

Steve Moore, LMFT, Calabasas, California
www.stevemoorecounseling.com License# MFT 23396
"A successful marriage is large enough to hold the dreams of both partners, and the only agenda is to encourage your partner to evolve into the person he/she came here to be."

Yvonne Wilson, Clinical Psychologist, LMFT, Corona, California
yvonnewilsonphd.com License# MFT26092 & Psy17078
"Two lovebirds can soar across the sky with limitless possibilities.
When out of love it is like a bird with a broken wing."

Nicole Story, Ed.S, LMFT, Jacksonville Beach, Florida
www.OceansideFamilyTherapy.com License# LMFT MT2208
"Champagne bubble baths (or showers) for two every weekend. Ways
to celebrate, indulge, seize the moment, relax, show appreciation, and
honor one another completely."

Peter Sholley, MFT Registered Intern (#57471), California
www.sholleysomatics.com Supervisor Frances Verrinder, MFT 11970
"Design a Relationship Constitution to set out your goals and
intentions clearly. Work on a document together that expresses the
hopes and courage (biggest heart/biggest life) of each spouse or
partner, something to return to that can help shape the mutual
imagination in the relationship. First draft a list of intentions each
partner has, including what they want to bring into being, how they
want to treat and be treated, what they would like to experience with
their mate, what brings them to a higher level of purpose and
connection. Coming up with questions to answer is part of the
exercise. Beyond marriage or partnership vows, this can be a
document designed to grow and breathe with the relationship through
time. Returning to this mutually devised 'constitution' can help a
couple weather storms, stay focused on positive intentions, and grow
together even as they grow independently."

Susan Addis, Ph.D., Gainesville, Florida
www.DrSusanAddis.com License# PY 5626
"Not only is it important to have your own needs met, but also it is just
as important to listen, really listen, to the needs of your spouse. Just
because you do not feel that something is important to you, if it holds
importance to your spouse, then it should be just as important to you.
You don't have to understand it or even agree with it. Just honor it and
respect it as well as you can."

Dr. Jack McInroy, Psychologist, Denver, Colorado

www.DrMcInroy.com License# CO 518

"Two farmers went to seed their crops. One threw them on the ground and left them for months to grow. The other fertilized, weeded, watered with tender loving care. Which grew the best crops? Obvious answer. We treat our most important relationships in the world like these 2 farmers. Only those with conscious, tender loving care flourish while the others die or remain stagnant. Which farmer are you?"

Kaerensa Craft, LCSW, New York, New York

www.kcraft.info

"Meeting with individuals for psychotherapy, I am struck by how often people feel compelled to act, to make decisions that have enormous consequences, as a result of feelings that are either transient or unclear; and based on situations that can, and often do, change with time. Emotions are a powerful thing for us humans, and we often experience them with such a sense of urgency, as if we need to act right away, to follow our hearts without delay, lest we miss out on something that we can never get again. I would like to offer couples the wisdom to give themselves and their relationships the benefit of time and exploration before making hasty decisions based on seemingly-urgent emotions. A favorite quote of mine, by Rainer Maria Rilke, is that 'No feeling is final.' I would also add that feelings are not facts. All too often, they are conflicted, confusing, irrational and illogical camouflage for deeper, often contradictory feelings, worthy of in-depth exploration with an unbiased, interested professional. Give yourself and your relationship an opportunity to really get to the heart of feelings and urges before acting upon them."

Lynn Saladino, Psy.D., Boston, Massachusetts

drlynnsaladino.com License# 9300

"Remember that your spouse is of primary importance in your life and remain aligned with them. By strengthening this partnership you will be able to better manage difficulties with your parents, children, and work conflicts. This will also help you both to continue feeling valued, supported, and important in your marriage."

J Kimbrough Benson, EdS, LPC, LMFT, Baton Rouge, Louisiana
www.rivercitypsychotherapy.co License MFT 767 License LPC 2291
"If you feel some sadness when your spouse leaves then counseling
may work. Hearing his/her car pull up in the evening brings out your
smile, then I'm encouraged. If you dance because he leaves, we have
lots of work to do."

Ellie Zarrabian, Ph.D., Spiritual Director, Los Angeles, California
www.centeronpeace.com
"When the good times end and there is conflict, that is when the
marriage begins. Most people think that's the end of the marriage.
That's wrong, that's just the beginning."

TL Holt, MA, Knoxville, Tennessee
tlholt.com
"In my experience with individuals and couples dealing with the
physical, emotional, and spiritual impact of substance abuse in their
marriage, I believe that it is vital to understand that the behavior is
many times linked to an internal struggle. In marriage, it is not enough
to simply ignore the behavior and hope that it dissipates with time. In
order for a marriage to be of success a couple must be proactive (with
all aspects of the relationship, not just substance abuse) in order to
foster a relationship of trust, safety, and open communication. So that
in those moments when struggles rise to the surface, the weight of
dishonesty and fear can fall to the ground, leaving the marriage
strengthened because the battle was not walked alone, but rather as a
unified pair."

Julie Uhernik, RN, LPC, NCC, Parker, Colorado
www.julieuhernik.com License# LPC 4714 & RN 110129
"Some great words of wisdom regarding marriage that I have found
come from Carl Whitaker MD, a psychotherapist and family therapist.
He offered succinct advice on establishing important boundaries in
marriages and families by suggesting… 'Enjoy your mate more than
your kids, and be childish with your mate'. Great advice to keep proper
perspective and attention focused on a healthy marriage."

Karen Stewart, Psy. D., Clinical Psychologist, Santa Monica, CA
www.drkrarenstewart.com
"When couples are from different religious backgrounds, certain problems can arise if they are not discussed in an open and honest format. As uncomfortable as these discussions can be, I highly recommend each spouse express EXACTLY what they want to bring to the relationship from their religious background so the couple can decide how both backgrounds can be honored in the marriage. For instance, if one spouse is Jewish and the other is Christian, it would be important to see how each partner feels about attending Christmas service, having a Menorah in the home, a Christmas tree, etc. These discussions are crucial to have when the couple is beginning to talk seriously about their future and ideally before they are married. If these issues arise while the couple is married, I would suggest that the couple create a compromise to honor both partners' feelings and family's religious background."

Wendi Svoboda, LCSW, Burbank, California
www.wsvobodalcsw.com License# LCS24639
"Do not comment or criticize your spouse's driving skills, or lack thereof. Remember that driving is about control. In a relationship, spouses are often seeking to reach a level of control that feels good for both. Trust that your partner knows where the destination is, and how to get there. As a metaphor for marriage, you will both take turns in the driver's seat; but the ultimate goal is to trust in your partner's ability, sit back and enjoy the ride, and arrive at your destination safely."

Elizabeth Boyajian, M.Ed, LCPC, Topsham, Maine
http://www.options-counseling.com/ License# 3300
"I would like to quote Thoreau who said, 'Our truest life is when we are in our dreams awake.' This speaks to mindfulness, being fully present for what life is offering to us, and remaining in our thinking parts of our brain, so our quest for our passions, and relationships will ebb and flow as in nature, marveling at all that is right here and right now."

Jeffrey Chernin, Ph.D. MFT, Los Angeles, California
www.jeffreychernin.com
"If someone goes to a restaurant and has a bad experience, they're
likely to tell 5 or 6 people about it. If someone has a good experience,
they're likely to tell 1 or 2 people. In other words, we have a tendency
to vent. When it comes to marriage, switch the ratio. For every
complaint or criticism you share with your spouse, share 5 to 6
compliments or words of appreciation. This will help make each of
you feel close to each other."

Joyce Thompson, MS, LCMFT, Wichita, Kansas
www.emotionaljourney.org License# 734
"Are you or your spouse a shopaholic? When you find yourself
shopping for 'things' that you really don't want or need, it's because
you are 'shopping' in all the wrong places. Stop, take a few deep
breaths, and try to figure out what's going on. Chances are, you have
unmet emotional needs, which is impacting your marriage. No matter
how many bags you carry home or how much you spend, you'll never
find the 'right' thing with money. With the help of a caring therapist,
you can find out what those unmet needs might be, so that you can
work towards making your marriage a success."

Sheryl Leytham, Ph.D., Psychologist, Des Moines, Iowa
Sherylleytham.com License# PSY 583
"If you have a selfish and self-centered spouse, it is hard to accept they
may never really understand your goals, feelings and opinions. That is
just not how they live in the world. You can successfully live in your
marriage by following a few guidelines. They are: 1) Understand that
their apparent lack of understanding of your position, feelings or goals
is due to the self-centeredness. Any efforts to force understanding by
pleading, lecturing or similar actions is likely to fail. 2) Waiting to
follow your goals until your spouse approves means you may never
reach your goals. Their goals will always come first 3) Love them for
who they are and accept their limitations 6) Learn how to
communicate boundaries about what is acceptable to you and what is
not."

Lynn Saladino, Psy.D., Boston, Massachusetts
drlynnsaladino.com License# 9300
"Make a set time during the week to check in with each other about your relationship. This should be a time that is free from distractions, such as cell phones, children, and work. Use this time to air annoyances or ways that would help you feel supported by each other. The intention of this weekly routine is to help you stay connected, avoid building resentment, and improve your ability to communicate directly about your relationship."

Dr. Stephen Trudeau, Psychologist, Westlake Village, California
www.HumansGuide.com License# PSY19669
"Invest EARLY. Couples therapy is not just for divorce anymore! Taking the time to invest in your marriage early is a strong predictor of future success. Pre marital counseling lays the groundwork for the future of dealing with the ups and downs that occur naturally throughout each relationship. Couples who have undergone some sort of pre marital counseling or marriage retreat report more satisfying marriages with less fighting, arguing, and hurt feelings. They also survive longer and avoid the bad behaviors that later are insurmountable in couples therapy. I have worked with many married couples that say if they knew then what they know now, they would not have behaved badly and ruined their relationship. Learning things like; overall sexual expectations, who takes the trash out, financial attitudes, arguing styles, negotiating strategies, leisure activities, shopping or sports addictions, etc. All of these can and should be discussed early on in the relationship and not just glossed over because we are 'in love.' We don't have to agree on everything, but being aware of the issues can give us realistic expectations for our relationship."

Larry L. Langford, MFT Intern (#60859) Fresno, California
www.larrylangfordtherapy.com Supervisor Brenda Kent, MFT 29581
"A successful marriage is an equilibrium of hearts and minds, a refusal to own or be owned, to conquer or be conquered, a willingness to give more than might be asked and to demand less than might seem needed."

Jaleh Donaldson

Cyndie Westrich, M.A., A.T.R.-BC, LPC, Marietta, Georgia
www.easel-arttherapy.com
"A successful marriage is one that has their priorities straight. Priorities: God, our marriage, our family. In that order…God, our marriage, our family…every time."

Stephanie Mihalas, Ph.D., NCSP, Los Angeles, California
www.askdrstephanie.com License# PSY 23268
"A child born with a developmental disability is a reminder that marriage takes hard work, dedication, and that your child is a little blessing to strengthen a marriage and force a couple to constantly remind one another what they love about their life together, and with their little angel."

Nicole Imbraguglio, Psy.D., Psychologist, Durham, North Carolina
www.lepageassociates.com
"Oh, the classic power struggle for the television remote (or who gets to decide what you're having for dinner or which way is the best way to get from Point A to Point B). The best way to deal with repetitive arguments that are far from life-or-death matters is on two levels. One level is to ask yourself, 'How important is this issue to me really?' If you rate the level of importance below a 7 on a scale of 1-10 (10 being most important), then let it go. (It's also okay to ask your spouse how important it is to them to get a better understanding of their take on the issue.) Part of participating in a mature adult relationship and making your marriage a success is recognizing that you will not get it your way all the time. The other level is the problem-solving level. Establish some ground rules around the issue if it continues to be a problem. If you watch some television with your spouse every evening, divide up the week where each person gets 2 nights to solely make TV choices and the remaining 3 nights are compromise nights (where neither of you get to watch what you *want* to watch but what you are both *willing* to watch). For the nights you aren't making the TV choices, take responsibility for your happiness and read a book, work on a crossword, browse the internet, or any other activity that makes you happy. If all else fails, spring for the DVR!"

Brittany Neece, LMFT-A, Austin, Texas
www.brittanyneece.com License# 201534
"Do you have the same argument over and over again? Is it always about the same issue? Don't be discouraged. Many couples have problems that seem unresolvable as they continue to communicate and argue the about the same problem they seem to be stuck on. The key is to start communicating about the problem differently, not necessarily to try to solve it. Once a couple can begin to see the problem from different angles and perspectives, it may naturally change the way they communicate about it, and ultimately shift the way they address the issue."

Dr. Jennifer A. Bennice, Licensed Clinical Psychologist, SC
www.wecharleston.com
"Accepting and loving your partner for his/her strengths and limitations, while also providing support and encouragement as he/she continues to grow as a person."

Hope Weiss, LCSW, Longmont, Colorado
www.HopeIsThere.com License# 34
"A successful marriage is one where conflict about raising your children takes place away from the children. Otherwise your kids will not respect you or your parenting authority, and they will use that conflict to play the two of you against each other."

Julie Nelligan, PhD, Licensed Psychologist, Portland, Oregon
www.julienelligan.com
"For women it is important to keep your girlfriends. I have often seen women abandon their friendships when they get married and start raising a family. It can be hard to fit in one more thing and friendships can sometimes seem a little too self-indulgent. But maintaining your friendships is well worth the effort. Girlfriends make your life richer by sharing their perspectives, listening when you need a shoulder, and for being there in ways that your husband and children can't be. You can't be all things to your husband and family and they can't be all things for you. Sometimes it takes a girlfriend (or two)."

Daniel L DeGoede, Ph.D, Clinical Psychologist, Pioneertown, CA
www.drdanieldegoede.com License# PSY9479
"Riding on a motorcycle together we learned 'It's not the destination, it's the journey' and, most importantly 'No Whining.' When you're riding you quickly learn it is dangerous to do anything other than 'pay attention.'"

Cristina Castagnini, Ph.D., Psychologist, Livermore, California
www.pathtohealtherapy.com License# PSY20435
"The most unfortunate thing I have found in our society is that we are all painted a picture of a 'Hollywoood-ized' version of love and romance that sets up for unrealistic expectations of what our spouse 'should' be, how love 'should' be, and how the 'perfect' relationships are. We constantly feel as if we are not in the 'perfect' relationship with the 'perfect-enough' person, which is why I believe many of us are so quick to either believe that we are not in a good enough relationship, with the 'not so good enough person', and feel unfulfilled in the relationships we have rather than working on the ones we are in. To help make your marriage a success I challenge everyone to try not to expect too much of one another, yourself or of your relationship. Instead, try to focus on what brought you together, what you appreciate about one another, and stop thinking that you will find some version of what you see on the big or little screen because you will be chasing something that does not exist."

Margaret Jordan, PhD, Houston, Texas
www.drmargaretjordan.com License# 31855
"A paradox of marriage is that it offers the potential for both people to grow and become the best they can be, but the relationship also allows the greatest possibility for the individuals' weaknesses and struggles to affect each other negatively. While marriage can facilitate growth and improvement, just being married does not heal psychological problems. It takes strength for a couple to acknowledge that they need or could benefit from help when problems emerge. This is not a sign of weakness or the end of the marriage, necessarily, but a start of a deepened connection and commitment."

Jennifer Ritchie-Goodline, Licensed Psychologist, Centennial, CO
www.drjenniferritchiegoodline.com
"Start each day with a kiss; say 'I love you' before you part; greet each other when you return home; find clear, concrete ways to communicate to your spouse that you care. Sometimes the little things really are the big things and set the stage for your interactions."

Diana J Bowen, LCPC, Gardiner, Maine
www.counselingpath.com License# CC2965
"Beginnings and Endings: Within the connections that people share there is inevitable discord, and misunderstandings that pull couples apart. Detaching from someone we love can feel like a death. With time and the giving of space, conflicts are healed. Relationship then contains within it moments of rebirth, of the commitment and affection that brought you together, and the choice to keep going forward."

Andrea Berry, MHR, ATR-BC, LPC, NCC, Laramie, Wyoming
www.wyomingarttherapy.com License# LPC 1049, NBCC 216654
"Consider carefully the motivation behind your beloved's behaviors before becoming enraged, hurt or frustrated. With reflection, conversation and an open mind you may find out that they had your best interest as their intention all along.

A couple entered my office for supportive counseling, after a lengthy guided discussion she learned that he washed her car every week because many years before she had said, 'it is so sweet you do these things for me …' She had long forgotten this comment; choosing to think he was making a weekly statement about her slovenly car habits. Once she realized his motivation she could enjoy the gift and love."

Joyce Dolberg Rowe, LMHC, Hull, Massachusetts
www.MentalHealthCounseling.biz License #91
"It is my firm belief that if we treat our family members as politely and respectfully as we would treat our boss's child, it is a win - win for all. As spouses, we must show the TLC to one another that we would extend to our best friend; after all, that is why we are together."

Valerie Chu, MA, ATR-BC, LCAT, Brooklyn, New York
www.artspringnyc.com License# 001304
"Switch places once in a while. Put yourself in the shoes of your
spouse for a day. It helps to increase your empathy for each other and
you might learn something about how your spouse might experience
you as well."

Jan Talen, LMFT, Grand Rapids, Michigan
www.funlifellc.com License# 4101006087
"In it to win it! This phrase points us in a number of directions! Are
you in your marriage to win for yourself or to win for your spouse?
The success in your marriage may depend on your willing attitude to
make a winning situation for both of you. So, be a great team player
and encourage, coach, support and teach yourself and your spouse the
ways that would make your life together a WIN!"

Genevieve Jacobs, M.A., Burlington, Vermont
http://wateranddreams.com License# 097 0000640
"I was chopping garlic for supper when he busted out 'It's all YOUR
fault that we are STUCK here!'

We had built and sailed together a small boat with our two black and
white 'tuxedo' cats across two vast oceans when we were in our
twenties. When he busted out with this accusation, we'd arrived to
anchor in utter paradise, Hiva Oa, Marquesas Islands, home of
hibiscus and sweetest smiles of pure love. Where your worst worry is
that you might get knocked by a coconut falling on your head on your
way to do the laundry in the fresh water river.

I chopped the garlic extra fine that night, considering his words. True.
Absolutely true, actually. Then I stepped up on deck and stripped and
jumped in the water. Let it all flow away, away. There are sharks in
that bay. But there are also sharks in the heart of your closest and most
trusted companion. Surrender. Victory over fear. Give yourself always
to the spiritual truth above the petty concerns of the ego. He threw me
a line and I came back aboard."

Tabi R.Upton, MA, LPC, Chattanooga, Tennessee
www.tabiupton.com and www.chattanoogacounselor.com
"Sharing a vision together can make a marriage a success. My parents shared a vision for their lives (they both wanted to be missionaries and to work in ministry together) and considered their marriage to each other to be an expression of God's love for his people."

Marcus Ambrester, M.A., Nashville, Tennessee
www.marcusambrester.com and www.newvisionworkshop.com
"My wife and I had placed our order at Noodles & Co. We were the only customers in the place. While waiting for our food, we were smooching and hugging and my wife says, 'You know we are doing this wrong.' 'What do you mean?' I said smiling. 'We are not acting like we are married.' 'Sweetie, we've been married five years. We are just acting like we are married to two *other* people.'"

Anna Valenti, LCSW (License# 11769), Phoenix, Arizona
www.annavalenti.com or www.SANEresources.org
"Get a little adventurous in the bedroom, as long as you're both feeling safe and mutually agreeable."

Elizabeth Boyajian, M.Ed, LCPC, Topsham, Maine
http://www.options-counseling.com/ License# 3300
"For marriage success, each person needs to be fiscally responsible. This means taking care of ones bills while considering the couple not just ones self. Responsibility for finances affords them with opportunities to grow together. Being able to rely on the other in a partnership for the basics of food, shelter etc. is critical. I have been in too many counseling sessions with couples that do not value this and it taints their relationship for the worse.

As a trained sensorimotor psychotherapist, being 'mindful' which is the art of *staying in the present moment*, right here right now, shedding, with practice, our former viseral reactions to people, places and situations, enables us to be fully in the moment with ourselves and our situations and live life to the fullest."

Peggy Halyard, BBA, MA, LPC (License# 14706), Houston Texas
http://www.couples-help.com and http://www.imagorelationships.org
"How you can make a marriage a success is demonstrating your love
during transition times throughout the day. For example, what do you
say to each other when you first get up in the morning, how do you say
good-by, what do you say when you first get home and what is the last
thing you say before you go to bed. Transition times are times you can
create!"

Dahlia Keen, Psy.D., Clinical Psychologist, Beverly Hills, CA
www.drdahlia.com License# 19992
"One of the criteria for a successful marriage is to 'fall in love'. We
often think that this means falling in love with our spouse, and the
various wonderful attributes and qualities that they possess. In truth,
relationships are more selfish than that, and the best marriages are
when we fall in love with OURSELVES. We may think that we are
preoccupied with the other, but a lot of what is really
happening involves loving the way we feel around our spouse. The
best marriage partners for us are individuals who love us best when we
are being who we want to be and doing what we want to do."

Faith Freed, MFT Intern (#IMF 61352), San Francisco, California
www.faithfreed.com Supervisor Dr. Sarah Villarreal, Psy D.
"Allowing a marriage to morph is one key. Just as the individuals that
comprise the couple are continuously growing and evolving, so too
must the relationship continuously grow and evolve. If we stay flexible
and willing to accommodate for expansion in ourselves, each other and
the marriage, we honor it as the fluid process that it is. Open-mindedly
embracing change also keeps life together juicy."

Andria Jennings, LCSW, Tucson, Arizona
www.andriajenningslcsw.com License# LCSW 3617
"When both spouses are committed to do anything necessary to
maintain the marriage, they will make it work. Commitment is the
basic foundation on which a marriage is based; from there a couple can
do anything together."

Jay Jameson, LMFT, Laguna Hills, California

jayjameson.com License# MFC 34802

"One of the main issues with busy couples, especially when they have younger children is the issue of sex. Specifically it is the lack of sex and where the couple will ever find the time or privacy to have sex. Like a good therapist I bring up the idea of scheduling sex dates into their weekly calendar. This is usually met with statements about how unromantic and non-spontaneous that makes sex. I typically respond with: 'What is less romantic, scheduling sex dates or not having sex?'"

Etan Ben-Ami, LCSW, Brooklyn, New York

http://www.effective-therapy-ny.com/

"If you want to have a happy marriage, remember to be kind. When all is well: be kind. When you're quarreling: be kind. When you're stressed out, hurt, and angry: be kind. Be assertive, be wise, set boundaries, don't give up fulfillment of your individual wants and needs, but remember to also be kind. You're not perfect, and you can't possibly be a perfect mate. Your kindness won't be perfect either. But whenever you have the ability: be kind."

Cheryl Krauter, LMFT, San Francisco & Berkeley, California

www.breastcancersurvivorsupport.com License# MFT14759

"Successful marriage, whether it is traditional or non-traditional, doesn't come with a guarantee or a warranty. If you're looking for that, buy a car."

Tania Henderson, LPC, Wheat Ridge, Colorado

www.sbscounseling.com License# 4115

"During difficult periods of depression or anxiety, partners may feel burdened down with added responsibilities that arise because the sufferer is struggling to function. For the depressed or anxious person, even mundane tasks are ten times harder when self-doubt and fear are bearing down. Resentment will stay at bay if you remember that your spouse is still hard at work- it is just effort directed towards the internal struggle. Get plenty of outside support so it is possible to be patient and compassionate."

Leah Danley, LPC, Edmond, Oklahoma
danleycounseling.com License# 2982
"Nothing spells love like really caring about another's well-being and personal preferences. For one woman this included buying him sunflower seeds even though the chewing and spitting irritated her. He knew the sacrifice she made and loved her all the more for it. Another woman was convinced she was loved when her husband cleaned up her mess after she had been sick and didn't complain."

Joan Levy, LCSW, LCS, ACSW, Kapaa, Hawaii
www.joanlevy.com License LCSW #3046
"Opposites attract because each person needs to come in towards center. So if you are way too tidy and find yourself in a relationship with someone who is way too messy - you may need to loosen up some while your spouse may need to tighten up some. If you are totally in the flow while your spouse has to have everything planned and accounted for - you may need to tie that camel, while your spouse might need to relax and trust more."

Marion Green, LMFT, EFT Therapist, Stamford, Connecticut
www.mariongreenllc.com License# CT 001251
"In moments of discord, couples tend to focus their energy on resolving the topic at hand that appears to be causing the emotional disconnection. Although this seems logical, couples forget to address the emotional significance of what is upsetting to each of them about the topic at hand. Going inward and asking ourselves "what is going on with me right now and how do I feel about this?" helps us to slow down and alter our reactive behavior towards our spouse that *attempts* to fix the problem. The problem lies less in the conflict at hand and more in the emotional interpretation we are experiencing in the moment. If each spouse could get to his or her own raw emotions on the subject and share from that place first, they could better understand one another and, in turn, be better able to make room for each other's feelings. By joining emotionally first, couples have a better chance of staying connected while they figure out a practical (logical) solution to their conflict at hand."

Octavia Carlos, LCSW-C, Largo, Maryland
www.octaviacarlos.com License# 05995
"Money, in-laws, sex, 'differences' don't break up a marriage but the inability to resolve the conflict about them does."

Dr. Denise Wood, M.A; Psy.D., Minneapolis, Minnesota
www.drdenisewood.com
"Look at your significant other like they are the only person in the room. Give them your undivided attention when they talk to you. Laugh like hell at anything funny they say, even if it's not funny, but they think it is. Make them your number one priority and your number one job. Be a lady in the street and a slut in the bed. Married for 16 years with two kids one step-son and a great dog, I'm telling you it works."

Dorian Mintzer, Ph.D.(LICD Psychologist, #2812), Boston, MA
www.dorianmintzer.com and www.couplesretirementpuzzle.com
"What if you are 'out of synch' with your spouse in terms of your energy and activity level? The key is for each of you to clarify what's important for you and to talk together about what you each need and want. You may benefit from changing your goals and dreams to incorporate the changes, and/or shift gears and re-evaluate your expectations of each other, especially regarding time together and apart. So, for example, if you still enjoy hiking and your partner can no longer hike and deal with high altitude, but can walk and ride a bike, either find places for wonderful walks at lower altitudes and/or plan a biking trip to do together, and also plan a hiking trip by yourself, with some friends, or with an organized group. Your spouse can make plans to do something special for him or herself at the same time, either at home or away. Often time apart can strengthen your relationship for the times you're together. If you give up all of your interests you risk resenting your spouse and your spouse may feel guilty that they're holding you back. The key is good communication, balance and respect. Strong and healthy relationships allow each partner to 'grow' and 'breathe,' while at the same time respecting and appreciating each other."

Dr. Sara Denman, Psy.D, Psychologist, Danville, California
drsaradenman.com License# Psy19808
"Watch your tone of voice. If you say something to your spouse in a defensive tone, he/she will match it. This is human nature. Once people become defensive, they stop listening and this will likely end in a fight. Kindness is usually met with kindness."

John Gerson, Ph.D., Katonah, New York
Relationship-repair.com License# 013534
"There is no better relationship in life through which to learn about oneself than marriage."

Charles K. Schrier, LMHC, CVE, LMAO, Albuquerque, NM
www.ckstherapy.com License# 0119401
"Never, never ever, be afraid of giving too much love, because the joy of being loved by another will never equal the joy of giving love to another. When couples come to me, I often hear one party lament, 'I don't know if I will ever be able to trust her/him again. And it may take a long time before I will be able to do so.' It seems as if they are expecting me to tell their partner something they must do, or change, so that they can re-earn their spouse's lost trust. I remind them that no one, not their spouse, nor I, nor anyone in the world can guarantee their partner's everlasting fidelity. I remind them that 'trust' is something they can choose to give or choose to withhold. By choosing to forgive and trust, one is taking the chance that they may one day be hurt again. But choosing to not forgive and not trust is choosing to withhold love. Choosing to not forgive and not trust is choosing to deny your happiness in the present in order to avoid the possibility of pain in the future. By choosing to not forgive and not trust, they punish themselves as well as their partner. Then I remind them, that if they end this relationship, they will have to make the same choice again in any new relationship they enter. It may seem unfair that an individual who was wronged has to take risks to save a relationship with the person that wronged them, but expecting that all things in life are fair is naïve and will ultimately leave one more disappointed than reality ever will."

Julia White, LCSW, Denver, Colorado
www.juliamwhite.com License# 992173
"When you are irritated with your spouse for NOT being romantic enough or leaving his clothes on the floor for the umpteenth time, ask yourself, if I get a cancer diagnosis tomorrow, will he be here for me to see me through this? If your answer is yes then the rest falls into perspective."

Wendy Dickinson, Ph.D., Psychologist, Atlanta, Georgia
www.growcounseling.com License# PSYCH 3256
"Do you ever find yourself with that sinking feeling when you know you are going to have to address a particular topic for the 17th time? How do you bring it up? I often suggest to my clients to give it a code name…and the more playful the better! 'Baby, you are doing that eggplant thing again.' Or 'It's about time to have an eggplant conversation' Not only will it bring a little levity to the conversation, but it gives you a way to sum up a topic or address it in public without others knowing. After all, we all have eggplants in our relationships."

Penn Barbosa, Ph.D., San Francisco, California
www.therapypenn.com License# PSY18949
"One of the most difficult emotions is to love your spouse not only for who he is, but also for who he is not. This is the fall we all experience, when you awaken one morning and realize that your husband is not Prince Charming. And of course, you are no longer a Sleeping Beauty. Life is asking you both to awaken to your ability of forgiving each other on a daily basis, from broken cups to broken promises."

George Kolcun, MFT, San Francisco, California
www.georgekolcunmft.blogspot.com License# MFC 46809
"Keeping your relationship strong and healthy can be a challenge after having children. Protecting the core relationship in your family is a key ingredient to positive family functioning. Make sure to find time to be a couple after becoming parents. Reserve some time to be alone with each other. Loving your spouse is the best parenting technique there is."

Mary-Michael Levitt, LMFT, DRCC, Hackettstown, New Jersey
www.riverviewcc.com License# LMFT 37F100153100
"Negotiate well and reap the rewards of understanding and closeness."

Jennifer Ritchie-Goodline, Licensed Psychologist, Centennial, CO
www.drjenniferritchiegoodline.com
"Making marriage successful after infidelity: If you have been
unfaithful to your spouse, recognize that it will take time to rebuild
and regain trust. In order to help do this, you need to be as open and
transparent as possible with your spouse, at least initially. Understand
that although the situation may be over for you and you are eager to
move forward, the situation might still feel fresh and new for your
spouse and will take time and a lot of concrete validations of trust to
begin to heal. If your spouse has been unfaithful to you and you have
decided to try to forgive him/her and remain in the marriage, after the
initial period, as you move forward and have concrete validations of
trust and commitment, you must try to allow yourself to believe in
your spouse and rebuild that trust or you will not be able to move
forward in a healthy, positive way. As your spouse works to rebuild
trust, you must be open to allowing him/her the opportunity to do so,
and give him/her the assumption of trust unless you have information
or indications of untrustworthy behavior. In other words, if you want
to get past the infidelity, you need to be willing to trust your spouse
again, unless he/she gives you a reason not to."

Wendi Svoboda, LCSW, Burbank, California
www.wsvobodalcsw.com License# LCS24639
"Remember to meet the needs of the little boy or little girl that is in
your spouse. Obviously I do not mean to treat your spouse as a child.
What I do mean is to indulge the vulnerable, innocent part of your
spouse. For example, after you have prepared a sandwich for your
spouse; slice it in triangles instead of halves, because your spouse's
early caregivers had prepared it that way. Or, watch a movie together
that was your spouse's favorite as a child. Remember that nothing says,
'I love you' like providing for your spouse something that was of
comfort as a child."

Jay P. Granat, Ph.D., LMFT, River Edge, New Jersey
www.StayInTheZone.com and www.DrJayGranat.com
"Always, let go of small conflicts."

Ellen Schecter, Ph.D., Clinical Psychologist, Hanover, NH
http://ellenschecter.com
"Choose your battles. How important is being right, or getting your way, in the short-term and over the long-term? On a scale from 1-10, how important is the particular issue you're disagreeing about? Will it matter in an hour, week, month or in a year? (Thanks to Suzy Welch for helping us think about the impact of our decisions.) Try to figure out why it matters to you, and share that."

Christopher Old, MFT, LPC, NCC, Truckee, California
www.mountainmentalhealth.com License# MFC 44697
"Often clients will come to me and say they think maybe they just haven't found the right relationship yet and that they really need to keep looking for it. This is particularly sad when they are currently married to someone who loves them. The one thing I always mention to them is, "remember that ideal relationships are made not found." Having the marriage of your dreams takes ongoing effort. It is not something that you stumble upon one day and then that is it."

Joan Levy, LCSW, LCS, ACSW, Kapaa, Hawaii
www.joanlevy.com License LCSW #3046
"It is important to transform your reality from Win/Lose to Win/Win for mutual connection and satisfaction in your relationship. If you are feeling resentful or guilty you have not yet found a way to negotiate a win/win with your spouse. In Win/Lose thinking we have only two choices: we sacrifice ourselves (be selfless), let our spouse win and inevitably feel resentful; or we do what we want (be selfish) with no regard for our spouse and inevitably feel guilty. Either way there is no real possibility for an open, loving and life-enhancing connection. A Win/Win reality invites mutual right action by balancing sacred self-care choices with sacred other-care choices, allowing both spouses to feel cared for and content."

Cyndie Westrich, M.A., A.T.R.-BC, LPC, Marietta, Georgia
www.easel-arttherapy.com
"We also learned early on that prayer is like super glue for a marriage... individually we may have Elmer's glue to mend a problem, but God is the super glue!"

Jeff Hutchinson, CPSAS, Houston, Texas
www.caribouministries.com
"Sex Addicts guide for making marriage a success: Avoid getting defensive when your spouse has questions. You're not a mind reader so ask your spouse how you can best support them. Also, keep in mind that your spouse is not your accountability partner. While he or she needs to be updated about your recovery your spouse cannot support you when you are struggling and need a pep talk. Above all your spouse isn't your cheerleader and six months of sobriety doesn't make up for years of acting out in the marriage. Instead try to understand things from their perspective."

Brad Nowlin, LCMFT, Overland Park, Kansas
www.bradnowlin.com
"Creating Positivity Spirals: Think several moves or stages ahead much as a master chess player would... but with your heart. Use the spirit of play to guide you to prepare a hot bath for your spouse with aromatherapy scents, then think about a warm towel fresh from the dryer. Chocolate and strawberries would enhance the evening and set the stage for more positivity spirals. Lovemaking could ensue with that same spirit of play and giving. Be creative and have fun!"

Mark Saindon, LMFT, Portland, Oregon
www.MarkSaindon.com License# T0376
"Be trustworthy. Keep your word. Have your actions match the promises and agreements you make with your spouse. The longest and most difficult road is the one to repair the damage from the loss of trust. I've heard it best described as a grueling and seemingly endless endeavor. Even when repaired, your relationship is never quite the same again. Be your word."

Joshua M. Simmons, PsyD, San Francisco, California
www.sftherapy.info License# PSY23334
"Don't compare your marriage to others. There is no one-way to be in a relationship. Like individuals, couples must find their own unique way and be guided by the consequences of their searching."

Tonya Ladipo, LCSW, Philadelphia, Pennsylvania
www.TheLadipoGroup.com License# CW015409
"Laugh together often. When you're walking around look at other couples. It's easy to spot those who are happy together, they're usually laughing or smiling. You don't know why they're laughing but you can tell that they're happy together. So find something that you both appreciate for its humor such as a movie, book, or your own silliness."

Dianne Greyerbiehl, Ph.D., LPC, PCC, Greenville, South Carolina
www.lifecoachinginstitute.net License# 4805
"You can help make marriage a success by developing a couple's life plan. This involves each person deciding what they would like in their marriage in certain life areas such as their relationship, finances, balancing work and personal life, and creating meaning in their marriage. They then compare their life plans and reach an agreement about what they want as a couple in each of those areas. For example, in the relationship area, they may agree to notice what the other is doing right and say something about it to their loved one. Or they may agree on how to parent their children in positive and loving ways. In any case, they turn what they want into goals and each begins to take small easy steps to make their life plan a reality. As a result, the couple is creating specific positive outcomes in their marriage over time, which in turn, tends to bring happiness and well-being."

Mary-Michael Levitt, LMFT, DRCC, Hackettstown, New Jersey
www.riverviewcc.com License# LMFT 37F100153100
"Unresolved conflicts eat away at marital bliss. Positive arguing works! Say the word 'I' not the word 'you'/ stay in the moment/listen to the other not what your own head is arguing back/make eye contact and use kind words."

Marilyn Wedge, Ph.D., Westlake Village, California
www.MarilynWedgePhd.com License# 23729
"Love Mrs. Godzilla! O.K., so your secret name for your mother-in-law is 'Mrs. Godzilla'. She doesn't remember your birthday, even though it comes around on the same date every year. She never has time to babysit the grandkids. On the rare occasions that she invites your family to dinner, she manages to forget that you are raising your children vegan (even though you've reminded her fifty times) and serves hamburgers. Even so, if you want to have a happy, successful marriage, NEVER criticize your spouse's mother or anyone else in your spouse's extended family. These criticisms can be deeply hurtful to your spouse (and to your children). Everyone has some good in them, so bite your tongue, and occasionally mention your mother-in-law's best qualities to your spouse. You will be glad you did."

Bob Brewster, LPC, Addison Dallas, Texas
www.brewstercounseling.com License# 19305
"The most consistent problem I see in marriages is one or both spouses do not act like they are married. Their behavior--staying out late, not calling their spouse when their schedule changes, communicating with old girlfriends/boyfriends--is more like that of a single person. My advice is to fully commit to your spouse for the rest of your life because divorce is an ugly process."

Stacy Paul, LPC, LISAC, Tucson, Arizona
http://www.stacypaullpclisac.com License# LPC-2397 & LISAC-1626
"Being part of the human race means that our unhealthy behaviors are motivated by fear. To some degree, all humans fear abandonment, rejection and lack of acceptance. These fears become more pronounced when we are in relationships. Often we react to each other not based on reality but based on our fears. In order to have a successful marriage, it is essential to be aware of when you are reacting out of fear. If you are having an extreme reaction to something related to your spouse, you need to identify the fear that is motivating your behavior. Walking through your fear will allow you to have a healthier and more intimate relationship with your spouse."

Judith Mathews MFT, Reno, Nevada
www.judithmathewsmft.com License# MFT 884
"I would like to offer my favorite marriage quote by David Schnarch PhD, the author of Passionate Marriage and The Sexual Crucible. He said, 'Most marriages are saved by the two or three things *not* said every day.'"

Marina Tonkonogy, MA., LMFT, Los Angeles, California
www.mtmft.com License #48252
"Acceptance of reality is one of the major contributors into making a marriage meaningful and fulfilling. We often don't allow ourselves to be who we truly are for the fear of being rejected or abandoned by our spouse, but then it creates a catch-22. When we try to make ourselves likable in order to be loved, then the love that we receive is not real, because we are not loved for who we are but for the image of ourselves that we present to our partner. It also makes us not accept our spouse as they are but to demand that they were what we want them to be. When both partners are willing to accept reality, this would greatly contribute into their individual growths and to the growth of their relationship."

Nicole Story, Ed.S, LMFT, Jacksonville Beach, Florida
www.OceansideFamilyTherapy.com License# LMFT MT2208
"Don't presume the other is using you, when they need to meet their own needs. What they need from you is important to them and a reason why they married you in the first place. Find a way to support and feel productive about it. It is possible to be energized by meeting the true needs of those we love."

Dr. Sara Denman, Psy.D, Psychologist, Danville, California
drsaradenman.com License# Psy19808
"Small jesters go a long way. Things like a post-it notes, saying I love you on the refrigerator or pillow can make your spouse's day. A hug when you or your spouse returns home from work can warm the mood for the evening. Taking those small easy steps will open your spouse's heart."

Nadim S. Ali, MA, LPC, ICCDP, GCADC-III, Atlanta, Georgia
Nadimali.com License# LPC 03775
"The keys to a happy marriage are based on four words. Two words get you in the union, and two words keep you in the union. The four words are I do and yes dear."

Raelene S. Weaver, Licensed Marriage Family Therapist, CA
www.raeleneweaver.com License# 46608
"Be mindful of expressing your love in various ways such as through words, actions and touch."

Cynthia Swan, M.A., C.M.F.T., L.P.C., Niwot, Colorado
www.cynthiaswan.com
"From my work with hospice, I have met so many women who experienced the sudden death of their partners....sometimes immediately after a phone conversation or shortly after they've left the house. Others watched as their partner toppled to the kitchen floor. (in front of them.) They are always glad they ended their time together in a positive and loving conversation, or took the time to express gratitude and love as they went their own ways for daily chores or work. So I would say that daily expression of love and gratitude even for the most mundane and smallest characteristic of your spouse supports a satisfying connection to your loved one."

Bert Epstein, PsyD, Petaluma, California
http://www.drbertepstein.com License# PSY21404
"Creating Successful Marriage Through Play: People say that a relationship needs 'work.' I disagree. A relationship needs 'play.' In the context of a relationship, 'work' is not fun, while 'play' is. Of course, there are times in a marriage where play is not appropriate. However, each spouse being his or her younger self can go a long way towards a successful marriage. And, the couple can be younger in a few years or many years. It is great to recreate times when the couple first began. In fact, it is important to keep alive the areas that attracted each partner to the other. In addition, child-like fun greatly enhances the quality of a relationship. So, live a little and have a great time."

Mark A. Foster, Ph.D., MFT, Sacramento, California
Askdrmark.com License# 22707
"If you want to die in a marriage, then choose to go to war with your partner. Emotional death is the only outcome to declaring war, and yet, people within their marriages openly do so all the time. Why do they do this? Because they want an experience and they say to themselves, 'you're not giving me the experience I want so I will fight you to get it'. Wow!!!!! What a winning strategy. Here is what is typically forgotten. Your partner chose you because they want to have an experience and it's not to die in war."

Kara Veigas, MSW, LICSW, Washington, DC
www.karaveigas.com License# LC50078142
"A couple of years ago my partner and I were updating our bathroom. We disagreed on what bathroom fixtures to purchase, based on my concern for what would be safe for our coming child. After a heated argument, my husband turned to me and gently explained that he agreed we should purchase the safer fixtures. What he was really yearning for, he discovered, was to have his preference respected, and to feel understood and appreciated for letting go of that wish for the sake of the family. A courageous effort by my husband to communicate his need for understanding, met with respect and validation, landed us on very solid ground together. We have realized that when you really feel heard and understood by your partner, your sense of safety in the attachment bond with each other deepens. Feeling more securely connected with each other, we found ourselves freer to be joyful, loving, creative and authentic."

Lorrie Crystal Eigles, MSED, LPC, PCC, Kansas City, Missouri
http://myauthenticlifecoaching.com
"Being open and learning from one another keeps a marriage fresh. My husband is a very generous person. As a result I've learned to be willing to share more of what's important to me, both in tangible and intangible ways. For example; I've now reached the point where I actually give him some of my really good dark chocolate. Now that's love!"

Suzanne Mallouk, M.D., Physician Surgeon, New York, New York
www.drsuzannemallouk.com
"In a successful marriage the husband and wife are aware that they are never responsible for the thoughts, feelings and behaviors of their spouse. A loving spouse tries to only validate and understand the thoughts, feelings and behaviors of their spouse, even if they don't agree with them."

Carmen Gloria Avendaño, LMFT, Wayzata, Minnesota
www.lifebalancetherapy.com License# 2104
"I love working out with my husband. It relaxes me and gives me energy for the day. It also reminds me that being married is like belonging to our favorite sports team and that we are both on the same side. The more we work together as a team, our satisfaction as a couple grows. You do not need to prove who is right or who is doing it better to score a goal; you need to work at it together. If I am not happy, you are not happy. To "win" at marriage, both players must be happy!"

Karen Hague, MBA, LMSW, ACSW, Ann Arbor, Michigan
www.boomersolutions.org License# 6801085338
"One of my favorite writers about relationships, Terrence Real, says, 'we marry our unfinished business.' The dynamics involved in marriage/partnership are fertile ground for triggering unresolved issues from the past. It's easy to project these issues onto our spouse and expect them to make things right. With appropriate support, however, this can be a wonderful opportunity for healing old wounds versus continuing to act them out. If both partners are willing to take responsibility for the baggage they bring to the relationship and resist blaming the other, true intimacy and connection can be fostered."

Joe Lowrance, Psy.D., Clinical Psychologist, Atlanta, Georgia
www.FinancialPsychologyCeus.com
"Money is an ongoing opportunity within a marriage to explore oneself, oneself in the world and in the context of a martial relationship."

Pamela Lipe, M.S., Licensed Psychologist, Saint Paul, Minnesota
www.PamLipe.com License# LP0268
"If you find that you do not have respect for your spouse (or your spouse doesn't have respect for you), your relationship may be in more trouble than you realize. You might disagree, argue a lot or even not like some things about your spouse, but that doesn't have to spell the end of the relationship. Disagreements, and many other issues, can be worked out. But if you have lost respect, many relationship experts predict a poor outcome for your relationship. Of course, respect and love go hand in hand but love alone will not carry you through. If you love but don't hold a high opinion of your spouse, it's time to get some help to bring back the respect."

Melinda Sharpe, LCSW, Wallingford, Connecticut
melindasharpe.com License# CT 001002
"I believe our spouses are our three-way mirrors. They show us sides of ourselves we can't view without help. We don't always like what they reveal, for often in their behavior we come to see what we think about ourselves, good and bad. This is because we have been teaching them how to treat us from the first moment we met them. If they treat us with respect that is because we required that, for we have been treating ourselves respectfully. If they don't, then we know that is an area we need to work on in ourselves. We are tempted to blame our partners and become angry for the unpleasant way they may treat us. The trick is learning what the spouse is showing us and using it to promote our own growth. In this way, a spouse is a great teacher, if we are willing to learn from this most intimate partner."

Trisha Swinton, LPC, LMFT, Denver, Colorado
www.trishaswintoncounseling.com License# LPC 4914 & LMFT 842
"From what I have observed while working with couples is that; couples who make it work are laid back and can go with the flow. Life is full of unexpected events and those who know you can't plan everything, such as when you're going to buy a house or have a baby; seem more able to adapt to new situations. If you do plan, remember that things do not always go according to our plans and that is okay."

Julie Uhernik, RN, LPC, NCC, Parker, Colorado
www.julieuhernik.com License# LPC 4714 & RN 110129
"It can be helpful to consider a good marriage or relationship like a cupcake. You are the delicious cake at the very base, which is wrapped in a special protective paper cover. You are stand alone great! A happy marriage or relationship is like the icing on the cupcake. The icing makes the cake even richer and more satisfying and complete. Some people are perfectly happy in their life being a delicious cake, and some choose to enjoy a little icing on their cake as well!"

Bette Levy Alkazian, LMFT, Thousand Oaks, California
www.BalancedParenting.com License# MFC 32747
"I have been interested in what makes a lasting marriage work for a long time. When I see older couples in the market or other various places, I ask them, 'To what do you attribute the success of your marriage?' Of course, I hear a lot about communication, not going to bed mad and being kind. However, the most common answer I have received is the one that intrigues and inspires me the most. When things get tough, you just don't leave!"

Angela R. Stern, LCPC, Crofton, Maryland
http://therapist.psychologytoday.com/44031
"Working with couples over the years, I have observed how trivial day-to-day conflict can become like a cancer to relationships. The cumulative effect of years of nagging can destroy love and intimacy, as resentments can snowball. A common relationship dynamic is when one of the partners takes on a parental-type role, and the other, a child-like role, with the parental partner constantly reminding his or her spouse to 'get this done' or 'don't forget ....'. The child-like partner learns to rely on the reminders, but also grows to resent the reminders; and it becomes a causally reciprocal cycle of nagging, dependency, and resentment. One way couples learn to break this cycle is for the parental-like partner to take a step back and allow the other partner to face the natural consequences of his or her forgetfulness or negligence. Of course, as couples establish this new pattern, they should begin with issues of less serious consequences."

Negar Khaefi, LMFT, Los Angeles, California
negarkhaefi.com License# MFC 45939
"After a night of lovemaking, communication can deepen, positive feelings toward one another are heightened, forgiveness is easier, tolerance levels go back up again. Hit reset, have sex."

AnnaLisa Derenthal, LPC, NCC, Roswell, Georgia
www.annalisaderenthal.com License# LPC004373
"Valuable questions. Whenever you are facing a tough decision, such as whether to end a marriage, you will inevitably be flooded with pros and cons, ifs and thens, and the fear of making the 'wrong' decision. When you find yourself in such a predicament, there are 3 valuable questions to ask yourself: What does your head say? What does your heart say? and What does your gut say? Your head gives you your logic, unencumbered by emotion, the plain facts and what you know to be true. These answers must be considered from a pragmatic point of view. Your heart gives you your feelings. It tells you what will hurt, what will feel good or right for you, and gives you information about your emotional needs. Your gut gives you your intuition, which may be a combination of the other two. You may not like what your gut says, but you can believe it; it is your truth. And most people say their gut is always right."

Sharon L. Thompson, LMFTA, Indianapolis, Indiana
www.talkwithsharon.com License# 85000045A
"Getting married means compromise and not getting your way all the time. If you want to have your way most or all of the time and do things your way all the time, *stay single*. There is nothing wrong with staying single. Marriage is a choice not to be taken lightly. It takes work, intentionality and compromise by both spouses."

Elayne Savage, PhD., Licensed Marriage Family Therapist, CA
http://www.QueenofRejection.com License# MFC 17077
"Focusing on enhancing what works rather than berating what doesn't work in the relationship will help many of the problems fall by the wayside."

Laurel Steinberg, LMHC, Licensed Psychotherapist, NY, NY
www.LaurelSteinberg.com
"'Don't let trying to conceive strain your sex life.' Some couples
wishing to conceive find themselves having a tough time getting
pregnant. Sex can lose its spontaneity when it is scheduled to happen
during a woman's fertile window. When month after month of
planning ends in regular disappointment, this planning can take a toll
on a couple's sex life. The key is to remember to fully enjoy each
other sexually, with the hope of conceiving that day, rather than just
the need to conceive. Complying with the demand puts tremendous
pressure on sex, leaving spouses so distracted that they are unable to
enjoy one of the most precious interactions they share. Parenting is
hard enough when relationships are not strained, so why damage them
at the inception?"

Joan Levy, LCSW, LCS, ACSW, Kapaa, Hawaii
www.joanlevy.com License LCSW #3046
"When you and your partner disagree do you feel that you are right
and somehow better? Judgment is hierarchical, disrespectful and
breaks connection. Discernment allows for differences of opinion
within an equal playing field while maintaining respect and
connection."

Sarah Pokorny, LCSW, Covington, Louisiana
www.pokornytherapy.com
"When upset with one another, remember that your spouse is just
trying to survive; doing the best he or she knows how. Deep down, we
all have a sensitive inner child that wants to please others. Patience,
patience, patience...and don't forget to have a little fun."

Cheryl Gerson, LCSW, BCD, New York, New York
www.cherylgerson.com
"Curiosity may be the most valuable trait to bring to a marriage.
Keeping a relationship fresh is mostly about realizing that the other is
unknowable."

Hadassah Ramsay, PsyD, Durham, New Hampshire
www.drhramsay.com
"While there will be disagreements and arguments, remember you and your spouse are on the same team."

Robert Weiss, LCSW, CSAT-S, Author, Los Angeles, California
www.sexualrecovery.com License# LCS-17610
"Now that you can be unfaithful via phone or webcam - how do you define cheating and infidelity in the New Media age? Does web-sex and online chat cause the same hurt as the lipstick stained collar and unplanned late nights of yore? Perhaps today infidelity is best defined as *The Keeping of Secrets in an Intimate Relationship.* More lies + more secrecy = less intimacy + less love. In this age of immediate access to endless Internet porn and Smartphone hook-ups. In order for couples to make marriage a success they need to clarify their definition of being unfaithful as clearly as they decide whether or not to have children."

Cindy Foster, LCSW, ACSW, NBCCH, Martinez, Georgia
mindbodystressreduction.com License# CSW002401
"Know and heal yourself. Invest the time and energy to heal emotional loss and wounds that you have experienced in your life. You can look at areas within yourself that need further growth, with both spouses supporting each other in this process they will make their marriage a success."

Dr. Ann Thomas, LMFT, Danville, California
dr-annthomas.com License# MFT12406
"Falling in love brings us together, providing the excitement and energy to take that huge step of connecting our life with another person. It's a shock for many couples when that intensity lessens until they realize that it's only when we're finished with the 'falling-in' phase do we have the necessary room for a deep and lasting love to develop. Marriages work when we're able to have the patience to allow the relationship to move through that first beauty to form strong and deep roots."

Wendy Becker, LCSW, Fort Collins, Colorado
www.FrontRangeCounselingandMediation.com License# 1007
"A marriage is work. If you start feeling like it isn't worth the effort
and think that the grass looks greener on the other side of the
fence, remember it is just grass. It takes the same amount of work as
the grass you already have."

Angela R. Wurtzel, MA, LMFT, Santa Barbara California
www.angelawurtzelmft.com License# 33686
"While there is no prescription for how to keep a marriage fresh like
the honeymoon phase, I do believe there are ways to improve the
longevity of a marriage. Creating meaning in the time a couple spends
together is essential. This can be at any time – while making coffee,
going for a drive, creating a project, shopping for clothes, venturing
out on a new hike, listening to music or snuggling up together
whenever it's possible. Each of these activities requires meaning for
the sustenance of a relationship. The meaning comes from being
attuned, that is to sense what another is feeling and respond
appropriately to those feelings, while quietly knowing what your own
experience means to you. Being attuned to another and feeling another
being attuned to you is the basis of trust that can bring freshness to a
relationship because each moment, no matter how simple, is shared
and new."

Terry Tempinski, PhD., Farmington Hills, Michigan
www.DrTempinski.com License# 6301002970
"In 30 years of practice, the overwhelming majority of cases, which
have presented to me for marital therapy involve relationships wherein
there is an IMBALANCE or INEQUITY in levels of consideration for
one another. Moreover, often this has been an enduring problem. If
you are in such a relationship wherein you feel your spouse just
doesn't seem to 'get it' when you try to elicit consideration for your
feelings, he/she is probably not just acting this way, but rather
struggling with genuine limitations best understood as psychological
deafness/blindness which can be understood and, in some cases,
resolved."

Tonya Ladipo, LCSW, Philadelphia, Pennsylvania
www.TheLadipoGroup.com License# CW015409
"Respect your spouse AND your marriage, both publicly and privately.
Most of us know that we should be respectful of our spouses and when
we're talking directly to our spouses. This is also true when our
spouses are not present. Frequently at parties and I have heard women
talking about their 'no good husbands' who 'can't even change a light
bulb.' If you have a complaint about your spouse then discuss it with
them privately."

Demarcus C. Davis, LPC/MHSP, Memphis, Tennessee
www.couples-n-families.com License# 2127
"Don't over-compartmentalize. It's inevitable that roles develop in a
family system based on individual talents and interests. However, we
run the risk of operating in individual silos when we don't live flexibly,
willing to switch roles even if temporarily. At minimum, we should
continue to engage our spouse in our endeavors with the same passion
and interest as we were dating."

Steve Sisgold, M.A., Certified Relationship Counselor, Novato, CA
www.onedream.com
"When I counsel couples, whether they are in a long term relationship
or newlyweds, I always suggest to enter their home or any space where
their beloved is as if it's a temple. If you were going to see the Dalai
Lama, how would you enter his space?"

Carol Marks-Stopforth, LMHC, Boston, Massachusetts
Carolmarksstopforth.com License# 6416
"Marriage is not for weaklings! It requires the courage to meet the
parts of yourself that might be unbeautiful and scary and to accept that
your spouse has them as well. This kind of recognition engenders
curiosity and acceptance and dispenses with the desire to change and
possess. Could anything be more intimate than to embark together on a
voyage of self-discovery with the aim of sharing that knowledge
thereby illuminating what is the same yet completely unique in each
other."

Tracy Gillette, Ph.D., LPC, NCC, Warrenville, South Carolina
www.gillettepsychotherapy-retreats.com License# 5050
"Let the other person 'win', give them what they want, agree with the
spouse, on at least one viewpoint. Then the spouse will likely be more
receptive to listening to the rest of what you have to say. Finding one
point to agree on, will get the spouse's attention."

Claudia Sinay-Mosias, MFT, San Francisco, California
www.sanfranciscocounseling.com License# MFC27519
"Sex, in a long-term marriage is much more than intercourse. Children,
illness, age, stress, can all get in the way. Sometimes we are just too
tired for the 'full Monty'. Everything counts toward a satisfying sex
life; cuddling, kissing, hugging, caressing, foreplay without the after
play. Stay physically connected even if circumstances keep you from
the kind of courtship sex you had in your 20's."

John Gerson, Ph.D., Katonah, New York
Relationship-repair.com License# 013534
"There is no better relationship in life through which to learn about
oneself than marriage."

Crystal Anzalone, MS, PLMHP, NCC, Omaha, Nebraska
http://www.thereflectioncenter.com http://arborfamilycounseling.com
"For those who ever wonder if their husbands will bail out on them for
another woman, please do not sit passively fretting. Rather, as women,
rediscover yourselves daily, weekly, annually and forever. Allow
yourself to enjoy your life in the presence of your husband. This can
create a mystique and interest that will keep the relationship alive. I
tease my husband and say, 'You will never have to find another
woman because of tiring of the one you have now. I plan on
continually evolving.' Speaking to our own ability to continue personal
growth sets the precedence that stagnancy in our relationship is not for
us. Rather than nag my husband to make changes that meet my needs,
I find ways to be fulfilled and thus I discover that he desires to remain
being the man that I long for. My own willingness to change and grow
spawns a by-product with a relationship of reverberating reciprocity."

Sandy McDermott, LCPC, NCC, Tranquility Counseling, IL
www.createtranquility.com
"Get your anger out of your system before you talk with your spouse. Writing your angry words out (so that you don't ever say them to your spouse), taking a walk or remembering all of the person's good qualities can help you to have a more fruitful discussion and make your marriage a success."

Dr. Joan R. Saks Berman, Clinical Psychologist, New Mexico
www.joanberman.com www.momentumandmemento.blogspot.com
"Taking a cue from Michelle Bachmann's appearance on 'Face the Nation' on Sunday, August 14, 'I respect my husband, he respects me,' she said. Mutual respect is very important. I believe that spouses should be equal, unlike Bachmann, who talked about wives being submissive to husbands. It's important for each spouse to see the other as a human being like themselves, not as an object."

Christa R. Surerus, MA, LPCC, Minneapolis, Minnesota
www.affinitasplc.com License# 186
"Inherent in humans is the drive to become whole. The essence of a relationship is to assist in this healing process as our partner is a mirror within which we catch glimpses of ourselves. If we are able to take in what we see through our partner's honest and loving reflection of ourselves, we are then able to grow from the feedback towards being whole. However, when we conceal our true nature from our partner, the image that's reflected back to us is distorted, thereby limiting our capacity for growth."

Shannon Byrnes, M.A., Psychotherapist, Los Angeles, California
www.shannonbyrnes.com
"Couples hear one another through their own life experience. In a successful marriage, they can identify their own filters allowing for an empathic space to emerge where they can feel validated and less defensive. Each partner longs to be known and understood. As they learn to quiet themselves, they make room for their partner's voice so theirs may also be heard."

Judith B. Taylor, LCSW, Lewiston, Maine
therapywithjudith.com
"Marriages begin to fail when the priority shifts away from the relationship. Daily check ins, weekly dates, quarterly getaways and at least a yearly vacation will help make marriage a success. You do not need a lot of money to do these things, just the desire and the time."

Donald Wallach, MFT, Petaluma, California
www.donwallach.com License# MFC34379
"Do you or your spouse have social anxiety and feel that your marriage can't be a success? Well it can. The challenge here is for the anxious spouse to push himself or herself outside of their comfort zone one small step at a time. One effective strategy is to start speaking more to strangers. If you are at the grocery store, ask a question about the groceries of the person next to you. If you are at a party, just say 'hi' to one more person than you usually would. If you are out on the street, just say 'hi' or smile at one more person than you usually would. Then just increase the amount of extra contact every day. Eventually, you will extend from saying 'hi' to a comment or two. Before you know it a full conversation can occur.

If you're the one who has a spouse that is anxious you can help by not leaving your loved one alone for too long. While they may need some time to challenge themselves try to reach out a little bit more than usual. Check-in and give them some relief from social stress, and reward them for their pushing outside of their comfort zone."

Jennica Jenkins, PsyD, LPC, Rocklin, California
Jennicajenkins.com License# LPC6072
"Grow together, regularly re-negotiate power points like money, sex, child rearing goals, and out of the home interests to make sure you are both on the same path. Discuss all matters that can impact your spouse's life -which means all matters that impact your life. Find joy and goodness in your spouse every day. Remember to be grateful for their personal characteristics that attracted you to them in the beginning of your relationship."

Jennifer Wilmoth, LAMFT, Atlanta, Georgia
www.growcounseling.com License# AMFT 000204
"Start marriage with an agreed upon financial plan you can both stick with and save yourself many future arguments. Money is one of the top issues couples argue about so having a pre-determined plan will help you navigate difficult financial decisions that often turn into power struggles. No need to re-create the wheel, you can take advantage of the wisdom of an established financial plan you both agree on and work hard to stick with the plan. Realistically there will be times as a couple you take detours off your financial plan, no worries just figure out how to get back on track or change the plan to make it work."

Igor Davidson, Ph.D., Clinical Psychologist, Brooklyn, New York
www.boutiquepsychology.com License# nys 016113
"Marriage is a personal 'commitment' to be part of a union with another person. You either make the commitment or you don't. Spouses who can and have made such a commitment are able to endure many trials and tribulations within their marriage. Those who don't have commitment are shaken and splintered by the most minor of differences. Both partners must be committed to the marriage for the union to last. The great majority of marriages are difficult, but only ones with "commitment" survive. Although this sounds simplistic, it goes a long in explaining why some marriages endure and others do not. This model is also quite positive, because commitment is not luck or superstition, it is a conscious choice that is under the control of each person."

Pamela Tinkham, MSW, LCSW, Greenwich, Connecticut
www.MindBodyFitnessLLC.com
"You have to be willing to do the work to make sure that the marriage is growing together and not apart. This involves an awareness and mindfulness that checks in on a moment-to-moment basis to ensure that your marriage is growing together. If it is not, you need to come up with a game plan together on how you can get the marriage to grow together before it becomes too late and falls apart!"

Lori Hollander, LMSW, MBA, Sex Therapist, Ann Arbor, MI
Realintimacy.com License# 6801087016
"Contrary to widespread stereotypes, men more than women say they long to hold hands, cuddle, and hug, especially when in a marriage with a 'low-sex' problem. Since more women experience 'low desire' for sex (33% of women compared to 16% of men)[i], a man will more often be the one longing for more sexual intimacy than his spouse wants. For that reason, he is especially disappointed when even hugs and quick kisses dwindle along with their sex life.

But pursuing her even for that light physical contact often just makes things worse. Instead of feeling the true gesture of his love, she will most often end up feeling pressure, 'that he is only doing this to get sex.' While sweet moments of loving words and caresses do stimulate and maintain sexual desire, they *only* work if these moments are completely *free of sexual expectations*.

In other words, common advice about creating time for sex, unfortunately, is rarely enough to resolve a low-sex problem. But with a concrete plan to create the *right kind of* time, a couple can start fueling real intimacy together - right now."

[i] Laumann, E., Michael, R. T., & Kolata, G. (1995). *Sex in America: A definitive survey*. Chicago: Grand Central Publishing

Jennifer Olden, Licensed Marriage Family Therapist, California
www.Jenniferolden.com License# 42693
"Historically, we believe that the more self possessed we are the better our marriage will be and so as therapists we help people to be stronger, happier, more evolved individuals and then a good relationship will just fall into place. However, the inverse is also true: The happier the relationship, the happier we will be as individuals. It sounds like a small difference but it's actually a paradigm shift because embedded in this statement is an understanding that we need relationships and our fears of loneliness and our need for connection isn't pathology but our birthright."

Florence Soares-Dabalos, LMFT, Chico, California
www.florencemft.com License# MFC40331
"Silent treatments can be difficult to manage in a marriage because communication requires two people to be engaged in the process. So what do you do if your spouse gives you the silent treatment? Know that this could be the way your spouse is handling stress, processing emotions, or dealing with the fear of resolving conflict and needs to feel safe before communicating. Know it is your spouse's responsibility to express how s/he feels (not yours) and let her/him know you'll be ready to talk when they are. Also pay attention to your own needs and feelings and take care of yourself accordingly."

Melissa Cramer, LCSW, CAP, Miami, Florida
GROWHEALLOVE.com License# sw9441
"In any long-term committed relationship, an individual must be wary of allowing their partner's limitations to become their own. They must constantly assess whether their experience of life is broadened through the union. If it is found that one is boxed into their partner's safety zone, the individual must make conscious effort to break free of this box. It is important to always make the space to honor and explore one's desires, hopes and true self."

Connie Studer, M.A. LMFT, Minneapolis, Minnesota
www.heteroflexibletherapy.com License# 1760
"It is important for couples to realize that in a relationship it is rare for each spouse to be giving exactly 50% at all times. Depending on circumstances one spouse may give 40% for a time and then there is a shift to 80% and 20%. If you look at the lifetime contributions for long term relationships it seems to balance out through time. Successful couples trust that this balance will occur and carry little resentment from those times when they were contributing a little or even a lot more than their spouse."

Anna Valenti, LCSW (License# 11769), Phoenix, Arizona
www.annavalenti.com or www.SANEresources.org
"Lighten up with each other."

Carey Laine, Psy.D., Grass Valley, California
http://drcareylaine.com License# PSY 21635
"Loving is easy to do, working at loving is also easy to do, however conscious loving is the foundation to understanding."

Michael Reeder, LCPC, Baltimore, Maryland
http://www.hygeiacounseling.com License# LC3624
"You can make marriage a success by reestablishing intimacy first before tackling problems. So, for example, if an employed spouse comes home to find that the stay-at-home spouse has not cleaned-up after the kids, the time to address this is *NOT* when the employed spouse first walks in the house. Relax a bit, eat dinner together, get a sense of how the day went, and tackle this later. It's important that one or both spouses not get in the habit of anxiously anticipating regular fights (such as a daily 'this house is a mess when I come home' fight). This poisonous anxiety does as much or more damage than the actual fight."

John Sovec, Psychotherapist, MA, LMFT, Pasadena, California
www.JohnSovec.com License# MFC 46376
"A foundation to building a strong relationship is to not make assumptions and take each other for granted. Many people fall into the trap of making assumptions about who the other person is and how they will react to any given situation. Frequent and honest communication is the key to getting out of this trap. It can be a great refresher for any relationship to listen and learn from each other. Surprise each other by being present enough to not let assumptions bring boredom and tediousness to a growing relationship."

Jenny Grace Shaw, LMHC, M.ED., Maui, Hawaii
www.jennyshawtherapy.com License# 256964
"Marriage is hard work---it means time, patience, energy, tolerance, compromise, willingness, openness, trust, loyalty, and yes, respect. But such elements seem so general. Truth is survival of marriage does not mean both parties have such characteristics, rather it means both parties share the same or, at least, similar definition of the above."

Nancy Cason, Psy.D., Licensed Clinical Psychologist, Denver, CO
www.insights-autism.com
"When you have a child with a developmental disability, it is easy for parents to get lost and overwhelmed with the constant therapies, research, meetings, and other demands on time. However, in any marriage it is important to prioritize the marriage. A child with disabilities, like any child, needs parents who have a strong marriage. Take time with your spouse; whether you get a babysitter and go out, or have a date at home after the child has gone to bed. Parents with a good, happy marriage are better, more effective parents."

Gloria Saltzman, MA, MFA, Psychotherapist, San Francisco, CA
www.GloriaSaltzman.com
"Keep in touch when you are apart. To feel as though there is at least one person in the world who always has your back increases happiness and well-being."

Heather O'Neil, Licensed Clinical Social Worker, Denver, CO
www.oneiltherapy.com License# 992331
"In my practice and my life I have found it extremely helpful to remember that relationships are constantly changing along with the people involved in the relationship. Therefore, remembering to look at what you as an individual are doing or not doing and how this impacts the other person is important. I like to refer to it as 'reacting less' and 'relating' more. When you stop to think about how you can respond rather than react, so many things become less complicated."

Dr. Suzanne Lopez, MFCC Licensed, Albuquerque, New Mexico
Dr. Suzanne lopez.com License# 0094281
"'Till death do us part' projects fear and no room to grow either more together or apart on the journey of life. Until love and Eros, respect, common goals, kindness, communication, caring and commitment no longer bind us would be more realistic at this time of our evolution. There is no room for love to grow if someone feels trapped, you must always feel as free to stay, as you are to go for love to keep expanding."

Bette Levy Alkazian, LMFT, Thousand Oaks, California
www.BalancedParenting.com License# MFC 32747
"One huge pitfall I see a lot with couples is jumping to conclusions
and then reacting. This, of course, falls under the communication
umbrella, but it's a dynamic that repeats itself and can be very
frustrating and destructive for couples. Rather than reacting, couples
need to: Stop, breathe and then ask..

It's easy to assume that a gesture or an expression means one thing,
when, in fact, your spouse doesn't mean that at all. Check in! Ask
what your spouse is thinking. Stay calm so you can both hear each
other."

Toppie Lincicome, Licensed Professional Counselor, Shawnee, OK
www.counselingoklahoma.com
"There are two points I try to make with clients already married and
want to make marriage a success: 1. Trust is the heart of every
relationship. 2. Jealousy is always about the one who is jealous and not
about your spouse so get over it."

Daniela Roher, PhD., LPC, Scottsdale & Carefree, Arizona
www.droherpsychotherapy.com
"When you feel most discouraged in your marriage, that's when you
are most open, able and motivated to work at making healthy
changes."

John Sovec, Psychotherapist, MA, LMFT, Pasadena, California
www.JohnSovec.com License# MFC 46376
"Strong relationships are built when each partner learns the vital skill
of asking for what they need. This intertwines with not making
assumptions that the other person can mind read and automatically
fulfill unspoken needs. When these unspoken needs are not met,
resentment can begin to build in the relationship, which can lead to
arguments and the degradation of communication. The best way to
address this is for partners to learn to share clearly their emotions,
fears, needs, and desires."

Risha London Nathan, LMSW, Wellness Counselor, Brooklyn, NY
www.rishalondonnathan.com
"Although marriage, or any romantic relationship is clearly about the couple, it is also about the individual. It's important for people to be able to look at their own behaviors, rather than just externalizing the situation and putting a general emphasis on working on the relationship. A relationship is about how people relate to each other, how they mirror each other, support each other, and find common ground. I would tell any client who was struggling in their relationship, to take a closer look at themselves. Your relationship can only be as good as how you feel about yourself, and where you're at in your own life. Communication barriers are often at the heart of marital and relationship problems. Although it's sometimes difficult for an individual to find a voice in a relationship, good communication is pertinent to its success."

AnnaLisa Derenthal, LPC, NCC, Roswell, Georgia
www.annalisaderenthal.com License# LPC004373
"There's a fine line between love and hate. Powerful emotions lead to actions that carry big consequences. So it behooves you to be cautious when expressing such things, especially regarding your significant other. The person you share your life with knows your buttons and can stir up these strong feelings. Be clear with yourself first about what you want to say before you speak. Chances are, you hate the behavior or the belief expressed by that person, but not the whole person."

Leide Porcu, PhD, LP, Psychotherapist, Anthropologist, NY, NY
www.leideporcu.com License# 000210
"Two thinking minds and two wanting bodies in a relationship—that takes a lot of rupture and repair. The fabric stretches, breaks and then it's mutually mended and reinforced. With all those patches it may not look all shiny and perfect, but this is what happens when there are two voices that struggle to be heard. This is how a relationship grows and hopefully strengthens, so that we may not have to fall from the sky one day: 'I was happy, so I thought you were happy too. You stopped nagging!' 'I just got quieter!'"

Julia White, Denver, LCSW, Denver, Colorado
www.juliamwhite.com License# 992173
"Here's a fun tip for settling marital disputes non-defensively. Have your discussion butt naked. It's hard to take the situation too seriously under those circumstances."

Randy M. Gold, Psy.D, MFT, Calabasas, California
www.randyandmichellegold.com License# MFC33303
"Play together. It seems to me that couples that play together, do well together. Remind yourselves, and show yourselves, that being together in play and fun is an elixir for a happy marriage. While it's one of a handful of important traits for a happy marriage, it's essential. Play and frolic like children. Hang out, relax, adventure, and explore. Kids do well when they have playtime and so do their parents."

Phillip Lowry, CAGS, LMHC, RYT, Providence, Rhode Island
www.philliplowry.com License# MHC 00137
"In order for a marriage to be a success the couple needs to identify judgments that are interfering with their marriage. Then work towards a higher level of consciousness as individuals and as a couple. A form of therapy that may help is yoga therapy. Yoga is not simply a form of exercise but it is a path to increase consciousness and awareness. The eight limbs of yoga proposed by Patanjali in the *Yoga Sutra* is a path the individual works on to reach the highest level of consciousness. By mastery of our interactions with the world, our physical self, then our mind. I propose that a couple needs to go through a similar process to have a higher level of consciousness and awareness in their marriage."

Alison Howard, Psy.D., Washington, D.C.
www.AlisonHoward.com License# PSY1000439
"When patients ask me why people get married, I have to think about it. My answer has become: in a committed relationship, where two people are actively working on being successfully in a relationship, each person is also actively working on being a good spouse. We are therefore working on being good people, and this work inevitably seeps into the other relationships in our lives."

Rachel A. Sussman, LCSW., New York, New York
www.rachelasussman.com License# 070997-1
"One of the biggest mistakes I see married couples make is to become careless with their sexual connection. Sexual intimacy is such an important factor in a relationship. It's the one thing that separates friends from lovers. Whether you've been married for one year or fifty, it is entirely possible to see your partner as a source of pleasure. No matter what your age, sex is exciting, fun, healthy, and it's a wonderful way to express yourself non-verbally. Sex is very intoxicating and erotic in the early stages of a relationship when the 'chemical love bath' is flowing from our brains, and naturally, some of that excitement and desire will wear off over time. Try not to yearn for or mourn the past – no one can go back in time. Instead, get busy, get creative and invent new ways to connect sexually that are more representative of who you and your spouse are today."

Mary Julia Klimenko, LMFT, Benicia, California
www.mjklimenko.com
"Take a moment, when it seems like your partner is attacking you and recognize that there is no such thing as an angry person who isn't hurting or afraid. Look past the anger to the person you fell in love with. He/she is still there, summon your courage, drop below your ego, see what your partner is hurting about and speak to the hurt instead of combating the anger. If you have the wisdom to do this, you will have a very effective way of connecting to the person you love and making things better for both of you."

Nicholas Kirsch, Ph.D., Washington, D.C.
Bethesdapsychotherapist.com License# 1000137
"Remember that with a couple there are always 3 entities present: 2 individuals and 1 couple. Its relatively easy to know what each individual needs, while its easy to ignore what the couple needs in order to thrive. That's an equation for disaster. Successful couples pay attention to and cultivate the couple's needs, and they often choose to suspend or compromise their individual needs. Easy to say, very difficult to practice."

Joyce Thompson, MS, LCMFT, Wichita, Kansas
www.emotionaljourney.org License# 734
"When one of you has Post Traumatic Stress Disorder, both of you struggle with PTSD. Although it can be overwhelming for each of you, together you can learn to understand what's going on. To help make your marriage a success read books, research on-line, and get into Couple's Therapy with a therapist who 'gets it'. Once both of you figure out the 'hows' and 'whys' of PTSD, you can begin to grasp the 'hows' and 'whys' of each other. This 'task' can offer both of you the opportunity to love, laugh, and find hope together as individuals and as a couple."

Brittany Dudas, Psychiatrist, New York City & Greenwich, CT
www.bdudas.com
"In the course of any long-term relationship, and particularly one so close as marriage, people will make mistakes, sometimes egregious mistakes with painful consequences. Only forgiveness, made possible by love, will see a marriage through these difficult times."

Peter C. Cousins, Ph.D., ABPP Houston, Texas
www.changebringshappiness.com License# 23052
"Realize that on bad days YOU will be confused with THEM, and on good days you will be asked to love them and honor them. Your partner may resemble them more and more as they age, so if you have trouble finding something you like about them, you are not really trying."

Rama Ronen, Ph.D, San Francisco, California
WWW.entelechywellness.com License# PSY 23043
"Your relationship with your partner will change dramatically after having a baby. You will view each other with a new set of eyes. In order to keep your marriage strong and real it is important to treat each other with compassion and respect. Give each other the time and space to adjust to your new reality. Try your best not to interpret a behavior or a comment as personal or as a rejection. Cherish this change that transformed you to become a family."

Diana Kirschner, Ph.D., New York, New York
www.lovein90days.com
"My husband, Sam, and I used to fight like crazy and it was killing our
marriage. So we used a signal with each other to transform an
incendiary exchange that was heading into battle into one that drew us
together.

We realized that reality is, in a sense, like a 'movie' we are making all
the time. If you want to make a great romance, you need to practice
'rewinding the tape' when you don't like 'the take.' We agreed that
either of us could call out **'Take Two'** whenever he/she was hurt or
offended. Then we would start the interaction all over again and
construct it in a more loving win-win way—as a happy improv. If Sam
had trouble saying the words I needed to hear on a Take Two, I would
teach him and vice versa. This technique has saved us many times!

The last time Sam and I were on a plane together we started snapping
at each other and then we did a Take Two. I wound up sitting on his
lap telling him a joke. The stewardess asked us how long we had been
going out together! She was shocked when we answered, 'Over 25
years!'"

Barbara Winter PhD, Boca Raton, Florida
www.drbarbarawinter.com License# PY4034
"Those who we bring into our lives typically mirror who we are. The
roots of our unhealed pain often attract those who will continue to feed
those wounds. We need to help heal the wounds of our spouse and not
keep them open. All those things that go into a loving relationship will
help heal."

Samantha Madhosingh, Psy.D., McLean, Virginia
www.kidsfirstdoc.com License# 0810003364
"Value your spouse's positive attributes, and express gratitude and love
in your marriage daily. Writing in a gratitude journal will allow you to
focus on all the things you appreciate about your spouse, family, and
life."

Teresa L. Oglesbee, Ed.S, NBCC, NBCCH, LPC, Rincon, Georgia
http://www.sccforu.com/ License# LPC004615
"Be Discreet: Got your attention didn't I? Be discreet with what you share about your marriage. Even telling your best friend or a trusted family member about certain information regarding your spouse is inappropriate and can ruin your marriage."

Michi Fu, Ph.D., Licensed Psychologist, Los Angeles, California
http://asianamericanpsych.blogspot.com/ License# CA PSY 19807
"A colleague of mine who specialized in working with couples and sex therapy once told me that the key to a happy marriage is realizing that the other person will never change. What does this really mean? It means accepting your spouse the way that they are, rather than secretly hoping that they'll change over the course of time, because they love you so much, etc. Therefore, it's more important to change your own perspective, rather than focusing on your partners' (mis)behaviors. Do you agree?"

Paula Chu, Ph.D., LPC, Farmington, Connecticut
www.paulachu.com
"The connection between two people in a good marriage is strong enough to bear each person's whole weight when it needs to. That is, you can be your whole self and the connection can still bear that. In fact that's how it grows stronger and stronger. The *freedom to be whole* comes from knowing that the other person is *a champion for your inner growth and well-being*. Trusting that, you can share all the difficult thoughts and feelings that come with being human. When inner struggles are shared in the space between two people who love and respect each other, the burden lifts and the darkness fades. It's essential t*o be able to repair* the inevitable nicks and tears in the connection, and it helps to delight in each other's company. But over the years, these things are sustainable only when you know the other person is actively safeguarding your growth and well-being.
As Augusten Burroughs wrote about his own marriage: 'Even when we fight, it is in a Container of Good.' A good marriage exists within a Container of Good."

Faith Freed, MFT Intern (#IMF 61352), San Francisco, California
www.faithfreed.com Supervisor Dr. Sarah Villarreal, Psy D.
"Lighten up! We need to be able to laugh at ourselves, laugh with our spouse and laugh about the relationship. Finding the humor in it all is a healing elixir. Recently, I texted my husband 'Say something funny.' And he wrote back 'Something funny.' Silly, sure. Yet I felt instantly heard, connected, reassured and charmed. Badabing Badaboom."

Christy Sorden, LPC, Colorado Springs, Colorado
www.SordenCounseling.com
"Over communicate! Just when a spouse has assumed something, this typically enlists a defensive response from their significant other. This will begin the downward spiral of negative communication and cause the same old arguments. If one takes the time to over communicate, they are being sure to communicate their needs, wants, desires, as opposed to assuming their spouse already knows. This extra communication provides information so the defensive reaction that follows assumption is prevented."

Michael G Quirke, L.M.F.T., San Francisco & San Mateo, CA
www.michaelgquirke.com License# MFC39030
"Sincere apologies go a long way. So many people wait silently hoping that their spouse will perceive the hurt that they feel and genuinely apologize."

Patti Geier, LCSW, Psychotherapist, Brooklyn, New York
www.pattigeier.com License# R031706-1
"A huge difference between marriages that succeed and those that don't have to do with the way a couple fights. Fighting can be destructive or constructive, depending on the way you engage with your partner. Destructive fighting is about blaming, shaming, criticizing, and assassinating each other's character, which can destroy a marriage. Constructive fighting means taking responsibility for the way you feel and expressing your feelings using 'I statements'. For example, 'I don't feel safe when the car is driven fast. I feel scared. I want the speed to be reduced.'"

Dr. Jeffrey Bernstein, Exton, Pennsylvania

www.drjeffonline.com

"Trying to improve your marriage without first being aware of your own toxic thoughts toward your spouse and challenging them is an exercise in futility."

Amy Serin, PhD., Psychologist, Peoria, Arizona

www.TheSerinCenter.com License# 3859

"It is important in a marriage to seek outside help before problems get to be too overwhelming. We live in a fast-paced, complicated culture and marital problems can spin out of control before spouses know what hit them. The result can be the end of a relationship that had the potential for greatness. Often little a change and hope that can be instilled by a professional are all a relationship needs to be put back on the right track."

Lora Hanna, LISW, Columbus, Ohio

www.lorahanna.com License# I 0007749

"Don't rely on your spouse to meet all of your needs. It is unrealistic to think that one person can be your lover, best friend, confidant, dance partner, etc. This puts too many expectations on your spouse and sets you both up for disappointment and frustration. Instead, be sure to stay connected to or cultivate other people and activities in your life to meet your social and emotional needs. Your life will be richer and your relationship will be stronger because of it."

Philip C. Hyde, Ph.D., Oklahoma City, Oklahoma

http://philipchydephd.com/

"Based on my clinical experience, I believe there are 3 keys to having a successful marriage. One, that couples work out a mutually agreeable way to 'manage' conflict without raging or just avoiding disagreements. Two, that couples find ways to have 'fun' together and not let conflict enter into their fun time. Three, that they develop a strategy and a time for listening to each other and having an opportunity to talk about relationship matters airing gripes, complaints, and appreciations."

Sandy McDermott, LCPC, NCC, Tranquility Counseling, Illinois
www.createtranquility.com
"Prior to discussing a problem that might cause conflict, try using a relaxation or guided imagery CD. When you are calm and at peace to start with, you can avoid lots of anger."

Jay P. Granat, Ph.D., LMFT, River Edge, New Jersey
www.StayInTheZone.com and www.DrJayGranat.com
"At times, it is best to just 'let things be.'"

Michael Keller, Ph.D., Licensed Psychologist, St. Paul, Minnesota
www.psychologicalserviceassociates.com License# MN LP 4821
"My experience in working with couples reveals that happy couples do not necessarily avoid conflict, but more so tend to handle conflict constructively. By doing so, they tend to use conflict to solve problems rather than to attack the other person, thereby actually building their relationship as a result of how they experience the conflict. Happy couples strive to be gentle and positive with one another during conflict by avoiding being particularly critical, defensive, or sarcastic. In doing so, they demonstrate respect and concern for their spouse as a person, while being able to still disagree or challenge their spouse's position on given matter."

Ari E. Fox, LCSW, New York, New York
www.copewithschool.com License# NYS 076234-1
"Couples often get bogged down with what is perceived as *fairness* in a relationship. I am doing A and B, so she better be doing the same. I am putting in the time, so it is not fair that he is not keeping up his side, a frustrated spouse might express. A couple in a healthy long term relationship may come to recognize that expecting complete and constant equality of responsibilities or energy is not realistic or useful. It is more helpful to think of a marriage as an ebb and flow in which each spouse contributes to the best of his or her abilities at any given time, with the understanding that roles could be reversed or situations could change at any moment. This fosters a more collaborative partnership that can reduce competition and negativity."

129

Christy A. Cole, LCPC, Kennebunk, Maine

www.christycolecounseling.com

"Each spouse writes down ideas for unique dates and puts them into a jar. Dates could range from dance lessons to going on a hot air balloon ride. Then one idea is pulled from the jar and the date is turned into reality."

Isadora Alman, LMFT, Alameda, California

www.askisadora.com License# ML24319

"No matter how many roles you have to play co-mortgage holders, parents, community members, workers, friends - never forget that you were once sweethearts and that relationship needs to be nurtured. So find time every week to spend 'sweetheart time' together doing what you did when you were first dating."

David Brandt, L.C.S.W., Upper Montclair, New Jersey

www.davidbrandtlcsw.com

"There is nothing like a relationship to bring out and push any existing buttons. The rewards of companionship and intimacy are wonderful but they usually don't come without compromising and negotiating on many subtle and not so subtle levels, especially over the long haul. But sharing space and time together does not have to mean totally giving up one's own space and/or identity. For some, the 'caretaker' part of themselves gets called upon. For others, 'fear of abandonment' may enter in. And, for still others, 'fear of confrontation' may arise. In any of these cases it is then difficult to disappoint the other (which is a normal thing to sometimes have to do), or 'matter of fact-ly' be firm regarding one's boundaries, as the imagined consequences may seem too dire. It is equally important to find the fine line between asserting one's needs and not treading too harshly on one's partner's needs and concerns. The only models we have in all of this are often our own (frequently dysfunctional) parents, siblings and family members and the dynamics we have watched and/or experienced with (and through) them. We certainly must eventually pick our battles carefully, find balance, mutual respect, empathy and compromise. This takes practice, interest and work!"

Weston M Edwards, Ph.D., Psychologist, Minneapolis, Minnesota
SexualHealthInstitute.org License# 3347
"Sexual satisfaction is an indicator of the level of overall health in a
relationship. Our biggest hopes, fears, joys and pains are often linked
to sexuality. Societal values typically limit sexual expression to a
primary relationship. It is imperative that you and your partner address
sexual desires, interests, needs, fears, limits, wants and hopes.
Anything you can't talk about, you need to be talking about with your
partner."

Marcel Schwantes, Life Design Coach, Chattanooga, Tennessee
www.marcelcoaching.com
"I want to give you an understanding of the core roles men and
women play in a complimentary relationship that brings success to a
marriage. Lets look at the core role of a wife.

Her design is that of a 'helper.' In Old Testament Biblical
tradition, God gave Eve (see Genesis 2:18) the job description of a
'suitable helper' for Adam. A fascinating term but widely
misunderstood because in modern society, a 'helper' is viewed as a
position of subordination--they have no authority. In reality, a 'helper'
in the Old Testament is a person of strength who supports and provides
assistance to people in need. In essence, there's no implication of
inferiority in the woman's role as 'helper.' It is a great compliment to
women as invaluable to their men, custom-made to help husbands be
and do what they can't be and do on their own."

Sara Lesser, LCSW, Oakland, California
www.saralesser.com License# LCS24539
"We all long for a secure connection to our spouse. At times, it can be
so hard to access or believe this. We can find ourselves stuck in the
same dynamics, frustrated, sad and blaming each other. Most couples
do some of this. In order to make marriage satisfying, we must find
our way to honestly expressing and understanding the impact we have
on each other and to knowing each other's more vulnerable feelings
and needs."

Rudy Rodriguez, LCSW; ADHD Coach, Asheville, North Carolina
http://adhdcenterforsuccess.com/blog License# C000238
"Attention Deficit Hyperactivity Disorder relationships can be fun, exciting and frustrating. To transform your troubled ADHD relationship, start by grounding yourselves in a clear and *accurate* understanding of adult ADHD. Acknowledge the strengths as well as the challenges and weaknesses of your ADHD spouse and modify unrealistic expectations. It is equally important to recognize the possible feelings, concerns and frustrations of the non-ADHD spouse. If more help is needed, don't hesitate to seek help from a 'trained ADHD professional'."

Olubukonla (Bukky) Kolawole, PsyD, New York City, New York
www.drbukkyk.com
"There are different paths to resolving fights in a relationship— the long route and the short route. You decide which route you take, whether intentionally or unintentionally. The long route is one where you focus on the content of the event that triggered the fight (i.e., the who, what, where, when and why) and systematically analyze it to see who gets what portion of the blame. The short route involves simply identifying the emotions beneath the content of the event (i.e., how your spouse was or is feeling) and addressing that in a compassionate way that communicates and promotes a sense of safety to your partner. You see, relationships rely on three main types of safety to thrive— physical safety, emotional safety and commitment safety. Always do your part to cultivate all three, especially during the most difficult times."

Carole Gauthier, NYS Licensed Psychoanalyst, New York, NY
www.carole-gauthier.com
"There is absolutely no recipe to make a marriage successful. It all depends on many parameters, which are dependent on context and personality. Above all, the 2 partners need the awareness, willingness and courage to be honest/authentic and deal with whatever comes up between them without hiding nor manipulating nor taking anything for granted."

Jason Hughes, MA Holistic Counseling, Beverly Hills, California
www.onemanslovestory.net
"Self-love lays the groundwork for creating a healthy and constantly flourishing marriage."

Alisa Ruby Bash, LMFT, Beverly Hills, California
www.alisarubybash.com License# 47733
"I think one of the most essential pearls of wisdom to remember when you are married is to follow my rules of the 4 C's on a daily basis. Everyday, we must: **Commit** to our relationship again by thinking about why you married your spouse or why you fell in love with them, **Communicate** about our day, our feelings, hopes, and fears, **Connect** in some way physically whether it is through sex or just a simple hug and kiss, or backrub, and, be **Considerate** of our spouse's feelings by gathering our thoughts before we say something hurtful we regret later, or by getting them their favorite dessert, or just being kind. At the end of the day, before you go to bed, reflect back consciously to see if there is any part of the formula you overlooked. There are no hard and fast rules and you can fulfill the 4 C's in 5 minutes if you don't have time, or make a whole day or vacation out of it. But, overall, it is an easy way to remember this recipe whose intention is to encourage kindness and appreciation in your marriage, and help prevent anger, hostility, and pent up frustration from building."

Christy Sorden, LPC, Colorado Springs, Colorado
www.SordenCounseling.com
"Children can bring absolute joy into a marriage as well as high levels of stress. Married couples will be strides ahead of this battle if they learn, early on, to tackle this obstacle as a team. By keeping boundaries between parent time, parent child time, and family time this will show children that although they are very important to the family dynamics that parents deserve equal time together. Children will also learn to not pin parents against each other if the parents front teamwork. In order to accomplish this task, have parental conversations when the children are not present. Even if you think they cannot hear you, because they most likely can!"

Leashia Moody-Miller, LPC, Birmingham, Alabama

www.moody-milllercounseling.com License# 2063
"When a spouse suffers from a mental illness such as depression, anxiety or bipolar they can go through periods of normal functioning and limited functioning. In these situations the marriage can be stressed to the point of irreparable damage due to the roles that develop. I encourage the spouse that is not ill by saying, 'Coping with the mental illness of your spouse involves taking care of yourself as you care for them. This will help you to not develop unhealthy roles with your partner that can lead to resentment. It is also important to separate them from their illness and remember that their illness doesn't define them or your relationship with them'."

Michael Luongo, LPC, Chaplin, Connecticut

www.michaelluongolpc.com License# 001182
"Real love is about more than just the initial infatuation. Infatuation is an extremely fun & exciting part of a relationship, but real love is about commitment and the desire to be with someone through the hard times, as well as the good times. Over the course of a long-term relationship, there are going to be potential pitfalls (i.e. financial difficulties, childcare issues, unforeseen medical issues, etc). If you work hard together, at your marriage, the feelings of infatuation that, initially, brought you together will remain a part of your marriage."

Ilene A. Serlin, Ph.D, BC-DMT, San Francisco, California

www.union-street-health-associates.com License# PSY 11092
"Live in abundance by encouraging each other to be creative, take reasonable risks for your dreams, and be each other's confidantes and best friends."

Nancy Simon, L.C.S.W. Evanston, Illinois

www.nancysimontherapy.com
"In a healthy relationship, each spouse knows who he/she is and what they need in order for both to be happy and safe. Accept your spouse and realize that nothing they do is ridiculous; just misunderstood. Empathy goes a long way."

Renae M. Reinardy, Psy.D., LP, Fargo, North Dakota
www.lakesidecenter.org License# 434
"Avoid perfectionism that leads to parenting your spouse. It is true that there is a correct way to fill the dishwasher, but if you are constantly correcting your spouse due to your own perfectionism, it can cause problems in your relationship. Let the small stuff go, even if your way is 'better'. This will allow your spouse to remain confident in their own skills which in turn will lead to more helping-out behaviors. When a spouse feels like they can not do it correctly, they will often stop doing the task completely. Good enough gets it done and you and your spouse remain equals in the relationship."

Kimberly Gist Miller, LMFT, Frisco, Texas
www.harmony-counseling.com License# LMFT 5212
"The key to a long, happy, healthy marriage is for both partners to allow for truth to be spoken. Finding the courage to lovingly and respectfully share your thoughts, feelings and needs allows your partner to know you intimately and creates a powerful attachment. Not speaking truth, in order to avoid conflict, leads to emotional distance. Distance creates detachment. Detachment creates resentment. Resentment creates indifference. Indifference leads to divorce."

Joe Lowrance, Psy.D., Clinical Psychologist, Atlanta, Georgia
www.FinancialPsychologyCeus.com
"Money is an ongoing opportunity within a marriage to explore oneself, oneself in the world and in the context of a martial relationship."

Peter Strisik, Ph.D., Psychologist, Anchorage, Alaska
http://www.strisik.com
"One of the most important skills is the ability to tell the difference between solvable and unsolvable problems in relationships. Relationship skills that couples learn can then be applied most efficiently to solvable problems with the benefit of encouragement and confidence from greater resulting success. Perhaps more difficult to master is loving acceptance when it comes to the unsolvable ones."

Larry Cappel, M.A., LMFT, Denver, Colorado
http://downtowndenvertherapy.com/ License# LMFT715
"Saying No, the Ultimate Act of Love
Saying 'NO' is an act of love. If you've got a spouse that is addicted to gambling, sex, or substances, the most loving thing you can do is say NO! No, you cannot continue to be a part of this relationship and this family unless you are active in a recovery program, are maintaining sobriety and are working to resolve the underlying problems that led to your addiction in the first place. Many spouses are afraid to make this stand out of fear that their partner will choose addiction over relationship. The truth is that you've already lost them. The addiction is like an affair. Your partner is carrying on with 'someone else.' Saying 'NO' is the only chance you have of getting your spouse back. If you continue to support them in their addictive behavior you are helping them to continue the 'affair' with their addiction."

Karen Bonner, MS, LPC, Madison, Mississippi
www.dreamcounselor.ms License# LPC 1293
"When two people get married, a third thing is created that is more important than the two individuals. That third thing is the marriage. It is a living, dynamic entity that the two individuals must yield to. If the spouses in the marriage can put the marriage first – not themselves or one another, the marriage will thrive. Putting oneself first in a marriage is obviously problematic but putting the other first all of the time is equally bad, leading to the resentment that always accompanies codependency. If both spouses agree to put the marriage first – always attempting to do what is best for the marriage, success is more likely."

Anthony Scheving, M.A., Psy.D., (#PSB 35759) Sonora, California
Supervised by Dr. Susan B. Day Ph.D. CA PSY # 23349
"One of my favorite sayings is, 'Underneath anger is hurt and underneath hurt is caring.' If you don't care about something then it is impossible to get hurt, and if you are not hurt then you are less likely to get angry. It is very easy to react in anger, but if one can express the hurt behind the anger, it creates understanding. If one can express why one cares in the first place then you are on your way to compassion."

Kelly Newbill, LMFT, Sacramento, California
www.kellynewbillmft.com License# 48465
"Find what works for the two of you, it might not be what works for
the couple next to you."

Laurie Monroe, Licensed Clinical Social Worker, Eureka, CA
www.healingtheinnergoddess.com License# LCS 21959
"One of my favorite quotes is by George Bernard Shaw: 'We don't stop
playing because we grow old, we grow old because we stop playing.'
A happy relationship (or marriage) is one in which play is prevalent
and does not only pertain to any children or pets in the home. Be
spontaneous! Have you done anything silly and unexpected this week?
Be creative. Use your imagination(s)! Challenge your spouse that you
will both do at least one spontaneous act every week. Be silly with one
another! Go to the toy store and buy 2 yo-yo's or 2 hula hoops (really
great exercise, by the way!), go to the adult toy store and buy some
grown up toys, spontaneously stop at the park and go for a hike, climb
a rock, look for whales, see an animated movie or make an emergency
ice-cream stop. The only boundaries are ones you impose. Who said
we are supposed to act like grown-ups? Grown-ups are boring!
Children play and laugh easily. Happy adults do, as well."

Monica O'Neal, Psy.D., Boston, Massachusetts
www.DrMonicaONeal.com
"A wedding is not some magical process...and while your officiant is
ordained with powers, those of sorcery are not one of them! In most
cases, you know who you are and you know who you are choosing to
be with, before you enter the marriage. Therefore, if you have some
serious considerations or concerns about your partnership before you
make the commitment of marriage, they will only continue to be there
once you say, 'I do.' They'll most likely become more challenging over
time. With this in mind, it is definitely worthwhile to do clinical
premarital counseling to decide if you're ready to commit yourself to
one another. And if you decide that you are ready to marry, it will at
least help you learn how to best nurture the warmth and joy within the
relationship."

Ginna Beal, LCSW, Austin, Texas

www.ginnabeallcsw.com License# 32880

"Our Way or The Highway: The quickest way to get your spouse to understand your complaints is to listen to him/her. When you really give up any need to be 'right' and 'win,' you are on the path to finding 'our' way, rather than 'my' way. Also, when you begin to admit your own mistakes, your spouse will feel much safer in admitting his or her own mistakes and the door opens for finding 'our way.'"

Julie Dubovoy, LCSW-R, Babylon, New York

http://www.juliedubovoy.com/

"Intimacy: The Remedy for the Inevitability of Change: Whether we like it or not, life is about change. Yet, embracing the inevitability of change does not mean you must sacrifice happiness in your marriage.

When a couple has a child, especially a first child, they are rarely prepared for just how dramatically the dynamics of the relationship change. There is less time and energy for one another, so they lose the intimacy that was there before the children, the marriage, the careers, and everything else.

I guide them back to the path by reminding them that if it were not for love, then nothing else would exist or will exist. If the relationship is not nurtured, the foundation upon which all else is built in the marriage will wash away. Find ways to re-establish intimacy: Set a date night. Do not allow your children to sleep with you. Lay with each other on the couch without a child in between you.

You will be surprised how something as simple as a sudden embrace or a private moment can rekindle the flame."

Rosemary Clarke, PhD, LPCC, Albuquerque, New Mexico

www.relationshipcoinc.com License# LPCC 94

"There are six competencies each with a set of skills that make a marriage a success. The competencies are: Commitment, Caring, Compatibility, Communication, Conflict Management and Change."

Judye G. Hess, PhD., Berkeley, California
judyehess.com License# PSY5553
"If you cherish your time alone, DON"T give it up in your marriage.
You may lose the most important part of you and then have nothing to
give yourself or anyone else. Whether you schedule a daily walk
alone, have your own study time, have a room or a wing of your own
in your home, or live in a separate domicile, it may well be worth the
extra cost or inconvenience.

As the famous poet Rilke has said, 'When a person abandons himself,
he is no longer anything, and when two people give themselves up in
order to become closer to each other, there is no longer any ground
between them and their being together is a continual falling'."

Debra Franklin, LCSW, Granby, & Hartford, Connecticut
www.progressivepsychotherapy.com
"Most relationships either fail or are unhappy. Why is this? It is
because most people enter into a relationship wanting to be fulfilled by
the other person. Unconsciously, they are seeking something that was
missing in their childhood. The truly happy relationships are those in
which people felt fulfilled before the relationship, already in gratitude
for what they have and naturally enjoying some service to their
community (in work for example). The relationship then becomes a
secondary, beautiful gift, not a 'need.' Healing the self can improve the
way we view ourselves, our work, and in turn, our relationships in
order to be much happier."

Karen Turner, LMFT, DAPA, Denver, Colorado
www.ElderWisdom.com License# 426
"The shared 'spiritual' basis of a marriage is essential to success or
failure. By spiritual, I mean that the 'spirit' of the marriage is based in
shared values of mutual respect, love and cherishing one another to be
and become the very best person possible. These values may or may
not be religion based, but must be shared. A strong spirit means that
the couple really likes one another as well as loves one another. They
are supported to thrive and not just survive."

Dr. Jeffrey Bernstein, Exton, Pennsylvania
www.drjeffonline.com
"In successful marriages, understanding is more important than love. I have never seen any divorced people reflect back and say that they felt totally understood by their ex spouse."

Steve Sisgold, M.A., Certified Relationship Counselor, Novato, CA
www.onedream.com
"It is said in the Hebrew tradition that when two people join in love, a voice from heaven announces the merging of the souls. In Hebrew your lover or spouse is your 'Bashert', which means destiny. We create sacred love when we remember that we are in the presence of the beloved and express unconditional compassion, honor and love.

And when something happens that shakes that feeling, breathe in and share your whole body experience with the intention of staying close, not being right."

Anna Stewart, MFT Registered Intern (IMF# 60886) California
Supervised by Darlene Davis, MFT (MFC# 40875)
"The monotony of everyday life can create feelings that you've married a business partner or a roommate who helps with the chores. At these times, look at your spouse and remember that they were once a fun-loving child who built couch cushion forts, finger painted, and spun in circles until they collapsed in dizzy laughter. Do something silly and playful with your partner to see that light and imagination shine again."

Dr. Rosalind S. Dorlen, Psy.D., Psychologist, Summit, New Jersey
www.drdorlen.com License# 1369
"There is a tendency for two people who fall in love to consciously or unconsciously wish that the other will complete them and make them whole. They then spend their lives trying to morph that person into being more like themselves. To find value, appreciation and humor in celebrating the differences between you and your spouse is an aspirational, but achievable goal."

Lova G. Njuguna, MC, NCC, LPC, LISAC, CCBT, Tucson, AZ
www.pimacounseling.com License# LPC 2171 & LISAC 11871
"I knew that my husband was a good fit for me when I realized he did not need me to create his happiness. He was already happy with his life. He just wanted to share it with me."

Kevin M Hallinan, LCSW, CAP, SAP, ICADC, Melborne, Florida
www.Kmhpsychotherapist.com License# SW6611
"Frame of reference: Although we all have unique frames of reference, we tend to believe others have the same frame of reference, as us. This is one of the primary obstacles in human communication and thereby, in human relationships, marriage in particular. No matter what the difficulty may be, it can not be resolved if the spouses are unable to communicate effectively with one another. Therefore, in order for a marriage to be successful it's essential for the couple to realize this, and not turn their referential assumptions into 'facts'. "

Lindsey Stewart Plumer, LMFT, Roseville, California
www.lindseyplumer.com License# MFC43983
"Couples are often quite surprised at how difficult having babies and small children are on the satisfaction within a marriage. Research shows that this time period is universally the most difficult for the majority of couples. Getting help during this time can keep a couple on track. It is also helpful to hold the attitude that the frustrations that come up around early childrearing are temporary and pass with time."

Philip C. Hyde, Ph.D., Oklahoma City, Oklahoma
http://philipchydephd.com/
"Based on my clinical experience, I believe there are 3 keys to having a successful marriage. One, that couples work out a mutually agreeable way to "manage" conflict without raging or just avoiding disagreements. Two, that couples find ways to have 'fun' together and not let conflict enter into their fun time. Three, that they develop a strategy and a time for listening to each other and having an opportunity to talk about relationship matters airing gripes, complaints, and appreciations."

Cyndie Westrich, M.A., A.T.R.-BC, LPC, Marietta, Georgia
www.easel-arttherapy.com
"Honoring another is not to be confused with submission. Holding whom your husband or wife is as a person dear to your heart is honoring him/her."

Yaji Tramontini, Licensed Marriage Family Therapist, California
http://yajitherapy.com License# MFC45878
"It is important to express your needs in a relationship; in fact the marriage is doomed without that expression. Expressing needs is not about putting the toilet seat down, taking out the trash, coming home to a lovingly prepared meal and or clean home. It goes beneath that. The needs I speak of are behind the reason you get so darn upset when the 'surface' needs aren't met. For example you might think, wow he didn't put the toilet seat down, he must not respect me very much. Flip this around and you get at the deeper need. I need to FEEL respected. You can take this even deeper. Why do I need to feel respected, because I need to feel loved, and when you don't put the toilet seat down, I don't feel loved. The following are 5 things you can do to reveal what your need is in order to accurately express what you feel, think and want:
1. Start with noticing your reactions.
2. Do you feel annoyed, irritated, angry, sad, frustrated, hopeless, etc?
3. Question why you are FEELING that way.
4. Go even deeper in your questioning, what is the NEED behind the feeling?
5. If you can, go even deeper with the questioning. Keep going until you hit the very basic needs. Love, support, safety, etc."

Julie Blackman, LCSW, Chicago, Illinois
www.julieblackmanlcsw.com
"A successful relationship is one in which each partner is authentic and whole while also feeling connected. There is enough trust for each to be vulnerable and enough space to keep evolving, even though it means going into unchartered territory. Only if they're engaged in each other's journey will they grow together rather than apart."

Julie Weiner-Dabda MC, NCC, LPC (License# LPC-13264), AZ

http://julieweinerdabdacounseling.community.officelive.com
"Marriage is and always will be a work in progress. There are hills and valleys, high points that start off as 'the facade of happily ever after' but at times can be, 'when will this be over, or why did I do this?' My pearl of wisdom, would be 'you get out of it what you are willing to put into it'. Marriage always requires work, just as any relationship does, however if it becomes more work then play, then it is time to reconsider your contribution. People talk about friendship, sex, passion, communication, trust, as being the foundation of marriage however if expectations are not clear and not communicated effectively, then the foundation becomes weak. Both parties must be 100% happy with their decision and roles in the relationship. The trick is knowing when the happiness starts to fade and what needs to be done to re- kindle the happiness."

Elayne Savage, PhD., Licensed Marriage Family Therapist, CA

http://www.QueenofRejection.com License# MFC 17077
"If one of you stays up much later than your spouse, consider tucking in the 'early-bird.' It's a nice ritual and a sweet way to connect at the end of the day."

Janet Holt, LPC, Hot Springs, Arkansas

www.janetholt.com License# P1007048
"We don't prepare people well for marriage in our society. Fairy tales end at 'happily ever after.' The lack of respect and the sarcasm that passes for humor in our popular culture models the exact opposite of skills needed. This oft-repeated line from the 1970's hit movie, *Love Story,* is a perfect example: 'Love means never having to say you're sorry.' Wrong, wrong, wrong. Love doesn't die of natural causes. It dies from abuse or neglect.

I've never agreed with the sentiment that marriage is work. Instead, I think of it as a life account that pays rich dividends if you invest regularly. Deposits take the form of kindness, fidelity, mutual respect, trust, honesty, flexibility, and, of course, romance."

Lara M Schwartz, M.A., MFT, Manhattan Beach, California

www.laraschwartz.com License# MFT35813

"A necessary and often overlooked piece of marriage is each person's individual path. Meaning, it is imperative that each person be willing to take 100% personal responsibility for themselves, specifically their own unique experience in each moment. If we don't inhabit our own experiences, we can't accurately share them with the one we love. And the whole point of marriage is to love and be loved deeply and fully. Without the courage to know ourselves without guard, we won't be present enough to share who we are with our spouse or be able to clearly see who they are. The rewards of marriage are found in bringing our open hearts to each other again and again."

Melissa Cramer, LCSW, CAP, Miami, Florida

GROWHEALLOVE.com License# sw9441

"In any long-term committed relationship, an individual must be wary of allowing their partner's limitations to become their own. They must constantly assess whether their experience of life is broadened through the union. If it is found that one is boxed into their partner's safety zone, the individual must make conscious effort to break free of this box. It is important to always make the space to honor and explore one's desires, hopes and true self."

Shelly Clubb, M.S., M.A., NCC, Denver, Colorado

www.transformativecounselingservices.com License# 12176

"Marriage must hold space for and allow our spouse to change course - perhaps in their work, their spiritual beliefs, and even some core values. If you really knew how much you and your spouse were going to change throughout your lifespan together, could you honestly commit to a lifetime of this sort of uncertainty? Yet, true intimacy requires that we take that risk. Ultimately the contradiction is that we must turn ourselves over to something bigger than either of us – the marriage itself – while at the same time, not forfeiting our own individuation work. The marriage, at its best, would hold us and reflect something back about who we are as a couple and individuals, as we change and grow."

Teresa Trower, M.A. LMHC, Jacksonville, Florida

www.stressbustercoach.com License# MH0002000
"Think before speaking and make sure your words are thoughtful and respectful."

Dr. Fredrick Woodard, LP, PhD, Milford, New Hampshire

Woodardhypnosisandpsychotherapy.org License# 1082 NH
"I believe marriages that are successful are ones that involve a commitment on the part of the couple to work together on issues with money with open communication and cooperation. Money is an important part of the relationship as it may determine one's ability to have further opportunities to develop a holistic life style that is either functional or dysfunctional."

Diane Renz, LPC, Boulder, Colorado

www.yourgatewaytohealing.com License# 4623
"Marriage is not the finish line. Often we see it as a final goal of finding a sense of belonging, connection, and safety, where we will not be alone in the world. The paradox of our interconnectedness and our being alone requires our attention and consciousness. We are born alone; we will die alone, in the sense that no one can do it for us. Moreover, the beauty of our lives and the myriad of emotions and meaning we find lives deep within us. We long to share this, and to some extent can, but the heartache of not fully being able to express to another our experience, is what art and poetry is made of. The point here is to enter relationship staying aware of our responsibility to our experience and not expecting anyone else to fill in the gaps, or keep us from our existential explorations. Relationship can help us to see the parts in us that are seeking healing. Take each disappointment, irritation, insecurity, satisfaction, ease, and confidence that comes from relating in marriage as your gateway to understanding yourself more and more. Your awareness will keep you conscious and responsible to your continual evolution versus becoming complacent waiting for a partner to alleviate any discomfort. With this awareness you might then find the security within yourself that allows you to be vulnerable and open to truly loving."

Catherine DeMonte, LMFT, Beverly Hills & Calabasas, California
www.catherinedemonte.com License# MFT 27623
"It is important to remember that when we enter into a relationship we are not entering it empty handed. We arrive into every relationship with our own baggage, our own stories, our own spoken and unspoken/conscious and unconscious beliefs, goals and desires, our own gender and role assignments, our parent's input and programming, and all of our experiences. That is **a lot** to bring. Although we THINK we are seeing our spouse with fresh eyes, we are really looking at him or her through a set of lenses; lens made out of past relationships and our whole belief system. How that shows up is, if for example your father abandoned your family when you were a child, you may believe all men eventually leave and leading you to be on the lookout for his departure. You look for it so you won't be side-swiped 'when' (not 'if') it happens and may look for cues and clues that aren't really there of your spouse's eventual departure. You might even unconsciously push him away so he will prove you right.

Whatever your 'wound' or story is – it is important to have enough self-awareness so that you know when your partner triggers you, you don't see it as 'proof' of your wound – such as 'I am not enough', 'I will be abandoned' 'I have to do everything myself", etc. Otherwise self-judgments turn into 'My SPOUSE is saying I am not enough', 'S/he is going to leave me.', etc."

Annie Schuessler, LMFT, San Francisco, California
www.annieschuessler.com License# 43865
"When couples argue about money, they tend to argue about particular issues such as whether or not they can afford to go on a vacation this year. These arguments often get gridlocked, because the real argument is not only about those particular decisions. Underneath arguments about money are much larger dreams and fears. Money can represent freedom, security, fun, or even love. Consider asking your spouse what his or her dreams and fears are about money. This conversation can help you get out of gridlock and lead to creating financial intimacy, the kind of relationship where you can talk openly about money."

Daniel L DeGoede, Ph.D, Clinical Psychologist, Pioneertown, CA
www.drdanieldegoede.com License# PSY9479
"After 45 years of marriage you realize it is much easier to see the beauty in your partner's body at 35 years old but much more important at 65 years old."

Nadine Winocur, Psy.D., Los Angeles & Sonora, California
DrNadineWinocur.com License# PSY15391
"Each spouse should get into the habit of practicing mindfulness, such as by doing a daily mindfulness meditation, so that you gain conscious awareness of your actions within the relationship and can take responsibility for them. While your spouse may be the one that precipitates your reactions, in almost every case, you are the one that's responsible for their severity. It's critical that you take responsibility for this intensity no matter how much the other person's words or actions may serve as the metaphorical match that lights the fuse. It's your fuse. Take responsibility for your underlying tendencies to feel hurt, ashamed, or angry by identifying your negative expectations, perceptions, and the beliefs that underlie them, and admit these to your spouse as quickly as they arise. If you do, you are likely to develop a robust and lasting bond. For even greater depth of intimacy, find an effective strategy to heal these negative perceptions, and your relationship will become increasingly easy and enjoyable over time."

Joyce Marter, LCPC, Co-Owner of Urban Balance, Chicago, IL
www.urbanbalance.org License# 180-002902
"Usually, that which initially attracts us to our mate is inevitably what drives us crazy about them down the road! For example, somebody might be attracted to a spouse who motivates them to be their best and helps to structure their life. Down the road, those same characteristics may be viewed as critical or controlling. Or, somebody might be attracted to a partner because of their sense of humor and spontaneity. Down the road, they may be irritated that their spouse does not seem to take life seriously enough. During times of relationship strain, it is important to remember the good ways in which those qualities of our partners impact our lives."

Dee Marcotte, MFT, LPC, Denver, Colorado
Www.deemarcotte.com License# 2704
"When your spouse says they need to speak to you about something that bothers them about you, don't take it personally. If we are listening to learn more about our spouse, we would be listening to find out about their preferences, not our defects. We would make it about them rather than getting self absorbed and making it about us. Keep a good boundary, decide what you can do for them, and don't take it personally."

Dr. Jill Zimmerman, LMFT, Hudson, Wisconsin
www.integracounselingservices.com License# LMFT 189-124
"Don't forget you are still individuals and support each others' dreams and aspirations. For example, if your spouse gets the opportunity to go abroad for three months and you can't go because you're working, the person should still go and have the experience. Being married doesn't mean you are joined at the hip and must do everything together--be interdependent."

Joan Rabinor, LCSW-C, Chevy Chase, Maryland
www.joanrabinor.com
"Empathize with and validate your spouse's feelings, even if you don't necessarily agree with his/her position. He/she will also be more likely to do the same for you. You will both thus minimize defensive communication and conflict, and promote intimacy and mutual understanding. Feeling heard by one's spouse goes a long way."

Barbara J Peters, LPC (License# LPC002758), RN, Cumming, GA
www.bjpcounseling.com and www.thegiftofalifetime.net
"Nothing is more important than the relationship between two people. It can outlast everything from jobs, kids, money and anything else surrounding marriage. But marriage takes work and it needs to be done on a daily basis. No day should go by without you making your marriage a priority. You may ask, 'How can I make marriage a priority?' Think of creative ways to say I love you and give a complement daily."

Lisa Hartwell, PsyD, RN, Honolulu, Hawaii
www.hidrlisa.com License# Psy800
"The values you both agree upon that are important in your marriage should be carried forth during your daily life and be a representation of your marriage and yourselves to others."

Jay Jameson, LMFT, Laguna Hills, California
jayjameson.com License# MFC 34802
"I came to the conclusion early in my life that 'I would rather you behave like you love me and never say it, than have you say that you love me but never engage in behaviors that show love.'"

Matt Borer, Ph.D., Licensed Marriage Family Therapist, Florida
www.mattborer.com and www.breakupplan.com
"Never use the word 'work' in regards to your relationship. People always say things like, 'relationships are hard work,' or 'we need to work on our relationship,' etc. If you can change the word from 'work' to 'focus' it can make all the difference in the world. People work hard enough in their careers to have to come home and work on their marriage. Focus is something that you can do all the time in very small ways. Maybe a text message to say hi, or picking up something small while you are at the store that your spouse might enjoy. If you can ask the question 'how will this effect my spouse' before making a decision, you will find that you are constantly 'focusing' not working on your relationship."

John Sovec, Psychotherapist, MA, LMFT, Pasadena, California
www.JohnSovec.com License# MFC 46376
"In building the foundation for a strong relationship it is vital to maintain not just the identity of the couple as a unit but also of the individuals involved. It is important for couples to remember back to when they first met and remain cognizant of the qualities each admired and was attracted to. Making sure to nurture those qualities in each other, while also nurturing and encouraging their own individual growth will help ensure that there is balance and respect in the relationship."

Dr. Joanne Vizzini, LCPC, NCC, Baltimore & Columbia, MD
http://freedomthroughtherapy.com/ License# LC 1091 & NCC 48509
"In terms of a successful marriage, my thoughts would be, 'A marriage
is a union of two souls who will function best with a balance of being
independent, dependent, and interdependent.' As spoken to me by the
late Dr. Joseph Ciarrocchi, 'Research demonstrates that those who play
together, pray together, and lay together, stay together (1995).' Success
is garnered by the ability of each party to have empathy for their
partner and the pain caused by human interaction in the relationship.
True empathy aids in containing one's defenses and allows the partner
to enter the other person's world. Empathic response is offered
whether or not the behavior is perceived as a cause for pain. The
perceived offending party is invited to notice their own behavior, even
if they do not agree that this behavior caused pain. Demonstrating love
and compassion by having an open, reflective listening stance which
focuses on the impact of behavior on their partner is essential.
Agreeing to disagree and focusing on managing one's own anxiety
instead of expecting one's partner to do so, adds to a template of
satisfaction and contentment. Listening and acting from the heart to a
partner's feelings offers the potential for success, and even happiness,
in marriage."

Nadine Winocur, Psy.D., Los Angeles & Sonora, California
DrNadineWinocur.com License# PSY15391
"Something that can help ensure a successful marriage is to create
levity during moments of disagreement or conflict. It's ideal if one of
you can successfully move from hurt or angry feelings into
compassion for the other, but often, humor is your only and best option
within reach. Keep in mind to only use a type of humor or playfulness
that engages your spouse versus alienates them. The point is to shift
the conversation from a highly charged negative emotional state,
where the two of you are at opposite poles, to one that is a bit lighter,
more positive and more joined. By doing so you might create a space
that permits just enough emotional distance from the pain, and enough
connection with each other, that your feelings and needs can be openly
discussed and resolved."

Joyce Dolberg Rowe, LMHC, Hull, Massachusetts

www.MentalHealthCounseling.biz License #91

"It is my firm belief that if we treat our family members as politely and respectfully as we would treat our boss's child, it is a win - win for all. As spouses, we must show the TLC to one another that we would extend to our best friend; after all, that is why we are together."

Shadia Duske, MA, NCC, Denver, Colorado

www.psychotherapy-healing.com License# NCC 279400

"Being a whole and complete person, comfortable and secure with oneself, allows one to be able to connect to another whole and complete person in a healthy and interdependent way. Only when one feels a sense of self-love and acceptance can one be able to fully embrace and receive the love and acceptance from her spouse as well as have the ability to love and accept her spouse in a healthy and genuine manner. The road to marital success and healthy connection begins with the process of discovering and embracing who we are."

Corinne Soares, LCSW, Fresno, California

http://therapistsdesk.blogspot.com/ License# LCS 24017

"When you marry someone you also marry his or her dreams and ambitions. One of the best ways to show your spouse you love them is by supporting them in achieving their goals. These goals could be educational, career or interpersonally based. Standing by your spouse through any challenges that may arise while accomplishing these goals can strengthen your relationship and make the achievement of the goal memorable for both of you."

Janice C. Hodge, LCPC, Chicago, Illinois

www.jchodge.com

"Pronouncing 'I Do' fuses your entire being to your beloved an entirety. Your enduring commitment will shape your family members and intimate friends as long as you live, too. Acceptance and honor of your Beloved is a sacred and tender trust. This gift of committed relationship is far beyond that of exclusive dating. Do not enter into it lightly or unadvisedly."

James S. Graves, PhD, PsyD, Pasadena, California
www.DrJimGraves.com License# PSY18196
"We usually marry because we 'love' our spouse. Maintaining and expressing that love is a key to a successful marriage. Maintaining love requires both partners to behave with integrity and trustworthiness in the marriage. Expressing love is about verbalizing and physically demonstrating one's deep affection for the other. Mutually saying 'I love you' maintains confidence in the love bond between partners, while physical expression, like hugging, kissing, cuddling, holding hands, causes the release of oxytocin, the 'love hormone.' Frequent release of oxytocin in the body helps to maintain 'that loving feeling,' which, in turn, promotes the desire to express our love. That's a positive feedback loop for marital success."

Melissa Swartz, LGPC, Shepherdstown, West Virginia
www.melissaswartz.com
"When our spouse's dark side offends us, we need to remind ourselves that we have a dark side too and our spouse has a light side as well. Our spouse is a whole person and so are we. One moment is not the sum of who we (or they) are. Keep this in mind to help your marriage to be a success."

Matt Zamzow, Behavioral Specialist, Houston, Texas
www.apolloleadershipsolutions.com and www.eddinscounseling.com
"One of the biggest challenges is learning how to communicate with our spouse. It is important to remember to be true to your own person while also being transparent with your spouse. Always remember to communicate your thoughts, needs, expectations, and desires."

Leah Schoen, LPC Intern, Portland, Oregon
www.schoencounsel.com
"I like what Buddhist philosopher Daisaku Ikeda said, 'Marriage is not made for a pair of lovers gazing fixedly into each other's eyes but for two people aiming at a mutual goal. I quite agree. We promised each other that no matter what adversity we encountered, we would encourage each other and overcome it.'"

Molly Kinser Douglas, ATR, LMHC (License# 001175), Iowa
"What can help make your marriage a success is writing vows for each other even after your married. My husband and I wrote personal vows to each other of how to keep the other happy. His for me included giving back rubs, foot rubs, and even popping my toes, and always promising to record my favorite shows. Mine for him included making pot roast at least once a year, winding up the vacuum cord and not screaming out when I see a deer near the road! These promises are still working well after 7 years. Since we have had our first child there have been a few more 'vows' added to the marriage such as: role-model the kind of parent/person you want her to grow up to be, always make time for play, teach no obvious wrong, and always make time for date nights!"

Laurie Monroe, Licensed Clinical Social Worker, Eureka, CA
www.healingtheinnergoddess.com License# LCS 21959
"I don't know why we don't teach people how to re-connect. We get so good at dis-connecting, we do it all the time, it's normal and natural, and should be expected. We are human beings. We are going to piss each other off. Unfortunately, by the time people get into marriage counseling they have sometimes spent years disconnected. Two people are living in the same house, but they may as well be in different states. How different marriages would be if we were taught to expect to disconnect from one another, taught that the most important thing is to become an expert at re-connecting, quickly, and as often as necessary, sometimes even several times in one day, so that we can STAY connected, which is what can help make marriage a success."

Dr. Sara Denman, Psy.D, Psychologist, Danville, California
drsaradenman.com License# Psy19808
"If you find yourself in conflict with your spouse, sometimes it is best to take a break if things are getting heated. Set a time to come back to it. When the emotions are calmer, a resolution is much more likely. I have learned through the years that during a fight no one is listening. One person speaks and while he/she is speaking the other is figuring out what they are going to say next. Clearly this is not productive."

Dr. Patricia W. Stevens, LPC, Louisville, Colorado
www.awarenessdynamics.com CO License #249
"There is nothing more important in a relationship than touch. Touch is the communication of the heart. We are not individuals who survive in isolation. While words transmit our normal messages, touch adds a dimension that seldom lies. So, touch each other as often as possible – you will find it beneficial to each of you individually and together."

Kara Veigas, MSW, LICSW, Washington, DC
www.karaveigas.com License# LC50078142
"A couple of years ago my partner and I were updating our bathroom. We disagreed on what bathroom fixtures to purchase, based on my concern for what would be safe for our coming child. After a heated argument, my husband turned to me and gently explained that he agreed we should purchase the safer fixtures. What he was really yearning for, he discovered, was to have his preference respected, and to feel understood and appreciated for letting go of that wish for the sake of the family. A courageous effort by my husband to communicate his need for understanding, met with respect and validation, landed us on very solid ground together. We have realized that when you really feel heard and understood by your partner, your sense of safety in the attachment bond with each other deepens. Feeling more securely connected with each other, we found ourselves freer to be joyful, loving, creative and authentic."

John Bogardus, Licensed Clinical Social Worker, Sonoma, CA
www.johnbogardus.com
"When it comes to young people who are contemplating marriage, remember two related ideas. Don't fall in love with someone just because they have 'potential.' While people can grow emotionally, it is not a good bet to marry someone without plenty of evidence that what you love about your partner is already on display. Another way of thinking about this is summed up by the expression, 'What you see is what you get.' In a reflective moment take a good look at your partner and see if you can imagine their flaws just as clearly as you see their strengths. When you are married, this is who you will be with for life."

Keri Cooper, LPC, Austin, Texas

www.coopercounselingpractice.com License# 17351
"Several years ago I took a year sabbatical from my counseling
practice to attend Le Cordon Bleu culinary school. While knee deep
in cake and icing (being neat wasn't one of my gifts) it occurred to me
that relationships are a lot like pastry. No two are the same; each one is
unique and special. While they take time and effort to create, they also
bring great joy. I would encourage couples to not only celebrate their
individuality but also their uniqueness as a couple. I would encourage
couples to embrace and appreciate all the attributes that make their
relationship as unique as they are. Bon Appétit!"

Dr. Jack McInroy, Psychologist, Denver, Colorado

www.DrMcInroy.com License# CO 518
"There was once a wise old man on his front porch rocking in his
favorite chair chatting with his son-in-law Jack. A car comes to a stop
in front of the house and a middle age man walks up to the porch and
asks the older man a question. 'What kinds of people live in this town?'
The older man responded, 'What kind of people live where you come
from'. He responded, 'they were unkind, judgmental, narrow-minded
and rednecks.'

'I'm afraid you will find we have the same people here,' the older man
replied and the guest returned to his car and left. An hour or so passes
when another car stops and the same conversation reoccurs except
when asked how the people were in his town the answer was the
opposite. 'The people in my town are all very nice, giving, friendly,
accommodating and a joy to be around.' The wise old man said the
people here are just the same here too.' The guest left with a smile on
his face.

Jack questioned his father in law, how can you tell the first man people
here are unkind and the second one the opposite?'

'Jack, the man said with kindness and affection, you see in others what
you want to see. Look for the best in people and you will find it!'"

Lindsey Stewart Plumer, LMFT Roseville, California
www.lindseyplumer.com License# MFC43983
"Your partner is NEVER the problem. He or she is your best friend, lover and spouse, but not the problem. If you can both ally together against the problem then not only is it more likely to be solved but it's way more likely you will retain intimacy and respect."

Sara Ruebelt, MFT, Ph.D., Sacramento, California
http://www.hopemore.org/ License# MFC 50059
"In my dissertation research on cross-cultural couples and successful cultural adjustment in intermarriage I have learned that what can make a cross-cultural marriage a success is when couples share a high degree of values, which I call the four pillars: Honesty, Trust, Loyalty and Respect. In addition what helps is for the cross-cultural couples who face cultural differences to adapt and acculturate to each other's cultural world in a way of making a third culture which unites both of their realities and identities in their marriage. Many of the couples I interviewed embraced a cultural integration in their cross-cultural marriage, which involved inviting the 'strengths' featured in their cultural backgrounds as a way to benefit from the richness of both cultures."

Carol A. Anderson, MS, MFCC, Fresno, California
www.acenter4relationships.com License# MFC29432
"I love the concept Harville Hendriz talks about in his book, *Getting the Love You Want*. In summary, marriage is wonderful, but God/Nature/The Universe has a Higher Purpose than for us to merely 'feel good!' In reality, we will almost always fall in love with the person who in the beginning feels so perfect, but in reality turns out to be least capable of meeting our needs! On the other hand, this is the 'Perfect' Partner for calling each other to Wholeness and Healing each others' wounds! As one partner makes requests of the other to meet their needs, the other must often stretch, grow and reclaim Lost Parts of the Self. As that process unfolds, that partner reclaims their Wholeness and as they unconditionally meet their partner's needs, their partner is healed."

Ruth D. Timmons, LCSW, Austin, Texas

ruthtimmons.com License# 53791

"'For better, for worse, for richer, for poorer, in sickness and in health, until death do us part.' So how does someone put this into action when a spouse becomes disabled or is diagnosed with a terminal illness? I think it is a decision, with no other alternative but to stick it out and do what you have to do, with equal parts of love, faith, commitment, and last but not least, humor. My father was a living example of this when my mother was diagnosed with ALS (Lou Gehrig's Disease). Even though he questioned why this happened, had bad days, and often cried, he never gave up on his marriage vows. Whether it was stroking her hair, singing to her, or being silly to make her laugh, my father demonstrated his love for my mother every day."

Anna Kumor, Licensed Marriage Family Therapist, Burbank, CA

www.annakumor.com License# Mfc41879

"Notice how often you attribute a feeling or need you have to your spouse. For example, if you feel angry you might assume that either it's your spouse's fault or it's his/her fault for not noticing and making you feel better. My advice is: take responsibility for your own feelings. Don't treat your spouse like a drug or pacifier who is supposed to comfort you at all times. If you have something to ask for or discuss, do so without blaming. You will increase the respect you have for yourself and for your spouse and at the same time improve your marriage!"

Marlo J. Archer, Ph.D., Psychologist, Tempe, Arizona

www.DrMarlo.com License# 3300

"You can't put two people in a house and not have any conflict. Conflict does not mean angry screaming and yelling, it just refers to a disagreement in which two people want slightly different things. The key to resolving conflict is for each party to let go of what they have already chosen for the solution and focus on what their spouse really needs to get out of a solution. If you each focus on meeting the needs of the other person, you'll come up with creative options neither of you have even considered."

Deborah Hecker, Ph.D, Washington, D.C.
www.drdeborahhecker.com
"The most successful marriages are those created by two-well-formed, secure individuals who come together for the purpose of enhancing one another. This model is in contrast to one that occurs too frequently, often ending in divorce, where spouses seek out marriage to complete their identity. It is not one's partner's responsibility to define them or to provide happiness. One must learn to do those for oneself. A happy marriage consists of 3 well-formed, well-nurtured, and well-balanced entities...the two individuals and the couple. Marriage should be thought of as a gift, not a necessity."

Shari Siegel, MA, CFT, LMFT, Merrick, New York
www.interpersonalsolutions.org
"QUALITY TIME means talking, connecting and looking at each other. It doesn't mean 'finding time' just to say you've spent time together. This is so important for couples to do as to NURTURE the relationship and not let it 'fall to the wayside' during our busy lives."

Jane A. Barton, Ph.D., Licensed Psychologist, Knoxville, TN
www.drjanebarton.com License# 2456
"When you or your spouse has had an affair, it is very challenging for the marriage to survive. I usually guide couples through several steps to begin healing. Steps include honest communication about what happened, sharing feelings about what happened, lots of active listening by both parties, and a clear idea of what it will take to rebuild trust. Lastly, the hardest step: forgiveness. In the process of forgiveness, spouses need to be aware when they are being punitive and be willing to practice stopping that behavior. Punitive behavior can consist of bringing up the affair repeatedly and/or passive-aggressive anger. Your spouse may have had an affair and damaged the marriage, but you will damage it further if you hang on to punitive thoughts and conduct. Hasn't he/she suffered enough? If not, when will it be enough? The truth is, it will probably never be enough. Even though it isn't fair, it is still up to you to forgive and let go in order to make the marriage a success."

Denan Burke, LMFT, MFC, Arizona & California
www.DenanBurke.com License# CA LMFT 10263 & AZ MFC 43415
"Dare to allow yourself to expose your tender, private feelings with one another. This may feel uncomfortable, unsettling, or perhaps embarrassing. Yet, it is when couples choose to risk emotional vulnerability with one another, to truly dare to face each other from a place of raw authenticity and allow their spouse to see their deepest, darkest places, that true bonding and partnership can arise. It is from that place that true strength and trust and emotional safety are woven in and continue to support and lift up the relationship. If there has been hurt, it is from that place that true healing may occur. To risk being emotionally vulnerable to the one that is most precious to you, is the vital step towards pulling your loved one close and creating a deep and lasting love."

Daniel Cowley, PsyD, Charleston, South Carolina
www.INGing.org License# 438
"In a successful marriage, the spouses negotiate openly about roles and functions—who does what and when—and compromise in ways that work for both, yet never compromise their integrity or ask the other to do so. Married individuals must honor their own individuality always, as well as their partner's, and recognize that spouses are like best friends—some last longer than others and then we move on, and that's okay—so enjoy it while it lasts, be gracious in letting go if it ends, and realize that they were like two ships meeting on the high seas, lashing together for awhile, then casting off and moving on their separate ways."

Rhonda Hidaji, Licensed Clinical Social Worker, Memphis, TN
lifevibration.com
"Our spouse is our most profound teacher. They are the ones that will really say, 'yes', the pimple on your nose is really big. Therefore, we must give feedback with love and compassion. When receiving feedback from our spouse our ego must take a back seat and adopt an attitude for gratitude. This is how we grow individually and together in our relationship."

Merrie Pearl, LCSW New Orleans, Louisiana
www.schematherapy-nola.com License# LCSW 9834
"A good marriage happens, in part, when you have a deep awareness of your partner's life story and the wounds they still carry. Each partner is cognizant of what behaviors trigger their partner's injuries, and are mindful not to do so. The marriage is the safe haven where empathy and safety is abundant."

Tom Edwards, Licensed Clinical Social Worker, Germantown, TN
tomedwardslcsw.com License# 1042
"Raising and appreciating a child who doesn't always adhere to social conventions can be a challenging experience for parents and their marriage. For example, there is so much discussion these days about Asperger's Syndrome. Parents can get quite anxious and disturbed, contemplating an uncertain future. Since optimism is what I strive for, I urge Moms and Dads to embrace their children's idiosyncrasies, keep their sense of humor about them, and hang on for what can be a fascinating ride. By doing this it can help generate a positive relationship with their child and make their marriage a success."

Travis E. Frye MA, LPC, Phoenix, Arizona
www.crossroadsfcc.com
"To help make your marriage a success play role reversal. When you and your spouse are having an argument that seems to be getting no where simply stop arguing and reverse roles. You would argue as if you are your spouse while your spouse argues from your perspective. For instance, you might say, 'Well, if I would just be more sensitive to you and help more around the house it would make a big difference.' You are making this statement as if you are your partner. Your spouse, who is arguing as if they are you, may respond with a statement like this: 'Maybe I can approach you differently, not give you so much grief.' What you will discover is that not only can this be fun, but it can also help you connect with your partner's experience and hear their needs in a new way. Finally, this is a step towards empathy, which is a necessary ingredient of a healthy and strong emotional bond with one another."

Dr Linda Olson, Licensed Clinical Psychologist, New Canaan, CT
www.americaslovedoctortherapy.com License# 002473
"You can help make marriage a success by interacting in a way that makes you feel competent and effective, not helpless and overly dependent."

Karen Hoving, Ph.D., Aurora, Colorado
www.drkahoving.com
"Arguments are a part of marriage, but if you get into a dead end argument try this exercise. Partner 1 expresses what s/he is feeling (just the basic points). When 1 is finished, Partner 2 repeats exactly what s/he <u>heard</u> Partner 1 say. THEN 2 responds to what 1 said. Partner 1 then repeats what they heard. This goes on back and forth. It slows the pace down, forces everyone to stop thinking about how they are GOING to respond without LISTENING to what the other is saying and feeling!"

Jay M. Seiff-Haron, Psy.D., #PSY23443, San Francisco, California
http://www.familytherapysf.com Licensed Psychologist CA
"Responsiveness is Key: Over the last few decades, different streams of research have converged upon the notion that emotional responsiveness lies at the heart of successful marriages. In Western cultures, we tend to prize independence and logic while demonizing dependence and heart connections, whereas tensions will arise in any culture when any of these are taken to extremes. Like head and heart, world-renowned couples therapist Dr. Sue Johnson sees independence and dependence as two sides of one healthy coin. In this context, responsiveness means that each spouse can feel that they are seen, valued, trusted and supported by the other as they have fun together and apart, manage conflicts in ways that bring them closer, comfort one another when they get upset, and depend upon one another at the levels of the logistical, the head, the heart and the spirit. More specifically, couples must have their eyes open; speak and listen with both head and heart; know (or learn) what is compassionate to both self and partner; and put that knowledge into action by walking the talk."

Dr. LeslieBeth Wish, Ed.D, MSS, LCSW, Sarasota, Florida
www.lovevictory.com License # SW 7132 Florida
"Making Marriage a Success as Empty Nesters. The kids are gone, their empty rooms seem to have grown larger over night, and now the space in the house echoes. To reignite your passion, do something together that is new, challenging--and even a little frightening. Doing new and difficult activities strengthens your sense of being a team. Learning how to ski, taking that long awaited trip to far-flung places, raising show dogs, building a house, taking a course, and doing just about any event that interests and challenges you will help create a feeling that "we are in this together." These experiences can help you find yourself laughing more, building new bonds and interests and seeing your spouse in a new light. Just in case you're wondering, my husband and I take our own advice. For example, we travel all over the world and collect art."

Dr Linda Olson, Licensed Clinical Psychologist, New Canaan, CT
www.americaslovedoctortherapy.com License# 002473
"Make a pledge to BE HAPPY NOW: I, _____ do so solemnly decide to adopt the Happiness Decision by being HAPPY NOW. Rather than reacting to my problems, I will use Happiness to Respond to them forsaking all negative thoughts. I choose happiness. So you are thinking how is that possible? Happiness is really up to you. When you think about negative things, you make yourself unhappy, which negatively impacts your marriage. Start acting like you are happy. What can help is by thinking about things you are grateful for. Happiness is controlling yourself so you can enjoy your marriage."

Eric Cassius LPC, MHSP, CHt, Memphis, Tennessee
Cassiusandassociates.com
"Just like an individual nurtures themselves, people must nurture their relationships. If one spouse looks to fulfill their spouse's needs it is more likely that person will try to reciprocate and meet their needs too. You scratch my back I scratch your back. Like the Rolling Stones song 'you can't always get what you want but if you try sometimes you get what you need'."

Jeff King, LSCSW, CSAT, CSAT, Newton & Wichita, Kansas
www.sexaddictionhelpks.com License# 3836
"Secrets kill; they eat you up inside and cause you to do things that are against who you know you are as a person. When in a committed relationship one starts to keep secrets, one starts to separate themselves from their spouse. This void only increases as the secrets start to build and take on a life of their own. Share your desires, fears, fantasies, feelings and perspectives. The more transparent your relationship is the stronger and more successful your marriage will be."

Joe Lowrance, Psy.D., Clinical Psychologist, Atlanta, Georgia
www.FinancialPsychologyCeus.com
"Money is an ongoing a topic and means of communication within all marriages. In order to support the health of the relationship, money must be discussed openly, honestly and directly."

Beverly Smallwood, Ph.D., Psychologist Hattiesburg, Mississippi
www.DrBevSmallwood.com
"Certainly the basic skills of honest and respectful communication and constructive conflict resolution in PRACTICE are essential. However, I think it's also critical that couples are truly WITH each other. This means sharing important values, supporting though not always agreeing, 'having each other's back,' and helping each other continue to learn and grow. It means trusting each other emotionally enough to be vulnerable, and always honoring that trust."

Madelyn Satz, Ph.D., Ann Arbor, Michigan
www.drsatz.com License# 6301007634
"Problems in a marriage are inevitable and useful. Our highest intention is to learn and grow. Our soul mate will help us by triggering our learning. As long as the triggers are in a basically loving and supportive relationship, they can be worked out productively. When you're feeling doubtful about your marriage, start by remembering back to what drew you to your spouse; reconnect with your deeper wisdom in choosing your relationship. Then ask yourself: what can I learn from this conflict; how can I turn this into something good?"

Sharon Morgillo Freeman, PhD, PMHCNS-BC, Fort Wayne, IN
www.centerforbrieftherapy.com License# 70000153A
"Start your morning with a promise to honor your marriage and
partner. Throughout the day practice acceptance and forgiveness. End
each day with words of love and commitment. By making these daily
efforts you will have a successful marriage."

Julie Dubovoy, LCSW-R, Babylon, New York
http://www.juliedubovoy.com/ License# R073412-1
"Committing to Commitment: Commitment is the cornerstones of any
successful marriage. Yet, there are many different shades of
commitment. A successful marriage requires that each spouse
establishes a mutually agreed upon understanding of the level of
commitment they both invest.

Both spouses must agree to what extent they will work to make their
marriage successful. Furthermore, as they grow and their lives change,
the married couple must periodically re-evaluate their commitment to
the relationship. When the couple regularly and openly discusses the
parameters of their commitment, they validate each other and even
establish a sense of emotional camaraderie as they work toward the
same goals. These are the marriages that survive.

Unfortunately, the marriages that I see fail are the ones where one
spouse is fully invested in the relationship, while the other spouse is
hopelessly and passively waiting for it to change on its own."

Jeanne Courtney, MFT, El Cerrito & San Francisco, California
www.FeministTherapyAssociates.com License# MFC29813
"Listen. Empathize. Show respect in your words, tone, and attitude (if
you can't, take a break and try again). Give yourselves permission
to take time apart, have differences, and say no sometimes. (For same
sex couples) if the law doesn't recognize your marriage yet, take even
more care to honor and celebrate it with your community, family, and
each other. Finally, make time to laugh and play together -- don't
stop going on dates with each other just because you're married!"

Keren Sofer, Psy.D., Philadelphia, Pennsylvania
drkerensofer.com License# PS016818
"Our lives, and our most intimate relationships, have become crowded with technology. It is commonplace to look around a restaurant and see couples looking at a glowing screen...rather than at each other. The truth is, we cannot be in two places at once - immersed in the latest news bit or text, and truly focused on our spouse. Choosing to turn off the technology means choosing to be completely and deeply present with the one you love."

Mindy Jacobson-Levy, MCAT, ATR-BC, LPC, PA & NJ
www.artb4words.com and www.thecenteraptt.com
"Marital success is determined by a matrix of intersecting principles established by the individuals in the partnership. The marital philosophy might embrace similar concepts related to friendship, respect, trust, love, the desire to maintain the relationship, ability to negotiate, ethics and values, conjoint dreams for the future, and the allowance of individual differences. Foundationally though, without creativity the opportunities for growth are stifled, leaving the relationship thirsty for nourishment. Creativity sparks resourcefulness and inspiration, which are key elements in a flourishing marriage!"

Carrie Eichberg, Psy.D., Licensed Psychologist, Boise, Idaho
www.dreichberg.com License# 202141
"When a couple moves into parenthood it is critically important that they continue to nurture their relationship with each other. It's too easy to fall into a cycle of working and taking care of kids while ignoring the marriage. This means the couple needs to make time to go out together by having regular 'date nights' without the kids. Without adult only time, the couple risks growing emotionally apart from each other. Happy parents lead to happy families."

Dr. Brian S. Canfield, LMFT, LPC, Bossier City, Louisiana
www.canfieldcounseling.com License LMFT #19 & LPC #120
"In traditional marriages – 'men provide and women prepare.' In successful contemporary marriages – 'couples share.'"

Shanna Moke, Certified Family Life Educator, Sioux Falls, SD
www.knappcounseling.com
"Find topics of mutual interest whether it be sporting events or theatrical performances. Keep in mind that divorce is NOT an option; it forces you to work on your marriage before giving up. Have date nights, have a picnic in your living room, write poetry to express yourself and be spontaneous! Set aside a day of the week to focus on intimacy and re-focusing on each other. If you think marriage and raising children together is tough, it is 10 times tougher when you are divorced!"

Jodi Blackley, LMFT, Orange County, California
http://www.jodiblackley.com
"Working on your marriage is important however, it is equally important to take care of yourself as individuals and never lose sight of who you were prior to the marriage. It's okay to occasionally take time for yourself away from your spouse. For example, go out with friends or get involved with a hobby. This time allows you to regain your identity separate from your relationship, and provides you opportunities to share more with your partner at the same time!"

Jesse Johnson, M.A., Portland, Oregon
www.vitalcollective.com
"As someone who will become a married person myself in the coming weeks, I have been putting significant thought and feeling into my intentions and beliefs around the concept of a relationship as it pertains to marriage and exclusive partnership. The strongest belief I hold about marriage is that, above all, I intend to leave my spouse better off than when I found her. In other words, a 'healthy' marriage, in my view, is one that seeks to serve the personal growth and development of each individual, thereby also serving the growth and development of the relationship. Cyclically, the growth of the dynamic can then serve the growth of each individual and onward. To be earnest in this pursuit, I think, takes a steadfast commitment to personal development, as well as the more familiar commitment to the partnership."

Marcel Schwantes, Life Coach, Chattanooga, Tennessee
www.marcelcoaching.com
"Husband: Understanding Your Wife

The man who really understands his woman knows how to meet four vital needs: friendship, security, value and affection.

Friendship. A woman needs a companion that she can share deeply with in a relationship. A man will never allow his woman to feel alone inside her own house.

Security. A woman needs to know that she is safe in the marriage, that her husband is being faithful, and that he would never sell out to fantasy.

Value. A woman's role as mother and wife can be a full-time job. She needs to know that she is valued for all those things.

Affection. A woman needs emotional responsiveness, intimacy, and affection. They need to be heard, and express their world to their spouses.

When a man learns to put these into daily practice, it states to his woman that he honors and cherishes her."

Deborah Klinger, M.A., LMFT, Chapel Hill, North Carolina
www.pizzadreams.com/dk License# 637
"Two key ingredients of a good marriage are safety and vulnerability. Both partners must be willing to be vulnerable, to expose to each other their inner worlds; their thoughts, emotions, ideas, hopes and dreams. And each must be safe for the other to expose him or her self to: they must treat the other's thoughts, emotions, ideas, hopes and dreams with respect and reverence. This vulnerability in a safe arena builds connective tissue between partners. The connective tissue bonds partners together, making their marriage a strong container that can weather the storms of life."

Ashley Seeger, LICSW, Washington, DC
www.DCCouplesCounseling.com License# LC303583
"The single most damaging behavior to a relationship is contempt.
Contempt is anger directed at someone you consider beneath yourself.
As a couples counselor, whenever I see contempt displayed - through
eye rolls, sighs or tone of voice - my radar goes off. These are the
couples that rarely make it."

AnnaLisa Derenthal, LPC, NCC, Roswell, Georgia
www.annalisaderenthal.com License# LPC004373
"Each person HAS to have his/her non-negotiables. Any relationship
has to have clear boundaries in order to function and thrive. Without
them you can lose yourself or give yourself away - a hefty price to pay
in the search for intimacy. At the same time, boundaries that are too
rigid are walls that keep people out and lock you in. To succeed in a
committed relationship, you have to be flexible and give in on some
things. But you have to know yourself to know what's most important
to you and what you will not sacrifice. Your conviction makes you a
more valuable partner and gives foundation to the relationship."

Kate Siner Francis, Ph.D., LMHC, Providence, Rhode Island
www.lifefulfillmentformula.com License# RI# MHC00438
"It can be challenging to be in a marriage with someone who has
experienced trauma. Here are three tools for staying healthy during
this difficult time. 1.) *It is not about you*: Even though your spouse
might be aiming his or her volatile emotions at you remember that you
are not the real target. 2.) *Get Educated:* Some of your spouse's
behaviors might seem mysterious or not even connected to the trauma;
reading about the effects of trauma will help you separate your spouse
from his or her issues. 3.) *Get your own support:* It is important that
spouses, of those suffering from the lingering effects of adult or
childhood trauma, get their own support --without this support, you
will likely not have enough reserve to navigate this difficult part of
your relationship. Remember, just like any other challenge in a
relationship, healing through your spouse's trauma can ultimately bring
the two of you closer together."

Susan Rua, CAC, LPC, Pittsburgh, Pennsylvania

positive-pathways.net

"What makes a marriage a success is to always stay playful and creative. Marriage can get a little stale with the same person day in and day out so think about things you both have never tried and do them together. For example, dress up a little in the bedroom or buy each other exotic clothes for intimate playtime. Stay young at heart the world is brutal and you will always need a partner you can go home to and relieve the tension to life not add."

Raelene S. Weaver, Licensed Marriage Family Therapist, CA

www.raeleneweaver.com License# 46608

"Don't take each other for granted. Even though your spouse may gladly do something for you--like fixing the computer--which is something you can't do--remember to say thank you, and how much you appreciate their help."

Guy D. Burstein, LCSW, Portland, Oregon

www.guyburstein.com License# 2931

"At our core, we carry a deep wound of being unlovable, unworthy, guilty and powerless. Marriage is an amazingly efficient cauldron in which these wounds can either fester or heal. When we live within our wound, expecting or coercing our beloved to make us well, we disown our own curative power. In the process, we constellate our spouse as either a hero or a villain but never an object of our compassion. There is no wounder like the wounded."

Ilene A. Serlin, Ph.D, BC-DMT, San Francisco, California

www.union-street-health-associates.com License# PSY 11092

"A successful marriage is one where the couple makes their home a refuge. With both adults working, it is easy to bring home stress. We really need our homes these days to be an oasis, a place we look forward to renewing ourselves. Take time after coming home from work to debrief, destress--take a walk, a few minutes to reflect on the day and leave it behind. Imagine entering a sacred space with a holy and loving atmosphere."

Adam Klein, Ph.D., Licensed Psychologist, Bethesda, MD
AdamKlein.net
"Marriage is very complicated. None of us gets all of what we want in childhood. The human quest for loving bonds is quite often driven by more hidden motives that revolve around wounds, deficits, longings and loss. Marriage offers a 'do-over' an opportunity to 'get it right', to heal the loss, to receive and give love in ways in which we experience ourselves as missed, unloved, hurt, mistreated or worse. Here's the rub: Our parents are our primary role-models in how to be in a marriage. It is at this point that marriages encounter the stage of disappointment; because our spouse cannot "heal" the deficits from our childhoods the marriage gets frozen in impasse. While more and more people tend to look for the escape hatch and turn to divorce, another possibility exists: Surrendering to the not knowing. Surrender in this way requires humility in the process of asking for help. Psychotherapy with a guide who knows how to offer advocacy for a better life with more intimacy offers a portal hole or a laser beam to many. At its best, new possibilities that heretofore did not exist become available. These possibilities revolve around how to create more and more intimacy, real caring, loving kindness in a marriage and in life."

Cheryl Gerson, LCSW, BCD, New York, New York
www.cherylgerson.com
"When you keep having the same conflict over and over, you know you're with the right person. Marriage is the ultimate 'do-over,' with the chance of actually doing better even if it does require growing up.

Michael DeMarco, PhD, LMFT, Bellows Falls, Vermont
www.mytherapist.info License# 0073062
"Marriage is a relationship dressed up in legal clothes, but it is a relationship just the same. Don't be afraid to create the relationship that you want to have, not the one you think you HAVE to have because that's what *normal* people do. *Normal* marriages, if you believe those statistics, end half of the time. You and your partner make up the rules as you go based on openness, honesty, empathy and love - and you'll get much further!"

Erica Morgan, MSW, LCSW, Covington, Louisiana

www.ericamorganlcsw.com

"A good marriage is where the level of negotiation is balanced. Whether it's dishes, TV channels, money, communication, or sex, it is about what you are willing to give up and what you are not. If it's a deal breaker, stand strong. If it's not, let it go. Relationships are about negotiating between the logic of your mind and the passion of your heart."

Melodie Anderson, MA, LMFT, Chico, California & Bellevue, WA

MelodieAnderson.com License# ML24320

"Every person wants to know he or she matters and is important to his or her partner. However, each individual feels a sense of 'mattering' in a different way. Ideally, each person has curiosity about what makes his or her partner feel loved, important, safe, or recognized. Then, he or she can make a commitment to demonstrate his or her love or recognition of his or her partner in this way. Oftentimes, a problem arises when the way someone's partner feels most acknowledged is not natural or easy for you to do. Therefore, the goal becomes taking the personal challenge to learn how to provide love or 'mattering' for a partner in the way they need it, in order to better the relationship or to negotiate for an alternative. This process helps one learn not only about one's partner, but also about one's self. Thus, this process becomes beneficial to both partners and deepens their relational intimacy."

Diana Longdon, LCSW, Helena, Montana

http://therapists.psychologytoday.com License# 121 MT

"In my years of experience, I have concluded that couples must have trust and respect for one another. They must be honest and genuine together and be able to communicate their feelings, thoughts, concerns and fears effectively. They must think in terms of 'we' rather than 'I' and make decisions based on what benefits the 'we.' Being in love is the icing on the cake but is not actually necessary for long-term success. Building a strong, loving foundation for a life together is a more effective predictor of stability."

Kari Marshall, Licensed Professional Counselor, Littleton, CO
www.karimarshall.com License# 3767
"It's the 'good stuff' in a relationship that makes the work that you
have to do worth doing: Being able to remember your partner's
strengths and positive qualities on a daily basis, taking time to relax,
play and enjoy is as necessary as water to a thriving plant."

Janet England, LICSW, Boston, Massachusetts
www.janetengland.com License# ma licsw#106771
"It is human nature to compare ourselves to others. This can be helpful
at times when we need a role model. The same is true of marriage. We
see couples we admire and aspire to be more like them. Perhaps they
are more affectionate towards each other or seem to communicate
better than we do. There is nothing wrong admiring but idealizing
another marriage can get you into trouble. When you notice yourself
comparing your marriage to someone else's marriage try to remember
that every relationship is unique and learn to appreciate the qualities of
uniqueness of your own marriage. Also, try to have a good laugh if
you or your partner find yourself feeling insecure about quirks or
eccentricities in your relationship."

Tina Edwards, LCSW, San Francisco, California
"When you find your spouse having a difficult time letting go angry
feelings related to you do everything you can to make them feel loved.
For example, a couple times a day say loving words to your spouse,
ask your spouse what you can to do make things better and do
something for your spouse that you know would put a smile on their
face."

Louise Mastromarino, Certified Counselor, Staten Island, NY
www.distantholistic.com
"Even in difficult times, communication is key. Married life with an ill
partner or seriously ill partner can be conquered with fearless tactics,
understanding, and constant surrendering to God. When we surrender
with fearless understanding we create healing, light and tranquility in
the midst of storms."

Dr. Lisa Cooney, MFT, San Francisco, California
www.leitheta.com License# MFT #38608
"How do you maintain love and connection with your beloved when a debilitating illness, tragedy, addiction or trauma occurs or is revealed? Especially, as the person you fell in love with becomes their wound? The short answer is compassion, love and continual practice in strong deflective boundaries so you don't take it personally or at least not so deep to harm your heart. The longer answer is for you to have a strong support system, as well for the spouse you may feel you lost to the issue. For each other, it's time together, physical contact and emotional connection that will open the heart and reconnect the soul of the person you fell in love with back to themselves and to you. When you remind your beloved of your love and the years of connection and those timeless personal stories only the two of you know, the neural pathways and love 'gene' will certainly be stimulated, and although the issue is still there, the connection will remain strongest. Never give up on a soul that is challenged."

Cheryl Krauter, LMFT, San Francisco & Berkeley, California
www.breastcancersurvivorsupport.com License# MFT14759
"Years ago I took a workshop from a family therapist I admired a great deal. He said something, which I have never forgotten, experienced myself and witnessed others go through too. 'I've been married and divorced 5 times to the same women.' This certainly speaks to the ebb and flow of a long-term relationship!"

Wendy Dickinson, Ph.D., Psychologist, Atlanta, Georgia
www.growcounseling.com License# PSYCH 3256
"Relationships often become mundane. After the sparkles of dating wear off, the mundane of life can settle in. Rather than longing for the magic of the early stages of the relationship, look for ways to find joy in the mundane. There is always something to celebrate if you are on the hunt for it. You might notice that you know how he likes his eggs, or what she likes in her coffee – these little things reflect contentment, settled-ness, and being known. These don't exist in the glitter of the new, but only in the depth of the mundane. Find joy in it."

Lisa M. Templeton, Ph.D., Psychologist, Broomfield, Colorado
www.interpersonalhealing.com License# PSY 3071
"As Sigmund Freud once said, 'sometimes my patients treat me as
though I am someone from their past.' This dynamic is not exclusive to
the therapeutic relationship, but really can occur in any dyadic
relationship, which involves intense closeness. Because of old wounds
that once occurred in past relationships, we can become much more
guarded in future relationships, almost expecting the person to treat us
as we have been treated in our past.

In a marriage, we have to be careful what internal baggage we are
bringing from our past and what our deeper expectations of our spouse
might be. We all protect ourselves in unconscious ways, ways that are
not always useful to ourselves or to our spouse. With these
expectations comes a subtle pull that can manifest others to act as we
expect them to. It can be a real bummer to be transformed by our
spouse into someone we are not, but it's easy to begin playing that role
once these expectations continue for a time. This is the dance of
relating – since both parties bring past experiences into the
relationship, it is difficult not to allow past hurts to seep into the
present. We must be mindful of our thoughts and feelings in the
moment and treat our spouse as though they are our first and only love.
In essence, love without fear of past hurts turning present."

Holly Gordon, DMH, San Francisco, California
drhollygordon.com License# PSY 8796
"Successful marriages are based on appreciation of our spouse's
individuality, and being curious about our spouse's experience,
especially their experience of us, of the relationship. This area is most
difficult to discuss, but has the most power to bring couples closer:
talk about what each finds difficult in the relationship, in the other.
This helps because each spouse's individual difficulties and needs
become engaged and 'hook onto' the other spouse's individual
difficulties and needs. Talking together about areas of personal
difficulty in the relationship helps couples to grow and become
closer."

Sharon Skelton, Licensed Marriage & Family Therapist, CA
www.midtown-counselor.com
"In this child-centered culture, where it's common for 'good parents' to invest most of their time and emotional energy in their daughter's pitch speed, or weather their son makes the singles tennis team by ninth grade, relating to a spouse gets taken off the stove completely. If mom and dad are driving around experiencing most of their joy and comfort from setting up their children to excel, instead of from one another, the family is out of balance. Children can't support the emotional needs of adults. Those are best met by your own self-care routines, and a good, fun marriage. Instead of spending your 'couple time' sitting side-by-side at the soccer field, or ordering the same thing at one of your four favorite restaurants once a month, and pretending that feels like a date, try a picnic and a make-out session on the back lawn at midnight. When you wake up, your good, fun marriage will be lifting up not only you, but your children as well, instead of the other way around. Your kids don't have the muscle to support your marriage anyway."

Sharon L. Thompson, LMFTA, Indianapolis, Indiana
www.talkwithsharon.com License# 85000045A
"Before you marry, get your own counseling. Every person can benefit *on some level* from counseling. We need a good sense of self to have a good, intimate relationship. A healthy and successful marriage happens when there are two emotionally healthy people in it."

Myles Downes, MFT, San Francisco, California
http://mylesdownes.com License# MFC48178
"In order to have a marriage or any other relationship be successful, it truly is essential to find a way to practice some amount of mindfulness, both about your own internal world and about your partner's. Mindfulness in this sense is a way of observing the world that is in the moment and non-judgmental, a way of practicing a more objective stance that is at the same time loving and engaged. All the rest of it -- good communication, being honest, being respectful -- will only take you so far if you're not also finding a way to be mindful about it all."

Dr. Mary Gresham, Licensed Clinical Psychologist, Atlanta, GA

www.doctorgresham.com

"Money is a major source of conflict in marriage and a great way to make marriage a success is to become a money team. Do all the money things together such as paying bills, deciding how to invest, deciding how much to spend in each category, deciding when to use credit, earning money, and writing your wills. It is not fair for one spouse to carry all the adult functions about money and the other to coast along. If you decide to divide the tasks, be sure to switch roles periodically so that you know how to do each task and can give your spouse help when needed. Make a values list before you get married and try to spend according to what you truly value. Have a money date monthly where you talk about where you stand financially as a team and then go out and do something fun afterwards. If needed, hire a financial planner or counselor to help you make choices and iron out conflicts."

George Kolcun, MFT, San Francisco, California

www.georgekolcunmft.blogspot.com License# MFC 46809

"Keeping your relationship strong and healthy can be a challenge after having children. Protecting the core relationship in your family is a key ingredient to positive family functioning. Make sure to find time to be a couple after becoming parents. Reserve some time to be alone with each other. Loving your spouse is the best parenting technique there is."

Dr. Cynthia Chestnut, Couple, Family & Sex Therapist, PA

www.drcynthiachestnut.com

"Intimacy is a mutual unguarded sharing and a vulnerability of self-allowing trust to rule and reign with confidence and security. It is the ability to know that your heart, mind and body will consistently be cared for and honored with dignity and respect. It is truly a dance of love.

Silence about the abuse will only keep you held hostage. Breaking the silence is the first step toward the fulfilling marriage you both deserve."

Leyla Mahbod Kenny, PhD, LICSW, Washington, D.C.
www.washingtondcpsychotherapy.com License# LC3000857
"Fall in love with each other not your fantasy of who you want the other person to be. If you expect your fantasy, you will constantly be disappointed with your spouse."

Cathy Chambliss, LMFT, Hermosa Beach, California
www.cathychamblissmft.com License# mfc39875
"Keeping Your Side of the Street Clean: Often times, we react to our spouse when they are not treating us nicely. We may fight unfairly, such as yelling, calling names, using sarcasm, withdraw emotionally or become disrespectful. Unfortunately, none of these tactics work when we are feeling hurt and often lead to more fighting or distance between you and your spouse. It is very important when disagreeing with your spouse to 'keep your side of the street clean'. In other words, just because they are using unfair fighting techniques, does not mean you have to because ultimately, it does not lead to resolving the problem, just making things work. The best thing to do when fighting gets out of hand is to tell your partner that you are taking a time out and will come back and talk to him/her when you are feeling calmer. Then go do something that will help you to calm down such as deep breathing, taking a walk, listening to music you like or journaling your feelings down on paper. You will always feel better about yourself when you have \"kept your side of the street clean\" and not engaged in unfair fighting."

Lynn Kennedy Baxter, BSN, LMFT, Colorado Springs, Colorado
www.BeConfidentToday.com License# MFT 939
"Respect is the most essential quality for a lasting relationship. Many relationship problems and negative interactions occur when partners are disrespectful of each other. Treat your partner as the most important person in your life, not the least significant. Respect and importance foster caring and devotion for each other, which in turn creates an atmosphere of more shared laughter. This is the circle of love that nourishes and renews the partnership every day. The Reader's Digest version? Be nice to each other."

Melissa Summers O'Neill, LCSW, Chicago, Illinois
www.melissaoneill.com
"The 70/30 Rule: I often tell young couples who are preparing for marriage that a good rule of thumb during good times and bad is that the ratio of love to hate should keep above 70/30. Understand I use the word 'hate' very liberally but that often really means the traits in our partner that provoke annoyance or frustration. There's two important pieces of wisdom in this rule. First, it's relieving and helpful to adjust your expectations, that your partner is not, nor will ever be, perfect. Second, it can be helpful in stressful times to focus on the pieces of your partner that you embrace and accept as well as figuring out a strategy to deal with the 'not so perfect' parts of them. In fact, it's often true that the parts that irritate us about our partner are connected to the parts we love. We may love their dependability but hate that they are not spontaneous enough; these traits come from the same place and we cannot change one trait without losing a piece of what we love about them."

Shari Siegel, MA, CFT, LMFT, Merrick, New York
www.interpersonalsolutions.org
"A successful marriage is one that has BALANCE. Having balance in our lives is very healthy. This means spending time with your spouse, your family and yes, time with yourself to self-care!"

Chasee Chappell Hudgins, Psy.D., Austin, Texas
ChaseeHudgins.com License# TX #33978
"Many couples deal with mental or physical illness in one or both partners. Taking care of our spouse during difficult times is part of being in a healthy, supportive relationship. To adequately support a spouse, however, the care giver must prioritize self care. Scheduling time for rest and relaxation, engaging in activities one enjoys, maintaining connections with support systems, exercise, healthy eating and sleep habits will help a caregiver maintain the stamina to care for another. It is important for a care giver to be able to acknowledge the inherent stress involved in caring for another and engage in self care without guilt."

Leslie Rouder, LCSW, CHT, Boca Raton, Florida
www.addadults.net License# SW5937
"Passion and romance are not the same as love. If you don't share
commitment affection, respect and loyalty to each other, you don't
have love."

Barbara Radin Fox, Licensed Clinical Social Worker, SC
www.bodyandsoultherapy.com
"A healthy, happy marriage, that is a marriage with two people who
love and care for each other, requires that both are healthy, mentally
and physically. I see a lot of couples in which one, or more commonly,
both individuals are not healthy. One common area of 'unhealthiness'
is an inability to manage anger appropriately. Most of these
individuals are also using alcohol or caffeine, either that can affect a
person's level of anger so the first thing I do is to find out what a
person is eating or drinking. After that I find out how many meals the
individuals are eating and how many hours they are sleeping. In most
cases, the couples whom I work with who reduce their stress level by
taking better care of themselves also begin to notice that they are just
not as upset with each other. The issues in the marriage that bothered
them before just aren't bothering them anymore or they were much
more able to discuss their issues with each other rationally. They often
find that they can regain the love and caring that they once felt and are
able to work out whatever differences they have."

Dr. Heather M. Browne, LMFT, Garden Grove, California
www.TheHealingHeart.net License# 34523
"If I choose you forever and decide you are the only one for my
lifetime, then I will view you as a partner and not an adversary. If I
choose to realize all my faults and shortcomings will be brought into
light being together and that my path is to grow myself instead of
criticizing you, then I will find why we are together. If this is my
responsibility and not your fault, I will continually have a journey of
learning and growing along side you. If happiness is not the prize,
but our desire to develop, mature, and learn to love deeper, we will be
rich within our marriage."

Geffen Liberman, CPC, LISAC, CRADAC, Gilbert, Arizona
www.glcounseling.com
"In my experience, marriage is like anything else in life. How good it goes depends on how much you (meaning both of you) are willing to grow it. A marriage is just as prone to getting stagnant as a job, a hobby, the place you eat at every other day, you name it. However, if you are willing to work at it, read books, seek growth, talk and be open and honest with your spouse, whatever it takes to grow the marriage, the sky is the limit! That is the key to a great marriage. That and a consistent, fun sex life."

Steve McCready, LMFT, Sacramento, California
www.counselingsacramento.com License# MFC43212
"Conflict is inevitable in marriage, and it's not inherently a bad thing for your marriage. You can't avoid it, you can only defer it - but deferring it has a significant emotional cost to you and your relationship and can create significant issues with trust later.

One of the most important things you can do for yourself and your marriage is to admit and take responsibility for your mistakes - at least if it's followed up by a genuine effort to change. That sends the message to your spouse that it's okay to make mistakes and be imperfect (i.e. human). This will make your marriage a safer and less stressful place where both of you feel more comfortable being yourself."

Brent O'Bannon, LPC, Certified Life Coach, Sherman, Texas
www.brentobannon.com License# 13223
"Love Works Together: Many couples say, 'I could never work with my spouse; we would kill each other!' That's true for some however research clearly shows that most emotional and physical affairs take place at work. Why? Because couples are designed to do what they love with the person they love. A surprising secret in my marriage of 27+ years is that working together in a business venture forces us to create a deeper partnership. Like Nietzsche said, "That which does not kill us makes us stronger."

Pat Wells, LPC, ACHT, Atlanta & Athens, Georgia

www.patwellstherapy.com License# LPC001800

"The goal of a sales pitch or a political speech is persuasion, while an intellectual debate seeks to prevail with the most valid opinion. In a marriage, however, trying to be right is the wrong approach and trying to win means everybody loses. Seek to understand. First, do this with yourself by sorting out what you are thinking and feeling and what part you are playing in the current situation. Then share this with the intention of listening to, and learning from, your spouse's perspective."

Louise Northcutt, MS, Atlanta, Georgia

www.louisenorthcutt.com

"For relationships to be successful, that is, be of benefit to each person, it is necessary to create environments that facilitate the highest unfolding of each. Each individual is responsible for creating that for themselves, and allowing the creation of that for the other. Each holds 100% responsibility for their experience of life, asking for what they want, and honoring the choice of the other. This likely means separate, as well as shared, friends and interests. When we honor the choice of the other, this is unconditional love, and not a love that is based on certain behavior. It doesn't mean we accept all behavior or never object to certain behaviors. It may mean that we step away, but never withholding love. This provides maximum space for individual unfolding, a way to maintain authenticity and individual integrity, while providing the honor and safety of a loving dyad."

Ellen Odza, LMFT, Alameda, California

therapyforaddictions.com License# MFC42947

"We are often attracted to the qualities we see in our spouse that we don't have. At first we admire them, and then are driven crazy by those very qualities. Introverts are often attracted to extroverts and then can't understand why they always want to spend time in the company of others. The easy going partner becomes the slug on the couch. The high achiever becomes the preoccupied, dismissing spouse. Understanding temperament can help to normalize and mitigate the conflicts these differences can create."

Kate Daigle, MA, NCC, Denver, Colorado

www.katedaiglecounseling.com License# 12442

"Eating disorders are devastating and deadly afflictions -- not only physically, but emotionally and relationally. These disorders can try to become your 'best friend', your 'primary relationship' and tear you away from your spouse and loved ones. Marriage is a sacred trust between two people, and the honest and deep love between these partners can overpower the grip of the eating disorder and promote recovery. Believe that healing is possible, and carry that hope with you every day. Communicate that wish to your spouse, and let him or her know that love can conquer every type of problem."

Michele Harris, M.Ed, LCPC, Boise, Idaho

wowcounseling.com License# LCPC 4110

"I have found that Forgiveness is essential in marriage. We are all imperfect and are often more likely to understand why we act the way we do, and to justify doing so, than we are able or willing to do for our spouse. Many couples get betrayed by their spouse, whether it be acts of sexual infidelity, emotionally disengaging, financial secrets or through other self-promoting acts. When we fail to forgive others we may remain full of grudges, which weigh us down emotionally. If we fail to forgive we may have a multitude of brief marriages, which leave us unfulfilled and wondering why others are able to sustain a life-long relationship while we are unable to do the same. Learning how to forgive, and then having the patience and faith to actively forgive is a key principle to maintaining a life-long marriage."

Jennifer Wilmoth, LAMFT, Atlanta, Georgia

www.growcounseling.com License# AMFT 000204

"Contrary to popular belief about marriage, it is better to put your spouse first and your children second. The whole family will be happier because the order of the family is known and consistent. Put your spouse first by making time for daily talks, cuddles, and occasional date nights consistently over time without the children physically or mentally present. Leaving your children might be hard at first but your spouse and children will thank you later."

Madeleine G. Boskovitz, Ph.D., Licensed Psychologist, Texas
www.mgboskovitz.com
"One of the most important things to do to assure a good marriage actually takes place before you get married. It is essential to go into marriage with open eyes, good judgment, and not wishful thinking. 'It' will not get better after you are married: courtship is the time when people are on their best behavior. If that behavior has major problems, they only get worse after the wedding. It is so important to look at the 'red flags' of your and the other person's behavior (red flags are behaviors that cause hurt feelings or even pain to the other). I advocate listening to friends and family—yes, even your parents -- about their opinion of the suitability of your match. They are usually more objective and not blinded by either person's charms. It is a lot easier to separate before the wedding, however painful or frightening that may be, than down the road, with potentially a couple of children who then experience the floor being dropped from under them."

Scott Haltzman, MD., Woonsocket, Rhode Island
www.DrScott.com License# RI7592 & MA77864
"The most common mistake that people make is to assume they know their partner. People color so much of their interactions with their own biases, that they often misunderstand more than they understand. That leads to frustration on everyone's part. By taking time to really know a mate, through judgment-free observation and good listening, a spouse can recognize how their partner's needs differ from theirs. Couples who are truly happy in their marriage are those who follow the simple rule of 1) figure out what pleases your spouse, 2) figure out what displeases him or her. Then, do more of (1), and less of (2)."

M. Dorsey Cartwright, LMFT, LPC, CCMHC, Austin, Texas
VoiceDialogueTrainings.com License# LMFT 4437, LPC 9934
"We each consist of a multitude of selves. Conflicts between couples are conflicts between parts of ourselves. The awareness that not all parts are angry, and that it not all parts are being attacked, can release us from the need to defend, and create the space and safety necessary to stay in connection and conversation with our spouse."

Abigail Natenshon, LCSW, Highland Park, Illinois
www.empoweredparents.com
"Anger needs to be recognized as a healthy human emotion that does not preclude loving. I am not a believer in the adage 'never go to bed angry,' because all feelings are legitimate and need to be allowed to run their course naturally. The time of day or night that they occur is irrelevant. Sometimes letting time elapse, or 'sleeping on it,' is helpful in allowing for clearer thinking, a more complete understanding of the conflict, and an increased awareness of additional insights and feelings (yours and your partner's) that might facilitate problem resolution and reconciliation. In addressing and resolving conflict, it is always more productive to understand and attend to the full complement of your partner's *feelings* which underlie his or her perspective, rather than to focus on the "facts" or logistics of the disagreement."

Letitia V. Haywood, MSW, LCSW, CYT, Indianapolis, IN
www.ellainc.com
"Equanmity & Marriage: As with this human existence, a successful marriage is a result of cultivating Equanimity (balance, contentment, peace, mindfulness) in life. One's ability to center self, let go of ego and be mindfully present to one's current existence and circumstance, improves insight that perceived challenges are not always what they seem. As we begin to do for our companion (spouse, partner) that which we wish to have, greater awareness evolves that what one needs and hopes to gain has to first be given, for change must begin with self."

David Olem, MFT, San Francisco, California
www.davidolem.com License# MFC40869
"I help couples look at how they can use humor in their relationship. Humor can create a deeper sense of intimacy and connection. The way the two of you have learned to laugh at an experience you shared, maybe even a really difficult one can remind each of you that you are not alone in this challenging world. Humor also serves to diffuse tension, makes it easier to discuss difficult topics and work through conflict."

Brooke Miller, Licensed Marriage Family Therapist, California
www.soapboxtherapy.com
"The person you married is in fact, a human being--a fact often forgotten. S/he can't be everything at all times, can't be your best friend and your lover and your supporter and your proofreader and your shopping partner--in every moment of everyday. Your spouse is a huge part of your life but you need friends, hobbies, and outside interests that fulfill you as well. There are three parts to every relationship, a 'you', a 'me' and an 'us', and each part deserves just as much attention and fulfillment as the other. In order to have a healthy marriage, the pressure of having a perfect spouse who is everything at all times needs to come off so that two *real human beings* can enjoy the journey together."

Christine D Moriarty, CFP, MBA, Bristol Vermont
www.MoneyPeace.com
"As part of a couple, the important thing is to be fluid and listen to each other's opinions. How do I practice what I preach? As two adults getting married, we each had our favorite insurance agent. Despite knowing that combining policies would save us money, I took care of the car insurance with my long time agent. He took care of the home insurance with his. Four years later, we finally put the whole insurance package out to bid and went with the lowest price. Not only am I a Certified Financial Planner, my husband is an accountant. We care about money savings, but needed to time to process so we were both comfortable."

Dr. Robert C. Allanach, LMFT, CGP, New Orleans, Louisiana
www.doctorallanach.com License# 697
"More than a few self made 'pop' psychologists have planted in a few minds a dangerous and divisive thought: 'If you believe that your spouse is cheating then (s)he probably is cheating.' Run the data. Can you find real evidence to support your possible faulty conclusion? You may be surprised to learn after securing ALL the data, your spouse's love may outweigh your suspicions. Maybe it's a trust issue and nothing more nothing less."

Carol A. Hicks, MA, LMFT, Pensacola, Florida
www.answerwithin.com License# LMFT 0120
"I had the unique opportunity to receive a marriage ceremony by the legendary Milton Erickson from his wheelchair in Phoenix, Arizona as we stood under his Palo Verde tree dangling with a parasite plant he referred to it as 'Arizona mistletoe'. He gazed steadily at us and began: *The first thing I want to do is admonish the two of you. You're both blind! But don't worry, it will clear up. You'll begin to see one another's faults. And when you do, don't either of you give up any of your faults because you are going to need them in order to understand and accept the faults of your partner.*"

Amy Meyers, PhD, LCSW, New York, New York
http://www.psychotherapynyc-healing.com/
"We have all heard that we marry our mother or father. This means that we often unconsciously seek mates who represent both good and challenging aspects of our relationship with our parents. What we hear less often is that we marry our brother or sister! We also recreate our sibling relationships in our spouse. Sometimes the choice in a partner may represent our best part of our sibling relationship and sometimes we may carry the strained or challenging parts of these relationships. Knowing yourself and your family dynamics, which includes your relationship with your siblings, will strengthen your relationship with your spouse. You must be able to distinguish who he/she is from your family-of-origin experiences."

Charmayne Alegria, MA LCPC, Meridian, Idaho
www.touchpointscounseling.com License# LCPC-4429
"Couples often relate their compatibility to shared interests and mutual attraction and rarely consider views of money, financial planning and spending habits; expectations and beliefs pertaining to family planning; career and/or education goals; sexual attitudes, values, and boundaries; etc. It is imperative that each individual have a strong sense of who they are as individuals and where they stand on these issues, otherwise they are vulnerable to losing themselves and the marriage. It takes two *whole* people to become a *whole* couple."

186

Kalila Borghini, LCSW, Yoruba Priest, New York
www.childofthestones.com License# 069524-R
"When you've been with someone for more than a decade and both of
you have gone through depression, life-altering experiences both
positive and traumatic, separations from one another, feelings of
wanting to move on, a strong need to go it alone, but you
remain because life without the other would seem diminished and less
fulfilling, then you know you are committed to the relationship and
that your love has transformed from conditional to as unconditional as
possible in adult life."

Teri McHugh, PhD, LMFT, Camarillo, California
www.drtmchugh.com
"In order to rebuild trust after an affair and reinvent your marriage
there must be open communication not only about the affair, but what
might have lead up to the affair. Affairs can be viewed as a symptom
of other things that are not right in the marriage. It's important to talk
about how you want your marriage now to be or to reinvent your
marriage rather than to fix or repair or to simply have damage control.
It is important to have an 'Open Book' policy of sharing information,
phone records and passwords. Have no secrets and work on building
trust again in the relationship. I recommend having a regular 'check in'
with your spouse to share each other's day, making plans for a couple's
night out on a regular basis and noticing the positive things about each
other and allowing for active listening for each to be heard."

KD Farris, M.A., Depth Psychologist, Santa Barbara, California
www.meshe.com and www.kdfarris.com
"What makes couples that have gone through infidelity successful, is
when the partner who did not cheat finds some personal material of
their own mirrored in the cheating partner's behavior. A mother
disconnected from her sexuality who turns away from that part of her
marriage, must look to herself and ask, 'Am I willing to step back into
my sexual self?' Is his cheating her fault? Of course not. Is his cheating
a wake up call? If she uses it as such, they just might have a chance to
put their marriage back together."

Robin A. Hubert, M.F.T, Los Angeles, California
www.HubertTherapy.com License# MFC 42452
"This is your precious life as well as your significant other's; along with the other people in your life, most importantly your offspring. This time will pass more quickly than you think. How can you create the most quality and joyful expansiveness with this precious time you have here on Earth? If you find yourself blaming others for all of your woes (and even relishing it), then you are indulging in victimhood and helplessness, which can negatively impact your marriage. Now, as an adult, it is your task to take responsibility for your well-being and the embetterment of this world. If you feel you are consistently victimized, you may have to swallow the bitter pill of awareness that you are in fact committing tyranny on yourself. The victim and the tyrant are intrinsically bound as one validates the other! Explore pathways to personal empowerment and well-being, and share that expansiveness with your loved ones."

Robert A. Moylan, LCPC, Naperville, Illinois
www.robertmoylan.com License# 180005037
"A marriage is like a business merger or acquisition. The best one can do is understand the deal at the outset. Lay all the cards out and go all in with your chips."

Jill Shugart, Licensed Marriage Family Therapist, Berkeley, CA
http://www.jillshugart.net
"Marriage researchers tell us that people who say they have happy marriages feel appreciated for what it is they do. It doesn't matter what the roles are...traditional or otherwise. What matters is that each person feels appreciated for his or her contributions. The tricky part is that people like to give and receive appreciations differently. Some prefer do to it by touch and physical affection, some by verbal acknowledgment, and some by action (when emptying the dishwasher feels sexy!) Since we tend to give in the way we like to receive, it is important to know what works for your spouse and do that so your appreciations can be received and enjoyed in the way you intend them."

Ellen Farrell, MA, LPC, EEM-CP, Savannah, Georgia
www.ellenfarrell.com
"I find some couples have never explored or discussed their goals and values in the relationship. Consider what makes a person healthy on all levels – and what are the deal-breakers? Have you chosen to heal unresolved pain of the past, changing negative habits and barriers to health? Then consider what matters to you at your core, and where getting support, and finding compromise is possible and appropriate. Remember, the dialog is a two way street! When we have a shared goal to be healthy, listen, clarify, and communicate with reverence, we can be better for knowing each other."

Claire Houston, LCMHC, Exeter, New Hampshire
www.wswcenter.com
"Marriage takes **courage** (to stay with it when it's hard, and to take a hard look at YOURSELF, to go down paths you've never gone before); **discipline** (to respond rather than react - with each word or action you are either contributing to or contaminating the relationship); **the long view** (marriage is a long-term commitment, and not every issue has to be addressed NOW. Develop patience for the right moment, or let it go completely); **personal responsibility** (to continue your own self-growth, to own your projections and immature eruptions, to laugh at your own insecurities, to deliberately treat this person as if they are someone you love, to apologize when needed, to STOP the ABCs - accusation, blame, criticism)."

Betsy Fredrickson, LCSW, Austin, Texas
www.wheatfieldtherapy.com License# 36895
"Money is a common issue among many marriages. What works for my marriage is combining our monthly income and each of us getting the same amount in an 'allowance' each month. The combined income pays all the monthly bills and all the things we do together. The 'allowance' gives each of us the flexibility to do with what we want. I am a spender and he is a saver. Having the stash of cash is always good when the communication breaks down and retail therapy is needed!"

Jennifer Lehr, LMFT, Orcas Island, Washington
www.weConcile.com License# MFC 41726
"Marriage triggers our deepest needs as well as our deepest wounds, yet a marriage can be a profound vehicle for healing. For a marriage to flourish, we must tend it, just as a garden must be planted, weeded, and watered to bloom."

Kimberly J Plourde, LCSW, Lisbon Falls, Maine
www.thetalkzone.net License# LC11517
"How to make a successful marriage work. Well in my personal and professional worlds I have experienced and observed both success and failures in this area. To be successful one needs to learn how to really love the other person. I mean a deep abiding love where one puts the needs of the other person above their own needs. Whether that is simply greeting one after a long day at work or engaging in an intimate experience. This deep abiding love is looking into your spouse's eyes and saying, without words, I love you deeply and you are all that matters at this very moment, nothing else in this world can come between us in this moment. Each moment builds upon that moment and you experience love that builds together not divides."

Cheryl Ades, LCSW, Louisanna, Kentucky
cherylades.com
"I believe from both my personal and professional experience the spouses know their inner landscape the better chance the marriage has to survive and thrive. Each of us has a myriad of parts and to pretend we are all monochromatic individuals deceives only our partners and even ourselves. Utilizing the Internal Family Systems approach developed by Richard Schwartz allows each spouse to take full responsibility for his or her desires and challenges, especially the unhealed wounds that trigger the extreme reactions that often cause friction in the marriage. By speaking for a 'part' of us rather than as the whole person feeling a certain way, a partner's defenses relax when confronted. The commitment to working any of our unhealed issues through is the greatest commitment we can make to a union blessed by God."

Lisa Hartwell, PsyD, RN, Honolulu, Hawaii
www.hidrlisa.com License# Psy800
"You and your spouse's values must be aligned to resolve differences. There cannot be an expectation that your spouse will accept your value as you see it and vice versa. When resolving an issue, the first step is to anchor which value you are both actually discussing (intimacy, careers, parenting, etc). You should both allow each person to discuss what they think about the value and how close you are aligned (versus polar opposites). From there, you both should apply how you would like this value represented in your marriage."

Paul Berkowitz, MD, FAPM; Scottsdale, Arizona
"Money, and its management, is as important in a marriage as virtually anything else you can think of. Money is a powerful element that is so easily swept under the rug when it starts to cause us pain and tension. So many facets of a relationship - honesty, trust, sense of worth and openness in communication to just name a few - go into how couples deal with money. A couple needs to keep their discussions about money management as open as possible. One practical method to achieve this end is for the couple to regularly attend to their financial affairs (pay bills, review expenses, make budgets, etc.) as a couple."

Melissa Swartz, LGPC, Shepherdstown, West Virginia
www.melissaswartz.com
"When making effective requests, it most important that you and your spouse are not in stress. We receive information differently based on our emotional state. Increase your chances of getting your needs met by asking at an optimal time."

Lorrie Crystal Eigles, MSED, LPC, PCC, Kansas City, Missouri
http://myauthenticlifecoaching.com
"Making the effort to tell your spouse that you love them even though it is sometimes difficult. My husband and I often time express how we feel by giving one another a card and writing thoughts like 'The sunshine of your love warms and lights my days and nights, reaches deeply into my soul and soothes me.'"

Jodi Milstein, LMFT, Los Angeles, California
www.JodiMilstein.com and www.RockStarTherapy.com
"Be present with each other whether you are enjoying a warm, positive moment together or resolving conflict through an argument. Being in the moment helps couples connect as well as resolve issues and to move forward from conflict."

Gary R. McClain, PhD, LMHC, New York, New York
www.JustGotDiagnosed.com License# 18-000355
"In sickness and in health... You could say that health is one of the wildcards in a relationship. It is subject to change over time, as heredity, environmental conditions, and lifestyle habits express themselves. In that regard, as we age, we may become more and more different from our partner. Couples can promote each other's wellness, and team up to live a healthy lifestyle so that they can be there in every way possible for each other. A lot of mutual encouragement, and a little gentle nagging, can go a long way: eat this, don't eat that, get your annual check-up. Take good care of yourself; encourage your spouse to do the same. Get active together. However, life is random. One partner may show the effects of the aging process sooner than the other, or may develop chronic, if not catastrophic, conditions along the way. Over time, caring can become caregiving. Live with passion and compassion, love each other inside out and outside in, live each day in the present moment, because tomorrow isn't guaranteed."

Ellen Farrell, MA, LPC, EEM-CP, Savannah, Georgia
www.ellenfarrell.com
"I find some couples have never explored or discussed their goals and values in the relationship. Consider what makes a person healthy on all levels – and what are the deal-breakers? Have you chosen to heal unresolved pain of the past, changing negative habits and barriers to health? Then consider what matters to you at your core, and where getting support, and finding compromise is possible and appropriate. Remember, the dialog is a two way street! When we have a shared goal to be healthy, listen, clarify, and communicate with reverence, we can be better for knowing each other."

James R. Iberg, PhD., Chicago, Illinois
www.empathywork.com License# 071.002641
"When emotions run high in a relationship, get clear what you really feel. Emotions need a three-stage process akin to childbirth prior to expression to your partner. It takes what can seem like an unbelievably long time in gestation (the first phase of thinking / interpreting) before the labor process — a second phase when bodily feelings are activated — gets underway. This is sometimes emotionally intense, but usually takes a shorter time than the first part. The third phase — the desired outcome — is the birth of deeper and more correct articulation of the important meanings the situation has for you. The third phase comes spontaneously and often in a very short time on the heels of the second. When this happens, it comes with relief, and with an increase in empathy for your spouse, as well as more confidence about what to say about yourself in words that don't defame your partner. If you stay with your inner process to get to this third phase before addressing the issue with your partner, you can speak authentically while still being able to listen with care."

Marilyn Earle, MSN, APRN-BC, Bluffton, South Carolina
scminddeva.com
"I believe the success of a marriage begins before the vows. If only couples would see a therapist and understand what each other's values, morals and family rituals are before diving in; a successful outcome is the probability."

Laura Carite, MA, LPC, RYT, Flanders, New Jersey
www.restoremindandbody.com License# PC1451
"Look at your spouse through a wide angle lens rather than a zoom. In marriage, perspective matters, and acquiring the skill of changing our perspective will not only circumvent problems but also enhance and enrich our relationships. Most marriages become overly 'zoom focused' on a handful of issues or personality flaws. Putting flaws into the context of the whole person, often reminds us why we married him/her in the first place. Zooming in is important and relevant, but never loose sight of wide angle viewpoint."

Nate Havlick, LCSW, Austin, Texas
www.AustinTherapist.com License# 29883
"The essence of marriage is the blending of lives, but not the blending of souls. Only two separate beings can join as one, but this joining is always a choice, not a given. It's grounded in a deep empathy with the other, a willingness to be open and vulnerable.

Respect for the other means looking past their behavior and their words to the heart of their experience and then, with compassion, speaking firmly of needs and limits, and exploring the choices that honor them both."

Tzu-Han "Lillian" Koskella, Registered Psychotherapist, CO
http://www.tlcpsychotherapy.com
"A successful marriage is one in which the couple makes marriage their top priority, by putting their rigid personal beliefs, preferences, and resistance aside and tries everything in the world to make sure it works."

Dr. Lisa Cooney, MFT, San Francisco, California
www.leitheta.com License# MFT #38608
"How do you maintain love and connection with your beloved when a debilitating illness, tragedy, addiction or trauma occurs or is revealed? Especially, as the person you fell in love with becomes their wound? The short answer is compassion, love and continual practice in strong deflective boundaries so you don't take it personally or at least not so deep to harm your heart. The longer answer is for you to have a strong support system, as well for the spouse you may feel you lost to the issue. For each other, it's time together, physical contact and emotional connection that will open the heart and reconnect the soul of the person you fell in love with back to themselves and to you. When you remind your beloved of your love and the years of connection and those timeless personal stories only the two of you know, the neural pathways and love 'gene' will certainly be stimulated, and although the issue is still there, the connection will remain strongest. Never give up on a soul that is challenged."

Elizabeth Boyajian, M.Ed, LCPC, Topsham, Maine
http://www.options-counseling.com/ License# 3300
"This above all: to thine own self be true,
And it must follow, as the night the day,
Thou canst not then be false to any man.
Farewell, my blessing season this in thee!"

"This quote was told to son Polonius who was in a hurry to flee from
his father's ways...but in reality we cannot be with another person, in
work, in love, in *marriage*, if we are not true to ourselves, our values
and our wants and needs. As a psychotherapist, and twice wife I know
that haste in any aspect of ones life makes for strife and
therefore honoring the process of learning about ourselves, keeping at
bay the noise of our friends and neighbors and our own yearnings to *be
true to oneself.*"

Rachel Eddins, M.Ed., LPC-S, CGP, Houston, Texas
http://www.eddinscounseling.com License# 19371
"Relationships can be fulfilling beyond your wildest beliefs and more
frustrating than anything you may have expected. The most important
thing to remember is to trust the other person and the relationship. In
those times when your first inclination may be to turn away from your
spouse (withdrawal, put up defenses, etc), do the opposite and turn
towards your spouse. It will reinforce your support for them so you
each know that you are not in it alone."

Colleen Quinn, PhD, Philadelphia, Pennsylvania
www.NorfordPsychology.com
"Listen First. When communicating with your spouse, whether in a
tense or intimate moment, be sure to let your spouse know that (s)he
was heard first *before* responding. Often what you think your mate is
saying is not at all the point trying to be conveyed. And often the
communicator does not want the problem to be solved. We all just
want to be understood. So before responding, look your spouse in the
eye and mirror back, 'So what I think you're saying is... Did I get that
right?' Feeling heard goes a long way to creating true intimacy."

Joan Ferdinand Keleher, MS, LCPC, Wilmette & Chicago, Illinois
www.joanferdinand.com License# 180005394
"A good marriage is that SAFE HARBOR of kindness and understanding where you both can retreat and recharge, ultimately becoming the catalyst for transformation into your very best selves."

Dan Hanneman, M.S. Clinical Psychology, Hebron, Illinois
www.blockbustyourpath.com
"When things get rocky and heated, it can be the most beautiful opportunity in a marriage. It is often a great opening to allowing old issues to be resolved from your past. Your spouse will trigger your deepest issues and they will be giving you the opportunity to work through your stuff. It is important to recognize that one of the functions they play in your life is to shake things up along the way. This is where the huge growth within yourself and your marriage can be realized. Anybody can enjoy marriage when things are sailing along. Your challenge is to take 100% responsibility for your issues under all circumstances."

Shannon Sprung, MA, LPC-Intern, Austin, Texas
www.shannonsprungcounseling.com
"The goal of any relationship between two people, whether romantic or not, is the same. I have discovered, not only through client work, but also through personal relationships, that we all strive for similar goals. We crave mutual respect from one another, we desire patience, understanding, and love. What we all have to remember is that the definition of love (and life) that we have created in our mind is just that. Each person has a different view of love and of the world, and we cannot expect anyone else's to look just as ours does. Love looks different for each individual; how you define it is based on your own needs, your own experiences, and what works best for you in your own life. Ideally, if we all came to a place where we can completely accept ourselves, hence making a more open space to accept others (keeping in mind that acceptance does not equal agreement), we can ultimately create more peaceful relationships with mutual respect and an understanding of our differences."

Harry Warner, MA LPC, Columbus, Ohio
www.ahlcounseling.com/Harry License# c.0800151
"Find in your partner that which you lack. Then, love and embrace that quality because it makes the two of you more powerful than one would ever be alone. Watch while the perfectionist becomes a guardian and the absent-minded becomes a dreamer."

Phyllis J. Bonds, MS, NCC, LMHC, LCAC, Indianapolis, Indiana
www.bondscounselingsolutions.com License# 39001570A
"My husband and I met at 15 in a Drivers' Education class. We were in class for the entire summer but spoke to one another only once during that time. However, I knew that he was 'the One.' On the last day of class I finally got up the nerve to start a conversation with him, hoping that it would spur more contact. We talked all of the way out of the building and were on our way downtown when a group of girls stopped him to talk. Not wanting to look like 'the fool,' I continued on my way. After about six blocks I heard someone calling my name and guess what; it was him.

That was 40 years ago and we have been married for nearly 35 years. The words of wisdom are two sentences:

1. Let the man do the chasing, and
2. Marry ONLY for love because nothing else will last."

Karen S. Waugh, Psychotherapist, LISW-S, Columbus, Ohio
www.waughcounseling.com
"I encourage couples that I work with to view their marriage as an innocent and separate entity...one that is outside of who they are as a couple, yet susceptible to their individual influence. The marriage is typically a target that couples focus on to avoid assuming personal and individual responsibility for what they have injected into the marriage. If both parties are willing to assume sole responsibility for their thinking, feelings, behavior and personal happiness, then this innocent entity that we call marriage will "thank you" by its reflection of trust, love, respect, and happiness. Things change when we do."

Jeff Goldman, LCSW, Denver, Colorado
JeffreyGoldmanPsychotherapy.com License# 986054
"The most common (and worst possible) strategy to keep a marriage happy is to decide not to talk about what's troubling you. The next worst strategy is to resolve to talk about everything that's troubling you."

AnnaLisa Derenthal, LPC, NCC, Roswell, Georgia
www.annalisaderenthal.com License# LPC004373
"Romance is fantasy, as in fairy tales and dreams come true. It satisfies a need we all have for emotional dependency. It is not unhealthy, and can be beautiful and wonderful, but its purpose is limited. It's fun, but it has a shelf life. When the thrill is gone, and she no longer takes your breath away, many spouses will say, 'I love him, but I'm not 'in love' with him anymore'. That's when the reality of the whole person, flaws and all, can no longer be denied, and we must work at our relationship. The luxury of fantasy only takes us so far. Deep and enduring love replaces 'bling' with a more mature form of fulfillment, which includes loyalty, team work, sacrifice and a true knowing of your reliable life partner through thick and thin. A good example is the scene in 'Fiddler on The Roof' where the father asks the mother 'Do you love me?'"

Hillary Glick, Ph.D., Clinical Psychology, New York, New York
hillaryglickphd.com License# 011217-1
"Naturally, the success of a marriage depends to a great extent upon one's choice of mate. As we all know, infatuation based on strong sexual attraction can blind people to other important characteristics, which will directly impact the long-term success of a relationship. It is extremely important to keep in mind early on the factors that make marriage work in the long run. Just for starters, consider your future mate's religious and political beliefs, financial philosophy, substance use, and social skills. Then you might wonder about issues of mood stability, tendencies toward rigidity or being controlling, jealousy, cleanliness and level of insight. These issues may be easy to overlook in the flush of romance, yet over time could become matters that cause deep rifts."

Ruth Wyatt, LMSW, MA, New York, New York
Www.ruthwyatt.com License# NYS 057890-1
"Don't Back Seat Drive! Co-parenting is like being a passenger in a car that your spouse is driving. Watching your partner drive can be torture at times! S/he either drives too fast or too slow, breaks too late or too soon, etc.. At these times, it is very hard not to say something critical or offer 'advice.' The problem is that when you do, your spouse feels undermined, less confident and drives more poorly.

Of course, if your partner really is driving dangerously, by all means say something. But if, as is more often the case, your spouse is driving not quite the way you would like, let it go. Don't back seat drive. Your spouse will feel calmer and more confident, drive better, and your ride will go a lot more smoothly!"

Molly Pierce, LPC, NCC, Leawood, Kansas
www.trueselfcounseling.com License# LPC: 2197
"A large part of marriage is about meeting each other's needs. Most spouses within a healthy marriage *want* to meet their spouse's needs, but they don't always know how. This is why it's so important not only to strive to meet your spouse's needs, but also to *voice* your own; therefore, giving your spouse the opportunity to meet your needs. For example, if you need comfort from your spouse, say to him or her, 'I am feeling vulnerable right now and I would like for you to give e me a hug.' Now your spouse knows exactly what you need, and they are able to provide that for you."

Cindy Foster, LCSW, ACSW, NBCCH, Martinez, Georgia
mindbodystressreduction.com License# CSW002401
"Rethink the purpose of your marriage. Having a conscious-based marriage will lead you to a higher love and a deeper emotional, physical, and spiritual connection."

Annie Fongheiser, MA, MS, LCAS Charlotte, North Carolina
"To achieve true-life balance and lasting satisfaction, place time with those you love at the top of your list."

Lind Butler, LPC, LMFT, Houston, Texas
www.lindbutler.com License # LPC 11187 & License# LMFT 2856
"Sometimes success in a marriage, involves a couple's willingness to get help when patterns of conflict seem repetitive or stuck. By getting a marriage counselor involved such as myself, the therapist can act as an interpreter helping filter out some of the raw emotion. By attempting to translate dialogue so that each can hear and comprehend in their own language, reactivity can be minimized. Marital counseling can provide a surface where couples can lay out all the pieces of a complex jigsaw puzzle; look at them and sort them according to size, shape, color, etc. With a different perspective, they are able to see the 'picture' and begin to create a joint vision of their marriage, by putting the pieces together collaboratively."

Tim Herzog, LCPC, Bozeman, Montana
www.reachingahead.com
"In good marriages, people are not afraid of an occasional conflict, and they incorporate good boundaries. For instance, one spouse might say, 'You seem pretty angry that I can't pick you up tonight… I care about you, and I have too much on my plate.' Notice that the statement validates the other person's position, while also validating one's own position and drawing a clear boundary. Ideally, each partner can tolerate it when the other is upset and can also calm his or her self. Setting good boundaries sets the stage for each spouse to independently feel solid on their own two feet."

Isadora Alman, LMFT, Alameda, California
www.askisadora.com License# ML24319
"Don't forget to make time for yourself no matter how hard it is to carve out that time. Taking time for you is not being selfish it is a *requirement* for being a much better companion, lover, parent, friend and all the other roles you have to play."

Dr. Victoria Boccanfuso, Psychologist, Tracy, California
www.vbpsyd.com License# PSY23177
"It's not enough to love each other, you must like each other too."

James Williams, LPC, Princeton, West Virginia
http://home.earthlink.net/~jameswilliams2/index.html License# 691
"Lean towards rational decision making to make your marriage a
success."

Frieda Ling, Licensed Marriage & Family Therapist, Arizona
www.psychologytoday.com License# LMFT-10199
"A genuine acceptance and embracement of your partner AS IS –
beyond ignorance or mere tolerance of his or her weaknesses – is the
foundation of a good marriage."

Lucy Papillon, Ph.D., Licensed Clinical Psychologist, California
drpapillon.com
"A close, intimate marriage requires that the two stay up-to-date with
each other. The best way these days to stay connected and current is to
text several times a day (some of them need to be humorous, things
must not be too serious, no matter what), speak to each other at least
once, and spend time after work and on weekends going out to eat at
least 3 times. A marriage is like a beautiful but quite delicate flower, it
takes loving attention and plenty of watering. (Speaking to it helps
too!) The contacts must be mutual, one can't do all the initiating of the
"how was that meeting at 10? Did you feel good about it?" Just a little
thought sent to the other says, 'I care about what you are up to.'"

Fran Ryan Ph.D., Kansas City, Missouri
www.psychologytoday.com License# PY01723
"The marital dyad must be the priority relationship in a family. The
husband and wife must model the appropriate roles of husband, wife,
mother, father, child or sibling for their children. This modeling, in
turn, readies children to play these roles in a healthy way as adults.

If children are seen as more important than the primary couple, the
marital relationship will suffer and, possibly, crumble. The children
may become manipulative, demanding, self-centered and even
narcissistic. Children grow up and create their own families using the
skills their parents have taught them through their example."

Nakeya Fields, LCSW, Pasadena, California
www.ffcounseling.com License# LCS 25754
"In a relationship, no matter the type, each person must learn how to
have a disagreement with the other. If you or your partner have no
working knowledge of how to effectively express negative emotions
such as anger or fear in the relationship, it will be difficult to move
forward into feeling the more desired emotions of love and caring.
Both parties run of the risk of remaining stuck in the negative if they
are unable to move forward together. Learn to fight, stomp your feet,
have your say and respect your partner's right to do the same. If
you worked hard enough to get to that space where it is possible to
talk, maybe even yell, and then forgive, you are most likely willing to
work at maintaining the bond with your significant other for the long-
term."

Rachel Greene, LMFT, Minneapolis, Minnesota
www.rachelgreenelmft.com License# 1215
"I believe that many aspects contribute to a successful marriage,
though I would summarize the big ones in two words. RESPECT and
BOUNDARIES. It is important that you respect each other as this
translates into your value for each other. Then there are boundaries,
which need to be clear and firm and surround the relationship. Without
firm and clear boundaries, many spouses find themselves drawn
outside of the relationship for a variety of reasons, primarily unmet
needs. With boundaries, unmet needs can be resolved within the
relationship through communication and respect. In my own
relationship, the respect and boundaries are essential to the core of the
marriage; everything else flows from there."

Olivia Mellan, MS, Therapist, Money Coach, Author, DC
Www.moneyharmony.com
"What I think makes my marriage work is endless amounts of
cuddling, reading a book to each other at night, laughter, humor and
regular doses of appreciative feedback. Holding each other in bed at
night, and curtailing impulses to criticize each other are great too!"

Hillary Goldsher, Psy.D, MBA, Beverly Hills, California
www.drhillarygoldsher.com
"When we think that we are fighting with our partner, we are actually fighting with ourselves. There is some underlying, unexamined issue of hurt, abandonment or pain from long ago. And one little action by our partner triggers those old feelings and while we think we are arguing with him or her about that thing he or she said or did, we are really arguing with those wounds from the past. A successful marriage requires us to look at those wounds of the past so we can understand and manage how they impact our present and future. How they impact how we move through our relationship with our spouse. It is only this knowing and this understanding, which allows us to shift and change things. It is a powerful tool."

Caroline E. Sakai, PhD, Licensed Clinical Psychologist, Hawaii
http://www.tftcenter.com
"Successful relationships require commitment, attention and work. Like tending a garden, relationships require daily attention and nurturing to bear the fruits of loving companionship, support, joy and understanding. Extra care is called for to weather storms and challenges, and working together to overcome these deepens and strengthens the relationship. Neglect and taking the relationship for granted can be withering and could even be fatal to the relationship when extended over time. Positive intentions need to become thoughtful and caring habits that enable partners to contentedly reap what they have sown and grown. Successful relationships take dedication and daily work."

Haylee Heyn, AMFT, Salt Lake City, Utah
wasatchfamilytherapy.com License# 7976237-3904
"Having a good relationship with your spouse starts with having a good relationship with yourself. Work on building your own self-esteem and confidence, and it will be easier to share that with the person you love."

Marino E. Carbonell, EdD, LMHC, CAP, ICADC, NCC, Florida
marinocarbonell.com License# MH6493
"A successful marriage is one that can separate being a couple from being parents. Do not let one rule the other. Set aside time for coupling without the need for parenting."

Molly Pierce, LPC, NCC, Leawood, Kansas
www.trueselfcounseling.com License# LPC: 2197
"A large part of marriage is about meeting each other's needs. Most spouses within a healthy marriage *want* to meet their spouse's needs, but they don't always know how. This is why it's so important not only to strive to meet your spouse's needs, but also to *voice* your own; therefore, giving your spouse the opportunity to meet your needs. For example, if you need comfort from your spouse, say to him or her, 'I am feeling vulnerable right now and I would like for you to give e me a hug.' Now your spouse knows exactly what you need, and they are able to provide that for you."

Risa Hobson, MA, LPC, Portland, Oregon
www.wtlcounseling.com License# C2656
"Parenting can put a lot of stress on a marriage, so it is important to remember that the marital relationship was there first, and needs to stay first priority. The stronger your relationship is as a couple, the stronger your relationship with the children can be. Consider what has helped you to feel connected and efficient as a couple before kids, and determine how to include your new family members in these same methods. When your marriage is successful, your kids will not only feel safe and secure in your care, they will learn far more from your modeling a healthy relationship than you could ever teach them directly."

M. L. Grabill, M.Ed., L.P.C., L.A.C., Colorado Springs, Colorado
mlgbehavhlth.com License# LPC 5825 & LAC 170
"What keeps my marriage a success is that after 30 years of marriage, it's still okay to talk to each other like we were in kindergarten."

Nancy McKelvey, LCSW, Fort Collins, Colorado
www.figureitoutcounseling.com
"We need to remember that a marriage relationship ebbs and flows, as it is a *living entity* that vacillates in its direction, its intensity, its purpose and needs. Without each spouse re-evaluating preconceived notions of what marriage *should* be a somewhat rigid set-up is that of unrealistic expectations, disappointments, and anger – leading to alienation and a vicious cycle. In the lyrics by Clint Black, 'Love is something that you do; love is not what you find, is not what you have, nor what you're in.' When we realize that 'love' is an action word, we can nurture the relationship and ourselves within it - allowing it to continue to develop, soften, deepen, and last. [I've been married 51 years.]"

Maren Gleason, LCSW, San Ramon, California
www.marengleason.com
"Couples can get caught in cycles of behavior and emotions and feel stuck. There is hope for changing this pattern and having a stronger sense of love and connection. Sometimes the patterns and feelings were learned in our families of origin. Even when there has been infidelity, couples can recover and reconnect in ways that they may have thought impossible. This process of change is not about learning to communicate better or learning to argue better, but with guidance, looking at the underlying feelings that drive the cycle of behavior. This pattern of behavior is sometimes referred to as a dance. As the couple learns about themselves and each other, the pattern or dance can be changed and bring a sense of secure, safe connection and love."

Andria Jennings, LCSW, Tucson, Arizona
www.andriajenningslcsw.com License# LCSW 3617
"You've heard the expression, 'Never go to bed angry,' but often, that only leads to long nights. It's okay to go to bed angry, but before you do, remind yourself and your partner that you love and are committed to each other and that 'this too shall pass'."

Jaleh Donaldson

Kathy Martone, Licensed Clinical Psychologist, Denver, Colorado
www.dreamagik.com License# 2441
"Marriage is a commitment made on two levels of consciousness. One level is the personal and conscious commitment whereas the other involves the soul's unconscious purpose for the holy union. Making this unconscious vow conscious is not only enlightening, but can also provide the essential 'glue' to keep the marriage stable. In order to craft such a conscious marriage, both spouses must understand that the unique challenges and stressors in their relationship offer them the opportunity to be both teacher and student, one to the other. This in turn creates a space for more open and constructive conversation and more effective problem solving."

Robyn Undieme, MA, LMFT, Tulsa, Oklahoma
License# 947
"Emotional intimacy and connectedness are unattainable without open communication and honesty with your spouse. All too often partners lack communicating what's really on their mind to their spouse because they assume their partner will be hurt, upset, closed off, or won't care. But shutting down won't solve anything and in turn, will affect a person's happiness, sex life, and relationship with their spouse and possibly their children. The problem is rarely what we think it is, rather, it's *how* we address the problem that is the real issue. Learning how to communicate and when, is one of the most important skills a person can have in life."

Tezlyn "Sam" Clark, M.Ed, LPC, Anchorage, Alaska
www.tezlynclark.com   License# 598
"Many people feel marriage is two people becoming one. If that were the case, you would lose one whole person . . . you would lose all of their delightful idiosyncrasies; their laughter; their wonderful, crazy daydreams, etc. Marriage works best when it's two separate individuals coming together to share one journey. "Love is when you may not see eye to eye, but can still walk hand in hand" (Unknown). "

206

Kim Leandre, CAGS, LMHC, NCC, East Greenwich, RI
www.kimleandrecounseling.com License# RI-MHC00412
"Couples, regardless of learned behavior, do best when each person gains insight into their thoughts, feelings, and behaviors. Couples need to take responsibility for their words, as well as non-verbal communication they display (eye rolling, sighing), and understand that human beings have a choice in their reactions despite provocation. Too often I hear 'Well, I yelled at her because she yelled at me!' It goes back to the timeless quote, 'Two wrongs don't make a right'. Someone needs to stop the circular pattern and in turn, others will react differently toward you. We, and only we, are accountable for our choices, our words and our behaviors as adults."

Shireen Oberman, LCSW, Beverly Hills, California
www.mytherapistshireen.com License# LCS 23843
"Don't take the daily frustrations of life out on your spouse."

Brittany Neece, LMFT-A, Austin, Texas
www.brittanyneece.com
"Don't wait to get professional help! So many couples wait until they have been experiencing disturbing and agonizing issues within their relationship for years and years before even considering therapy. When this happens, it is likely that one or both spouses has actually already given up mentally or emotionally in the relationship and may just 'go through the motions' of counseling as somewhat of a last attempt to repair it. When couples begin marriage/relationship counseling before their issues get to this point, there is generally a greater likelihood that both people will be more motivated and willing to make the changes needed to strengthen and improve their relationship."

Seeking Services of an Expert

When seeking the services of a Psychotherapist or any type of professional relationship please make sure to learn that they are meeting their State, Local and National regulations regarding their services before making an appointment. This will help you to decide if who you are seeking help represents their educational specialization. Feel free to inquire about the number of years practiced. Be an informed consumer so your decision to utilize their services provides a baseline of legitimate information. You can also check with your state to make sure any representation made is accurate and reliable.

State Resource Directory

The psychotherapists and other professionals listed in this resource directory have a wide range of credentials (certificates, degrees, licenses, etc.), which appear in the form of abbreviations following their name. To help interpret the credential abbreviations below are some meanings.

ALMFT	Licensed Marriage Family Therapist Associate
CAP	Certified Addictions Professional
CCBT	Certified Cognitive Behavioral Therapist
CPC	Certified Professional Counselor
CRADAC	Certified Reciprocal Alcohol and Drug Counselor
CSAT	Certified Sex Addiction Therapist
LCMHC	Licensed Clinical Mental Health Counselor
LCSW	Licensed Clinical Social Worker
LISAC	Licensed Independent Substance Abuse Counselor
LMFT	Licensed Marriage Family Therapist
LPC	Licensed Professional Counselor
M.Ed	Master of Education
MA	Master of Arts
MC	Masters of Counseling
MFCC	Marriage Family Child Counseling
MFTI	Marriage Family Therapist Intern
MS	Master of Science
MSEd	Master of Science in Education
MSW	Master of Social Work
MSSW	Master of Science in Social Work
NCC	National Certified Counselor
NCSP	Nationally Certified School Psychologist
PhD.	Doctor of Philosophy
PsyD	Doctor of Psychology

Making Marriage a Success in Alabama

Kenneth J. Wade, Ph.D., LPC, Birmingham, Alabama
1-205-933-3695 License# LMFT 119 & LPC 461
Page(s) 48

Margie Slaughter, ALMFT(# A115), Birmingham, Alabama
http://therapists.psychologytoday.com/rms/email_prof.php?profid=972
16
Page(s) 46

Leashia Moody-Miller, LPC, Birmingham, Alabama
www.moody-milllercounseling.com License# 2063
Page(s) 134

Dr. Poppy Moon, License Professional Counselor, Tuscaloosa, AL
www.poppymoon.com
Page(s) 15, 56

Making Marriage a Success in Alaska

Peter Strisik, Ph.D., Psychologist, Anchorage, Alaska
http://www.strisik.com
Page(s) 135

Tezlyn "Sam" Clark, M.Ed, LPC, Anchorage, Alaska
www.tezlynclark.com License# 598
Page(s) 206

Making Marriage a Success in Arizona

Geffen Liberman, CPC, LISAC, CRADAC, Gilbert, Arizona
www.glcounseling.com
Page(s) 180

Frieda Ling, Licensed Marriage & Family Therapist, Glendale, AZ
www.psychologytoday.com License# LMFT-10199
Page(s) 25, 44, 70, 201

Amy Serin, PhD., Psychologist, Peoria, Arizona
www.TheSerinCenter.com License# 3859
Page(s) 5, 128

Lynn Hoyland, Licensed Marriage & Family Therapist, Phoenix, AZ
www.lynnhoyland.com License# 0346
Page(s) 24, 26, 74

Anna Valenti, LCSW (License# 11769), Phoenix, Arizona
www.annavalenti.com or www.SANEresources.org

Kavita Acharya Hatten, MS, LPC, Phoenix, Arizona
www.phoenixcounseling.net License# LPC-0952
Page(s) 54

Denan Burke, LMFT, Phoenix, Arizona
www.DenanBurke.com License# 10263
Page(s) 159

Paul Berkowitz, MD, FAPM; Scottsdale, Arizona
Page(s) 191

Daniela Roher, PhD., LPC, Scottsdale & Carefree, Arizona
www.droherpsychotherapy.com
Page(s) 13, 16, 120

Alison Gamez, MA, NCC, LPC, Surprise, Arizona
Contact: 1-623-203-0696 License# LPC-13402
Page(s) 21

Marlo J. Archer, Ph.D., Psychologist, Tempe, Arizona
www.DrMarlo.com License# 3300
Page(s) 20, 157

Tracy G. Epstein, MS NCC LPC, Tucson, Arizona
www.arizonafamilycounseling.com
Page(s) 32

Andria Jennings, LCSW, Tucson, Arizona
www.andriajenningslcsw.com License# LCSW 3617
Page(s) 90, 205

Lova G. Njuguna, MC, NCC, LPC, LISAC, CCBT, Tucson, Arizona
www.pimacounseling.com License# LPC 2171 & LISAC 11871
Page(s) 141

Julie Weiner-Dabda, MC, NCC, LPC (License# LPC-13264), Tucson
http://julieweinerdabdacounseling.community.officelive.com
Page(s) 21, 143

Stacy Paul, LPC, LISAC, Tucson, Arizona
http://www.stacypaullpclisac.com License# LPC-2397 & LISAC-1626
Page(s) 100

Making Marriage a Success in Arkansas

Kenneth Joe Heard, LPC, LCMHC, Bryant, Arkansas
www.kjoeheard.com License# P8012118
Page(s) 10, 30

Janet Holt, LPC, Hot Springs, Arkansas
www.janetholt.com License# P1007048
Page(s) 15, 143

Brittany Smith, LCSW, Little Rock, Arkansas
www.EatHappy.org License# AR-1984C
Page(s) 55

Making Marriage a Success in California

Isadora Alman, LMFT, Alameda, California
www.askisadora.com License# ML24319
Page(s) 130, 200

Ellen Odza, LMFT, Alameda, California
therapyforaddictions.com License# MFC42947
Page(s) 181

Merrill Powers, MSW, LCSW, Auburn, California
www.powerstherapist.com License# LCS 19451
Page(s) 11, 53

Mary Julia Klimenko, LMFT, Benicia, California
www.mjklimenko.com
Page(s) 123

Elayne Savage, PhD., Licensed Marriage Family Therapist, Berkeley
http://www.QueenofRejection.com License# MFC 17077
Page(s) 30, 69, 107, 143

Judye G. Hess, PhD., Berkeley, California
judyehess.com License# PSY5553
Page(s) 139

Cheryl Krauter, LMFT, Berkeley, California
www.breastcancersurvivorsupport.com License# MFT14759
Page(s) 91, 173

Jill Shugart, Licensed Marriage Family Therapist, Berkeley, California
http://www.jillshugart.net
Page(s) 188

Jason Hughes, MA Holistic Counseling, Beverly Hills, California
www.onemanslovestory.net
Page(s) 133

Lucy Papillon, Ph.D., Licensed Clinical Psychologist, Beverly Hills
drpapillon.com
Page(s) 201

Hillary Goldsher, Psy.D, MBA, Beverly Hills, California
www.drhillarygoldsher.com
Page(s) 203

Dahlia Keen, Psy.D., Clinical Psychologist, Beverly Hills, California
www.drdahlia.com License# 19992
Page(s) 90

Jill Pomerantz, Licensed Clinical Social Worker, Beverly Hills, CA
www.jillpomerantzlcsw.com License# 24287
Page(s) 20

Alisa Ruby Bash, LMFT, Beverly Hills, California
www.alisarubybash.com License# 47733
Page(s) 133

Shireen Oberman, LCSW, Beverly Hills, California
www.mytherapistshireen.com License# LCS 23843
Page(s) 207

Catherine DeMonte, LMFT, Beverly Hills, California
www.catherinedemonte.com License# MFT 27623
Page(s) 146

Rene Lewellyn, LMFT, Brentwood, California
www.renelewellynmft.com License# MFC42173
Page(s) 45

Anna Kumor, Licensed Marriage Family Therapist, Burbank, CA
www.annakumor.com License# Mfc41879
Page(s) 157

Wendi Svoboda, LCSW, Burbank, California
www.wsvobodalcsw.com License# LCS24639
Page(s) 81, 96

Randy M. Gold, Psy.D, MFT, Calabasas, California
www.randyandmichellegold.com License# MFC33303
Page(s) 122

Steve Moore, LMFT, Calabasas, California
www.stevemoorecounseling.com License# MFT 23396
Page(s) 77

Catherine DeMonte, LMFT, Calabasas, California
www.catherinedemonte.com License# MFT 27623
Page(s) 146

Teri McHugh, PhD, LMFT, Camarillo, California
www.drtmchugh.com
Page(s) 187

Melodie Anderson, MA, LMFT, Chico, California
MelodieAnderson.com License# ML24320
Page(s) 171

Florence Soares-Dabalos, LMFT, Chico, California
www.florencemft.com License# MFC40331
Page(s) 10, 117

Stuart A. Kaplowitz, Licensed Marriage Family Therapist, Chino, CA
www.encouragingyourlife.com License# MFC 36347
Page(s) 61

Yvonne Wilson, Clinical Psychologist, LMFT, Corona, California
yvonnewilsonphd.com License# MFT26092 & Psy17078
Page(s) 51, 78

Cliff Crain, Licensed Marriage Family Therapist, Danville, California
www.4creativeliving.com License# LMFC 30798
Page(s) 42

Dr. Ann Thomas, LMFT, Danville, California
dr-annthomas.com License# MFT12406
Page(s) 109

Dr. Sara Denman, Psy.D, Psychologist, Danville, California
drsaradenman.com License# Psy19808
Page(s) 45, 94, 101, 153

Jeanne Courtney, MFT, El Cerrito, California
www.FeministTherapyAssociates.com License# MFC29813
Page(s) 164

Charlyne Gelt, Ph.D., Clinical Psychologist, Encino, California
www.drgelt.com Phone# 818-501-4123 License# PSY22909
Page(s) 76

Scott Lloyd Sherman, LMFT, PCE, Eureka, California
shamanicvisionpsychotherapy.blogspot.com License# MFT14936
Page(s) 33

Jaleh Donaldson

Laurie Monroe, Licensed Clinical Social Worker, Eureka, California
www.healingtheinnergoddess.com License# LCS 21959
Page(s) 137, 153

Larry L. Langford, MFT Intern (#60859) Fresno, California
www.larrylangfordtherapy.com Supervisor Brenda Kent, MFT 29581
Page(s) 83

Carol A. Anderson, MS, MFCC, Fresno, California
www.acenter4relationships.com License# MFC29432
Page(s) 156

Corinne Soares, LCSW, Fresno, California
http://therapistsdesk.blogspot.com/ License# LCS 24017
Page(s) 151

Dr. Heather M. Browne, LMFT, Garden Grove, California
www.TheHealingHeart.net License# 34523
Page(s) 17, 25, 27, 179

Dr. Suzanne Lopez, MFCC Licensed, Glendale, California
Dr. Suzanne lopez.com License# MFC 21623
Page(s) 119

Carey Laine, Psy.D., Grass Valley, California
http://drcareylaine.com License# PSY 21635
Page(s) 118

Cathy Chambliss, LMFT, Hermosa Beach, California
www.cathychamblissmft.com License# mfc39875
Page(s) 177

Jay Jameson, LMFT, Laguna Hills, California
jayjameson.com License# MFC 34802
Page(s) 23, 70, 91, 149

Cristina Castagnini, Ph.D., Psychologist, Livermore, California
www.pathtohealtherapy.com License# PSY20435
Page(s) 29, 86

Linda Nusbaum, Licensed Marriage & Family Therapist, Long Beach
www.lindanusbaum.com License# 45519
Page(s) 27

Michi Fu, Ph.D., Licensed Psychologist, Los Angeles, California
http://asianamericanpsych.blogspot.com/ License# CA PSY 19807
Page(s) 126

Ellie Zarrabian, Ph.D., Spiritual Director, Los Angeles, California
www.centeronpeace.com
Page(s) 38, 50, 64, 80

Robert Weiss, LCSW, CSAT-S, Author, Los Angeles, California
www.sexualrecovery.com License# LCS-17610
Page(s) 109

Robin A. Hubert, M.F.T, Los Angeles, California
www.HubertTherapy.com License# MFC 42452
Page(s) 188

Sari Fine Shepphird, Ph.D., Clinical Psychologist, Los Angeles, CA
DrShepp.com License #PSY20922
Page(s) 74

Negar Khaefi, LMFT, Los Angeles, California
negarkhaefi.com License# MFC 45939
Page(s) 107

Stephanie Mihalas, Ph.D., NCSP, Los Angeles, California
www.askdrstephanie.com License# PSY 23268
Page(s) 84

Jodi Milstein, LMFT, Los Angeles, California
www.JodiMilstein.com and www.RockStarTherapy.com
Page(s) 66, 192

Marina Tonkonogy, MA., LMFT, Los Angeles, California
www.mtmft.com License #48252
Page(s) 101

Jeffrey Chernin, Ph.D. MFT, Los Angeles, California
www.jeffreychernin.com
Page(s) 82

Nadine Winocur, Psy.D., Los Angeles, California
DrNadineWinocur.com License# PSY15391
Page(s) 147, 150

Shannon Byrnes, M.A., Psychotherapist, Los Angeles, California
www.shannonbyrnes.com
Page(s) 113

Lara M Schwartz, M.A., MFT, Manhattan Beach, California
www.laraschwartz.com License# MFT35813
Page(s) 144

Jonathan Mahrer, Ph.D., Mill Valley, California
www.BlueMountainCounseling.com License# PSY 14351
Page(s) 56

Dr. Sarah Villarreal, Psy.D, Mill Valley, California
www.entelechywellness.com
Page(s) 10, 55, 62

Miranda Palmer, LMFT, Modesto, California
http://counselingmodesto.com License# MFC 42393
Page(s) 73

Steve Sisgold, M.A., Certified Relationship Counselor, Novato, CA
www.onedream.com
Page(s) 111, 140

Sara Lesser, LCSW, Oakland, California
www.saralesser.com License# LCS24539
Page(s) 131

Jodi Blackley, LMFT, Orange County, California
http://www.jodiblackley.com
Page(s) 31, 44, 166

Dr. Sarah Villarreal, Psy.D, Palo Alto, California
www.entelechywellness.com
Page(s) 10, 55, 62

James S. Graves, PhD, PsyD, Pasadena, California
www.DrJimGraves.com License# PSY18196
Page(s) 152

John Sovec, Psychotherapist, MA, LMFT, Pasadena, California
www.JohnSovec.com License# MFC 46376
Page(s) 57, 118, 120, 149

Nakeya Fields, LCSW, Pasadena, California
www.ffcounseling.com License# LCS 25754
Page(s) 202

Bert Epstein, PsyD, Petaluma, California
http://www.drbertepstein.com License# PSY21404
Page(s) 102

Donald Wallach, MFT, Petaluma, California
www.donwallach.com License# MFC34379
Page(s) 114

Daniel L DeGoede, Ph.D, Clinical Psychologist, Pioneertown, CA
www.drdanieldegoede.com License# PSY9479
Page(s) 59, 86, 147

Gary Lange, Ph.D., Marriage & Family Therapist, Rancho Mirage, CA
www.GaryLangePhD.com License# 25633
Page(s) 44

Michael Kuiper, PhD., Licensed Psychologist, Redding, California
www.buildingjoy.net License# 14346
Page(s) 18

Jennica Jenkins, PsyD, LPC, Rocklin, California
Jennicajenkins.com License# LPC6072
Page(s) 114

Ken Siegmann, Roseville, LMFT, Roseville, California
http://www.insight-counseling.org License# MFC41274
Page(s) 43

Lindsey Stewart Plumer, LMFT, Roseville, California
www.lindseyplumer.com License# MFC43983
Page(s) 141, 156

Kelly Newbill, LMFT, Sacramento, California
www.kellynewbillmft.com License# 48465
Page(s) 137,

Dr. Andrew Mendonsa, Clinical Psychologist, Sacramento, California
www.DrMendonsa.com License# PSY23208
Page(s) 72

Sharon Skelton, Licensed Marriage & Family Therapist, Sacramento
www.midtown-counselor.com
Page(s) 175

Peter Gaffney, Psychiatrist, Sacramento, California
www.psychiatricadvice5cents.com
Page(s) 65

Ce Eshelman, LMFT, Sacramento, California
www.attachmentandtraumatreatmentcenter.com License# MFC27146
Page(s) 58

Steve McCready, LMFT, Sacramento, California
www.counselingsacramento.com License# MFC43212
Page(s) 180

Mark A. Foster, Ph.D., MFT, Sacramento, California
Askdrmark.com License# 22707
Page(s) 103

Sandra Reishus, Clinical Sexologist, Sacramento, California
sandrareishus.com
Page(s) 5

Anna Stewart, MFT Registered Intern (IMF# 60886) Sacramento, CA
Supervised by Darlene Davis, MFT (MFC# 40875)
http://hope-counselingcenter.org/Counselor8.html
Page(s) 140

Sara Ruebelt, MFT, Ph.D., Sacramento, California
http://www.hopemore.org/ License# MFC 50059
Page(s) 156

Jennifer Olden, Licensed Marriage Family Therapist, Sacramento, CA
www.Jenniferolden.com License# 42693
Page(s) 116

Sylvia Pritchett, MFT Intern BBS #63454, Sacramento, California
Page(s) 29

Aimee Vadnais, Psy.D, LMFT, San Diego, California
www.cvpsych.com License# PSY 21368 & MFC 39973
Page(s) 36

Diane DuBois, LMFT, San Francisco & East Bay, California
www duboistherapy.com License# MFC30808
Page(s) 26, 74

Juli Fraga, Psy.D., Licensed Psychologist, San Francisco, California
www.drjulifraga.com License# PSY20718
Page(s) 71

Joshua M. Simmons, PsyD, San Francisco, California
www.sftherapy.info License# PSY23334
Page(s) 99

Victoria Zurkan, Licensed Marriage Family Therapist, San Francisco
http://www.zurkan-therapy.com/ License# 43872
Page(s) 11

Peter Sholley, MFT Registered Intern (#57471), San Francisco, CA
www.sholleysomatics.com Supervisor Frances Verrinder, MFT 11970
Page(s) 78

Holly Gordon, DMH, San Francisco, California
drhollygordon.com License# PSY 8796
Page(s) 174

David Olem, MFT, San Francisco, California
www.davidolem.com License# MFC40869
Page(s) 184

Faith Freed, MFT Intern (#IMF 61352), San Francisco, California
www.faithfreed.com Supervisor Dr. Sarah Villarreal, Psy D.
Page(s) 90, 127

Claudia Sinay-Mosias, MFT, San Francisco, California
www.sanfranciscocounseling.com License# MFC27519
Page(s) 23, 112

Steve Orma, Psy.D., San Francisco, California
http://www.drorma.com License# PSY 23785
Page(s) 8, 10

George Kolcun, MFT, San Francisco, California
www.georgekolcunmft.blogspot.com License# MFC 46809
Page(s) 95, 176

Ilene A. Serlin, Ph.D, BC-DMT, San Francisco, California
www.union-street-health-associates.com License# PSY 11092
Page(s) 41, 134, 169

Gloria Saltzman, LMFT, San Francisco, California
www.GloriaSaltzman.com License# 22460
Page(s) 52, 119

Vanessa B Tate, LMFT, San Francisco, California
www.VanessaBTate.com License# MFC 48163
Page(s) 27

Dr. William I. Perry, Psychologist, San Francisco, California
www.drbillperry.com License# PSY10384
Page(s) 29

Rama Ronen, Ph.D, San Francisco, California
WWW.entelechywellness.com License# PSY 23043
Page(s) 124

Myles Downes, MFT, San Francisco, California
http://mylesdownes.com License# MFC48178
Page(s) 175

Gal Szekely, LMFT, San Francisco, California
MindfulLifeCenter.com License# 50301
Page(s) 22, 59

Michael G Quirke, L.M.F.T., San Francisco, California
www.michaelgquirke.com License# MFC39030
Page(s) 12, 50, 127

Cheryl Krauter, LMFT, San Francisco, California
www.breastcancersurvivorsupport.com License# MFT14759
Page(s) 91, 173

Jeanne Courtney, MFT, San Francisco, California
www.FeministTherapyAssociates.com License# MFC29813
Page(s) 164

Jonathan Mahrer, Ph.D., San Francisco, California
www.BlueMountainCounseling.com License# PSY 14351
Page(s) 56

Michael T. Halyard, LMFT, MBA, San Francisco, California
www.SFtherapy.com License# MFC42122
Page(s) 52, 70

Penn Barbosa, Ph.D., San Francisco, California
www.therapypenn.com License# PSY18949
Page(s) 95

Annie Schuessler, LMFT, San Francisco, California
www.annieschuessler.com License# 43865
Page(s) 146

Dr. Lisa Cooney, MFT, San Francisco, California
www.leitheta.com License# MFT #38608
Page(s) 173, 194

Dr. Sarah Villarreal, Psy.D, San Francisco, California
www.entelechywellness.com
Page(s) 10, 55, 62

Sally Broder, Psy.D., San Francisco, California
www.drsallybroder.com License# PSY 22229
Page(s) 40

Jay M. Seiff-Haron, Psy.D., San Francisco, California
http://www.familytherapysf.com Licensed Psychologist CA
PSY23443
Page(s) 161

Yaji Tramontini, Licensed Marriage Family Therapist, San Francisco
http://yajitherapy.com License# MFC45878
Page(s) 142

Brooke Miller, Licensed Marriage Family Therapist, San Francisco
www.soapboxtherapy.com
Page(s) 185

Raelene S. Weaver, Licensed Marriage Family Therapist, San Jose
www.raeleneweaver.com License# 46608
Page(s) 47, 55, 58, 102, 169

Denan Burke, MFC, San Luis Obispo, California
www.DenanBurke.com License# CA LMFT 10263
Page(s) 159

Angela R. Wurtzel, MA, LMFT, San Luis Obispo, California
www.angelawurtzelmft.com License# 33686
Page(s) 110

Michael G Quirke, L.M.F.T., San Mateo, California
www.michaelgquirke.com License# MFC39030
Page(s) 12, 50, 127

Maren Gleason, LCSW, San Ramon, California
www.marengleason.com
Page(s) 205

KD Farris, M.A., Depth Psychologist, Santa Barbara, California
www.meshe.com and www.kdfarris.com
Page(s) 187

Angela R. Wurtzel, MA, MFT, Santa Barbara, California
www.angelawurtzelmft.com License# 33686
Page(s) 110

Karen Stewart, Psy. D., Clinical Psychologist, Santa Monica, CA
www.drkrarenstewart.com
Page(s) 31, 81

Frieda L. Ferrick, Licensed Marriage Family Therapist, Santa Rosa
www.friedaferrick.com
Page(s) 68

John Bogardus, Licensed Clinical Social Worker, Sonoma, California
www.johnbogardus.com
Page(s) 154

Anthony Scheving, M.A., Psy.D., (#PSB 35759) Sonora, California
Supervised by Dr. Susan B. Day Ph.D. CA PSY # 23349
www.susanbdayphd.com
Page(s) 136

Nadine Winocur, Psy.D., Sonora, California
DrNadineWinocur.com License# PSY15391
Page(s) 147, 150

Bette Levy Alkazian, LMFT, Thousand Oaks, California
www.BalancedParenting.com License# MFC 32747
Page(s) 106, 120

Dr. Victoria Boccanfuso, Psychologist, Tracy, California
www.vbpsyd.com License# PSY23177
Page(s) 200

Christopher Old, MFT, LPC, NCC, Truckee, California
www.mountainmentalhealth.com License# MFC 44697
Page(s) 34, 75, 97

Shoshana Kobrin, LMFT, Author, Walnut Creek, California
www.kobrinkreations.com License# MFT 23716
Page(s) 76

Jill Shugart, Licensed Marriage Family Therapist, Berkeley, California
http://www.jillshugart.net
Page(s) 188

Dr. Stephen Trudeau, Psychologist, Westlake Village, California
www.HumansGuide.com License# PSY19669
Page(s) 83

Marilyn Wedge, Ph.D., Westlake Village, California
www.MarilynWedgePhd.com License# 23729
Page(s) 100, 193

Making Marriage a Success in Colorado

Tzu-Han "Lillian" Koskella, Registered Psychotherapist, Arvada, CO
http://www.tlcpsychotherapy.com
Page(s) 194, 228

Pam Snyder, LCSW, Arvada, Colorado
www.pamsnyderlcsw.com
Page(s) 66

Karen Hoving, Ph.D., Aurora, Colorado
www.drkahoving.com License# 10245
Page(s) 38, 161

Diane Renz, LPC, Boulder, Colorado
www.yourgatewaytohealing.com License# 4623
Page(s) 145

Lisa M. Templeton, Ph.D., Psychologist, Broomfield, Colorado
www.interpersonalhealing.com License# PSY 3071
Page(s) 174

Trudy M. Johnson, LMFT, Buena Vista, Colorado
www.missingpieces.org License# 755
Page(s) 47, 69

Kwai Kendall-Grove, Ph.D., Centennial, Colorado
www.drkendallgrove.com License# 2321
Page(s) 6

Jennifer Ritchie-Goodline, Licensed Psychologist, Centennial, CO
www.drjenniferritchiegoodline.com
Page(s) 87, 96

Lynn Kennedy Baxter, BSN, LMFT, Colorado Springs, Colorado
www.BeConfidentToday.com License# MFT 939
Page(s) 177

M. L. Grabill, M.Ed., L.P.C., L.A.C., Colorado Springs, Colorado
mlgbehavhlth.com License# #5825 & License# 170
Page(s) 48, 204

Christy Sorden, LPC, Colorado Springs, Colorado
www.SordenCounseling.com
Page(s) 42, 127, 133

Jeff Goldman, LCSW, Denver, Colorado
JeffreyGoldmanPsychotherapy.com License# 986054
Page(s) 198

Kate Daigle, MA, NCC, Denver, Colorado
www.katedaiglecounseling.com License# 12442
Page(s) 182

Julia White, LCSW, Denver, Colorado
www.juliamwhite.com License# 992173
Page(s) 49, 95, 122

Larry Cappel, M.A., LMFT, Denver, Colorado
http://downtowndenvertherapy.com/ License# LMFT715
Page(s) 62, 136

Karen Turner, LMFT, DAPA, Denver, Colorado
www.ElderWisdom.com License# 426
Page(s) 139

Shadia Duske, MA, NCC, Denver, Colorado
www.psychotherapy-healing.com License# NCC 279400
Page(s) 151

Dr. Jack McInroy, Psychologist, Denver, Colorado
www.DrMcInroy.com License# CO 518
Page(s) 79, 155

Nancy Cason, Psy.D., Licensed Clinical Psychologist, Denver, CO
www.insights-autism.com
Page(s) 119

Heather O'Neil, Licensed Clinical Social Worker, Denver, Colorado
www.oneiltherapy.com License# 992331
Page(s) 119

Kathy Martone, Licensed Clinical Psychologist, Denver, Colorado
www.dreamagik.com License# 2441
Page(s) 206

Taryn Bostwick, LPC, Denver, Colorado
www.TheButterflyWithin.com License# 6214
Page(s) 18

Shelly Clubb, M.S., M.A., NCC, Denver, Colorado
www.transformativecounselingservices.com License# 12176
Page(s) 41, 75, 144

Trisha Swinton, LPC, LMFT, Denver, Colorado
www.trishaswintoncounseling.com License# LPC 4914 & LMFT 842
Page(s) 105

Marne Wine, M.A. LPC, CST, Denver, Colorado
www.btid.com
Page(s) 57

Dee Marcotte, MFT, LPC, Denver, Colorado
Www.deemarcotte.com License# 2704
Page(s) 148

Bridget Engel, PsyD, Erie, Colorado
FrontRangePsychology.com License# 2909
Page(s) 9

Wendy Becker, LCSW, Fort Collins, Colorado
www.FrontRangeCounselingandMediation.com License# 1007
Page(s) 110

Nancy McKelvey, LCSW, Fort Collins, Colorado
www.figureitoutcounseling.com
Page(s) 205

Kate Feldman, MSW, LCSW, Hesperus, Colorado
www.consciousrelationships.com
Page(s) 53

Kari Marshall, Licensed Professional Counselor, Littleton, Colorado
www.karimarshall.com License# 3767
Page(s) 172

Hope Weiss, LCSW, Longmont, Colorado
www.HopeIsThere.com License# 34
Page(s) 85

William Hambleton Bishop, MA, Longmont, Colorado
www.thoughtsfromatherapist.com License# 6156
Page(s) 64

Dr. Patricia W. Stevens, LPC, Louisville, Colorado
www.awarenessdynamics.com CO License #249
Page(s) 154

Cynthia Swan, M.A., C.M.F.T., L.P.C., Niwot, Colorado
www.cynthiaswan.com
Page(s) 15, 102, 232

Julie Uhernik, RN, LPC, NCC, Parker, Colorado
www.julieuhernik.com License# LPC 4714 & RN 110129
Page(s) 80, 106

Amy Jones, LPC, DCC, Westminster, Colorado
www.growthworks.net License# CO 2693
Page(s) 43

Tania Henderson, LPC, Wheat Ridge, Colorado
www.sbscounseling.com License# 4115
Page(s) 91

Making Marriage a Success in Connecticut

Heather Hanlon, MS, LMFT, Bethel, Connecticut
http://www.heatherhanlon.com
Page(s) 37

Michael Luongo, LPC, Chaplin, Connecticut
www.michaelluongolpc.com License# 001182
Page(s) 134

Paula Chu, Ph.D., LPC, Farmington, Connecticut
www.paulachu.com
Page(s) 126

Debra Franklin, LCSW, Granby, Connecticut
www.progressivepsychotherapy.com
Page(s) 139

Brittany Dudas, Psychiatrist, Greenwich, Connecticut
www.bdudas.com
Page(s) 124

Pamela Tinkham, MSW, LCSW, Greenwich, Connecticut
www.MindBodyFitnessLLC.com
Page(s) 115

Lori Carpenos, LMFT, Hartford, Connecticut
www.3Principlestherapy.com License# LMFT000551
Page(s) 12, 34, 76

Debra Franklin, LCSW, Hartford, Connecticut
www.progressivepsychotherapy.com
Page(s) 139

Dr Linda Olson, Licensed Clinical Psychologist, New Canaan, CT

www.americaslovedoctortherapy.com License# 002473
Page(s) 161, 162

Brittany Dudas, Psychiatrist, New York City, Connecticut
www.bdudas.com
Page(s) 124

Beth Honey, LMFT, Somers, Connecticut
www.therapeuticconnections.vpweb.com License# 000996
Page(s) 36

Marion Green, LMFT, EFT Therapist, Stamford, Connecticut
www.mariongreenllc.com License# CT 001251
Page(s) 92

Melinda Sharpe, LCSW, Wallingford, Connecticut
melindasharpe.com License# CT 001002
Page(s) 105

Making Marriage a Success in Delaware

Dr. Cynthia Chestnut, Couple, Family & Sex Therapist, Middletown
www.drcynthiachestnut.com
Page(s) 58, 176

Natalie A. Cherrix, LCSW, DVS, Seaford, Delaware
www.nataliecherrix.com
Page(s) 50

Dr. Debra Laino, DHS, M.ED, MS, ACS, ABS, Wilmington, DE
www.delawaresexdoc.com
Page(s) 5, 12, 47, 57

Angela Tatum Fairfax, LPC, BC-DMT, NCC, Wilmington, Delaware

www.goodfruitexpressivearts.com License# PC0000438
Page(s) 35

Making Marriage a Success in Florida

Leslie Rouder, LCSW, CHT, Boca Raton, Florida
www.addadults.net License# SW5937
Page(s) 23, 61, 179

Barbara Winter PhD, Boca Raton, Florida
www.drbarbarawinter.com License# PY4034
Page(s) 45, 125

Susan Addis, Ph.D., Gainesville, Florida
www.DrSusanAddis.com License# PY 5626
Page(s) 78

Teresa Trower, M.A. LMHC, Jacksonville, Florida
www.stressbustercoach.com License# MH0002000
Page(s) 57, 145

Matt Borer, Ph.D., Licensed Marriage Family Therapist, Jacksonville
www.mattborer.com and www.breakupplan.com
Page(s) 19, 149

Nicole Story, Ed.S, LMFT, Jacksonville Beach, Florida
www.OceansideFamilyTherapy.com License# LMFT MT2208
Page(s) 78, 101

Kevin M Hallinan, LCSW, CAP, SAP, ICADC, Melborne, Florida
www.Kmhpsychotherapist.com License# SW6611
Page(s) 48, 141

Marino E. Carbonell, EdD, LMHC, CAP, ICADC, NCC, Miami, FL

marinocarbonell.com License# MH6493
Page(s) 204

Melissa Cramer, LCSW, CAP, Miami, Florida
GROWHEALLOVE.com License# sw9441
Page(s) 117, 144

Deborah A. Bruno, MSW, LCSW, Miami, Florida
www.mindbuild.net License# 6832
Page(s) 38

Carol A. Hicks, MA, LMFT, Pensacola, Florida
www.answerwithin.com License# LMFT 0120
Page(s) 186

Lynda K. Tyson, PhD, Pensacola, Florida
www.mmtmentalhealth.org License# LMHC 9018 & CMHP 50608
Page(s) 46

Chrisanna Harrington, M.A., R.D., L.M.H.C., Port Charlotte, Florida
www.nutegra.com
Page(s) 11

Scott Keller, LCSW, Tampa, Florida
www.scottkeller4u.com License# SW 9501
Page(s) 14

Thomas L. Tobias, M.Ed., LMHC, NCC, Tavares, Florida
www.triadpsychologicalservices.com License# MH1516
Page(s) 57

Dr. LeslieBeth Wish, Ed.D, MSS, LCSW, Sarasota, Florida
www.lovevictory.com License # SW 7132 Florida
Page(s) 162

Making Marriage a Success in Georgia

Janis R. Cohen, MSW, LCSW, Atlanta, Georgia
www.cohenfamilycounseling.com
Page(s) 71

Jennifer Wilmoth, LAMFT, Atlanta, Georgia
www.growcounseling.com License# AMFT 000204
Page(s) 115, 182

Wendy Dickinson, Ph.D., Psychologist, Atlanta, Georgia
www.growcounseling.com License# PSYCH 3256
Page(s) 9, 95, 173

Joe Lowrance, Psy.D., Clinical Psychologist, Atlanta, Georgia
www.FinancialPsychologyCeus.com
Page(s) 17, 104, 135, 163

Lauren Crawford Taylor, LCSW, Atlanta, Georgia
www.laurencrawfordlcsw.com License# 02831
Page(s) 27

Nadim S. Ali, MA, LPC, ICCDP, GCADC-III, Atlanta, Georgia
Nadimali.com License# LPC 03775
Page(s) 77, 102

Louise Northcutt, MS, Atlanta, Georgia
www.louisenorthcutt.com
Page(s) 181

Dr. Mary Gresham, Licensed Clinical Psychologist, Atlanta, Georgia
www.doctorgresham.com
Page(s) 176

Pat Wells, LPC, ACHT, Atlanta & Athens, Georgia
www.patwellstherapy.com License# LPC001800
Page(s) 181

Barbara J Peters, LPC (License# LPC002758), RN, Cumming, GE
www.bjpcounseling.com   www.thegiftofalifetime.net
Page(s) 30, 148

Dee Desnoyers, M.Ed., LPC, Decatur, Georgia
www.atlantacounseling.org License# LPC005453
Page(s) 66

Sharman Colosetti, LCSW, PhD., Decatur, Georgia
www.drsharman.com License# GA 2559
Page(s) 19

Cyndie Westrich, M.A., A.T.R.-BC, LPC, Marietta, Georgia
www.easel-arttherapy.com
Page(s) 38, 50, 84, 98, 142

Cindy Foster, LCSW, ACSW, NBCCH, Martinez, Georgia
mindbodystressreduction.com License# CSW002401
Page(s) 62, 109, 199

Teresa L. Oglesbee, Ed.S, NBCC, NBCCH, LPC, Rincon, Georgia
http://www.sccforu.com/ License# LPC004615
Page(s) 12, 22, 126

Kimberley L. Benton, Psy.D., Roswell, Georgia
www.peachtreepsychology.com License# PSY003416
Page(s) 26

AnnaLisa Derenthal, LPC, NCC, Roswell, Georgia
www.annalisaderenthal.com License# LPC004373
Page(s) 107, 121, 168, 198

Ellen Farrell, MA, LPC, EEM-CP, Savannah, Georgia
www.ellenfarrell.com
Page(s) 70, 74, 189, 192

Making Marriage a Success in Hawaii

Lisa Hartwell, PsyD, RN, Honolulu, Hawaii
www.hidrlisa.com License# Psy800
Page(s) 8, 72, 149, 191

Caroline E. Sakai, PhD, Licensed Clinical Psychologist, Honolulu, HI
http://www.tftcenter.com
Page(s) 203

Joan Levy, LCSW, LCS, ACSW, Kapaa, Hawaii
www.joanlevy.com License LCSW #3046
Page(s) 44, 92, 97, 108

Jenny Grace Shaw, LMHC, M.ED., Maui, Hawaii
www.jennyshawtherapy.com License# 256964
Page(s) 40, 118

Making Marriage a Success in Idaho

Nicole Eaton, LCSW, CCHT, Boise, Idaho
www.nicoleeaton.com
Page(s) 34, 54, 72

Carrie Eichberg, Psy.D., Licensed Psychologist, Boise, Idaho
www.dreichberg.com License# 202141
Page(s) 165

Michele Harris, M.Ed, LCPC, Boise, Idaho
wowcounseling.com License# LCPC 4110
Page(s) 182

Susan Reuling Furness, M.Ed., LCPC, LMFT, PTR, Boise, Idaho
jeffersonstreetcounseling.com License# LMFT 39 & LCPC 70
Page(s) 52

Kevin Rhinehart, LMFT, LCSW, CSAT, Meridian, Idaho
www.kevinrhinehart.com License# LCSW 612 & LMFT 2705
Page(s) 31

Charmayne Alegria, MA LCPC, Meridian, Idaho
www.touchpointscounseling.com License# LCPC-4429
Page(s) 186

Making Marriage a Success in Illinois

Leslie Karen Sann, MA, LCPC, Chicago, Illinois
http://www.lesliesann.com
Page(s) 73

Joan Ferdinand Keleher, MS, LCPC, Chicago, Illinois
www.joanferdinand.com License# 180005394
Page(s) 196

Nikki Lively, MA, LCSW, Chicago, Illinois
www.nikkilively.com License# 149.010124
Page(s) 19

Janice C. Hodge, LCPC, Chicago, Illinois
www.jchodge.com
Page(s) 151

Eleanor Laser, Ph.D, Chicago, Illinois
www.laserhypnosis.com
Page(s) 41, 73

James R. Iberg, PhD., Chicago, Illinois
www.empathywork.com License# 071.002641
Page(s) 193

Melissa Summers O'Neill, LCSW, Chicago, Illinois
www.melissaoneill.com
Page(s) 178

Joyce Marter, LCPC, Co-Owner of Urban Balance, Chicago, Illinois
www.urbanbalance.org License# 180-002902
Page(s) 22, 147

Julie Blackman, LCSW, Chicago, Illinois
www.julieblackmanlcsw.com
Page(s) 142

Nancy Simon, L.C.S.W. Evanston, Illinois
www.nancysimontherapy.com
Page(s) 134

Leslie Karen Sann, MA, LCPC, Geneva, Illinois
http://www.lesliesann.com
Page(s) 73

Dan Hanneman, M.S. Clinical Psychology, Hebron, Illinois
www.blockbustyourpath.com
Page(s) 196

Abigail Natenshon, LCSW, Highland Park, Illinois
www.empoweredparents.com
Page(s) 184

Melinda Yachnin, LCPC, Lagrange, Illinois.
http://www.melindayachnin.com License# 180-005280
Page(s) 42, 77

Robert A. Moylan, LCPC, Naperville, Illinois
www.robertmoylan.com License# 180005037
Page(s) 21, 60, 188

Sandy McDermott, LCPC, NCC, Tranquility Counseling, Springfield
www.createtranquility.com
Page(s) 113, 129, 242

Joan Ferdinand Keleher, MS, LCPC, Wilmette, Illinois
www.joanferdinand.com License# 180005394
Page(s) 196

Making Marriage a Success in Indiana

Sharon Morgillo Freeman, PhD, PMHCNS-BC, Fort Wayne, Indiana
www.centerforbrieftherapy.com License# 70000153A
Page(s) 65, 164

Dawn K. Kozarian, LMHC, NCC; Indianapolis, Indiana
www.KozarianCounseling.com License# 39001738A
Page(s) 63

Keith Magnus, Ph.D., Indianapolis, Indiana
www.woodviewgroup.com License# 20041351A
Page(s) 14

Letitia V. Haywood, MSW, LCSW, CYT, Indianapolis, IN
www.ellainc.com
Page(s) 184

Sharon L. Thompson, LMFTA, Indianapolis, Indiana
www.talkwithsharon.com License# 85000045A
Page(s) 107, 175

Donna Pollard-Burton, MA, LMHC, NCC, BCC, Indianapolis, IN
www.cairncottagecounseling.com License# 39002176A
Page(s) 12, 49, 61

Phyllis J. Bonds, MS, NCC, LMHC, LCAC, Indianapolis, Indiana
www.bondscounselingsolutions.com License# 39001570A
Page(s) 197

Making Marriage a Success in Iowa

Sheryl Leytham, Ph.D., Psychologist, Des Moines, Iowa
Sherylleytham.com License# PSY 583
Page(s) 82

Molly Kinser Douglas, ATR, LMHC, Des Moines, Iowa
mkinserdouglas@msn.com License# 001175
Page(s) 153

Dr. Don Gilbert, LMHC, Ankeny and West Des Moines, Iowa
www.newlife-counseling.com License# 00178
Page(s) 46

Greg Febbraro, PhD, Licensed Psychologist, Windsor Heights, Iowa
www.counselingforgrowthandchange.com License# 00896
Page(s) 60

Making Marriage a Success in Kansas

Molly Pierce, LPC, NCC, Leawood, Kansas
www.trueselfcounseling.com License# LPC: 2197
Page(s) 199, 204

Dawn Gilner, LPC, Lenexa, Kansas
www.DawnGilner.com License# LPC 2076
Page(s) 25, 54

Jeff King, LSCSW, CSAT, CSAT, Newton, Kansas
www.sexaddictionhelpks.com License# 3836
Page(s) 163

Brad Nowlin, LCMFT, Overland Park, Kansas
www.bradnowlin.com
Page(s) 98

Joyce Thompson, MS, LCMFT, Wichita, Kansas
www.emotionaljourney.org License# 734
Page(s) 9, 50, 56, 76, 82, 124

Donna Botinelly, DMin, LCMFT, Wichita, Kansas
www.actscounselingcenter.com License# 147
Page(s) 38

Jeff King, LSCSW, CSAT, CSAT, Wichita, Kansas
www.sexaddictionhelpks.com License# 3836
Page(s) 163

Making Marriage a Success in Kentucky

Thomas L. Volker, Ed.D., LMFT, Florence, Kentucky

www.thomaslvolkeredd.com License# 0406
Page(s) 16

Steven Smith, Psychologist, Lexington, Kentucky
Wisdomoftheheartinc.com License# 0559
Page(s) 6

Cheryl Ades, LCSW, Louisanna, Kentucky
cherylades.com
Page(s) 190

Making a Marriage a Success in Louisiana

David Earle, LPC, business coach, author, Baton Rouge, Louisiana
LAhttp://Therapists.PsychologyToday.com/rms/34753 License# 1834
Page(s) 67

J Kimbrough Benson, EdS, LPC, LMFT, Baton Rouge, Louisiana
www.rivercitypsychotherapy.co License MFT 767 License LPC 2291
Page(s) 80

Dr. Brian S. Canfield, LMFT, LPC, Bossier City, Louisiana
www.canfieldcounseling.com License LMFT #19 & LPC #120
Page(s) 36, 165

Sarah Pokorny, LCSW, Covington, Louisiana
www.pokornytherapy.com
Page(s) 108

Erica Morgan, MSW, LCSW, Covington, Louisiana
www.ericamorganlcsw.com
Page(s) 171

Dr. Robert C. Allanach, LMFT, CGP, New Orleans, Louisiana
www.doctorallanach.com License# 697
Page(s) 54, 185

Merrie Pearl, LCSW New Orleans, Louisiana
www.schematherapy-nola.com License# LCSW 9834
Page(s) 160

Making Marriage a Success in Maine

Diana J Bowen, LCPC, Gardiner, Maine
www.counselingpath.com License# CC2965
Page(s) 87

Christy A. Cole, LCPC, Kennebunk, Maine
www.christycolecounseling.com
Page(s) 130

Judith B. Taylor, LCSW, Lewiston, Maine
therapywithjudith.com
Page(s) 114

Kimberly J Plourde, LCSW, Lisbon Falls, Maine
www.thetalkzone.net License# LC11517
Page(s) 190

Elizabeth Boyajian, M.Ed, LCPC, Topsham, Maine
http://www.options-counseling.com/ License# 3300
Page(s) 81, 89, 195

Making Marriage a Success in Maryland

Adam Klein, Ph.D., Licensed Psychologist, Annapolis, Maryland
AdamKlein.net
Page(s) 170

Stephen Clarke, M.S., LGPC, Baltimore, Maryland
www.presenceproject.net License# LC4084
Page(s) 51

Dr. Joanne Vizzini, LCPC, NCC, Baltimore, Maryland
http://freedomthroughtherapy.com/ License# LC 1091 & NCC 48509
Page(s) 150

Michael Reeder, LCPC, Baltimore, Maryland
http://www.hygeiacounseling.com License# LC3624
Page(s) 118

Adam Klein, Ph.D., Licensed Psychologist, Bethesda, Maryland
AdamKlein.net
Page(s) 170

Joan Rabinor, LCSW-C, Chevy Chase, Maryland
www.joanrabinor.com
Page(s) 148

Dr. Joanne Vizzini, LCPC, NCC, Baltimore, Maryland
http://freedomthroughtherapy.com/ License# LC 1091 & NCC 48509
Page(s) 150

Angela R. Stern, LCPC, Crofton, Maryland
http://therapist.psychologytoday.com/44031
Page(s) 51, 106

Elizabeth Sloan, L.P.C., L.C.P.C., Glenn Dale, Maryland

www.CaringCouples.com
Page(s) 68

Octavia Carlos, LCSW-C, Largo, Maryland
www.octaviacarlos.com License# 05995
Page(s) 16, 93

Laurel A. Fay, M.S., LCMFT, Silver Spring, Maryland
www.laurelfay.com License# LCM167
Page(s) 21

Making Marriage a Success Massachusetts

Lynn Saladino, Psy.D., Boston, Massachusetts
drlynnsaladino.com License# 9300
Page(s) 79, 83

Carol Marks-Stopforth, LMHC, Boston, Massachusetts
Carolmarksstopforth.com License# 6416
Page(s) 111

Monica O'Neal, Psy.D., Boston, Massachusetts
www.DrMonicaONeal.com
Page(s) 137

Dorian Mintzer, Ph.D.(LICD Psychologist, #2812), Boston, MA
www.dorianmintzer.com www.couplesretirementpuzzle.com
Page(s) 49, 93

Maria Mellano, LICSW (License# 111055), Boston, Massachusetts
WWW.MariaMellanoTherapy.com WWW.LivePassionatelyNow.com
Page(s) 7, 55

Janet England, LICSW, Boston, Massachusetts
www.janetengland.com License ma licsw#106771
Page(s) 172

Joyce Dolberg Rowe, LMHC, Hull, Massachusetts
www.MentalHealthCounseling.biz License #91
Page(s) 87, 151

Making Marriage a Success in Michigan

Madelyn Satz, Ph.D., Ann Arbor, Michigan
www.drsatz.com License# 6301007634
Page(s) 163

Karen Hague, MBA, LMSW, ACSW, Ann Arbor, Michigan
www.boomersolutions.org License# 6801085338
Page(s) 104

Lori Hollander, LMSW, MBA, Sex Therapist, Ann Arbor, Michigan
Realintimacy.com License# 6801087016
Page(s) 116

Terry Tempinski, PhD., Farmington Hills, Michigan
www.DrTempinski.com License# 6301002970
Page(s) 110

Jan Talen, Licensed Marriage Family Therapist, Grand Rapids, MI
www.funlifellc.com License# 4101006087
Page(s) 22, 39, 88

Making Marriage a Success in Minnesota

Rachel Greene, LMFT, Minneapolis, Minnesota
www.rachelgreenelmft.com License# 1215
Page(s) 202

Dr. Denise Wood, M.A; Psy.D., Minneapolis, Minnesota
www.drdenisewood.com
Page(s) 93

Connie Studer, M.A. LMFT, Minneapolis, Minnesota
www.heteroflexibletherapy.com License# 1760
Page(s) 117

Weston M Edwards, Ph.D., Psychologist, Minneapolis, Minnesota
SexualHealthInstitute.org License# 3347
Page(s) 131

Christa R. Surerus, MA, LPCC, Minneapolis, Minnesota
www.affinitasplc.com License# 186
Page(s) 113

Pamela Lipe, M.S., Licensed Psychologist, Saint Paul, Minnesota
www.PamLipe.com License# LP0268
Page(s) 105

Michael Keller, Ph.D., Licensed Psychologist, Saint. Paul, Minnesota
www.psychologicalserviceassociates.com License# MN LP 4821
Page(s) 6, 129

Carmen Gloria Avendaño, LMFT, Wayzata, Minnesota
www.lifebalancetherapy.com License# 2104
Page(s) 62, 104

Making Marriage a Success in Mississippi

Beverly Smallwood, Ph.D., Psychologist Hattiesburg, Mississippi
www.DrBevSmallwood.com
Page(s) 163

Karen Mori Bonner, MS, LPC, Madison, Mississippi
www.dreamcounselor.ms License# LPC 1293
Page(s) 136

Patricia Brawley, PhD, LPC, McComb, Mississippi
http://www.PatriciaBrawley.com License# 0608
Page(s) 52

Making Marriage a Success in Missouri

Lorrie Crystal Eigles, MSED, LPC, PCC, Kansas City, Missouri
http://myauthenticlifecoaching.com
Page(s) 103, 191

Fran Ryan Ph.D., Kansas City, Missouri
www.psychologytoday.com License# PY01723
Page(s) 60, 201

Making Marriage a Success in Montana

Tim Herzog, LCPC, Bozeman, Montana
www.reachingahead.com
Page(s) 200

Diana Longdon, LCSW, Helena, Montana
http://therapists.psychologytoday.com License# 121 MT
Page(s) 171

Making Marriage a Success in Nebraska

Crystal Anzalone, MS, PLMHP, NCC, Omaha, Nebraska
http://www.thereflectioncenter.com http://arborfamilycounseling.com
Page(s) 35, 112

Making Marriage a Success in Nevada

Judith Mathews MFT, Reno, Nevada
www.judithmathewsmft.com License# MFT 884
Page(s) 101

Making Marriage a Success in New Hampshire

Dr. Fredrick Woodard, LP, PhD, Milford, New Hampshire
Woodardhypnosisandpsychotherapy.org License# 1082 NH
Page(s) 145

Hadassah Ramsay, PsyD, Durham, New Hampshire
www.drhramsay.com
Page(s) 28, 32, 109

Claire Houston, LCMHC, Exeter, New Hampshire
www.wswcenter.com
Page(s) 189

Ellen Schecter, Ph.D., Clinical Psychologist, Hanover, NH
http://ellenschecter.com
Page(s) 97

Making Marriage a Success in New Jersey

Laura Carite, MA, LPC, RYT, Flanders, New Jersey
www.restoremindandbody.com License# PC1451
Page(s) 193

Mary-Michael Levitt, LMFT, DRCC, Hackettstown, New Jersey
www.riverviewcc.com License# LMFT 37F100153100
Page(s) 59, 96, 99

Mindy Jacobson-Levy, MCAT, ATR-BC, LPC, Oaklyn, New Jersey
www.artb4words.com and www.thecenteraptt.com
Page(s) 165

Jay P. Granat, Ph.D., LMFT, River Edge, New Jersey
www.StayInTheZone.com and www.DrJayGranat.com
Page(s) 15, 97, 129

Dr. Rosalind S. Dorlen, Psy.D., Psychologist, Summit, New Jersey
www.drdorlen.com License# 1369
Page(s) 37, 140

David Brandt, L.C.S.W., Upper Montclair, New Jersey
www.davidbrandtlcsw.com
Page(s) 130

Making Marriage a Success in New Mexico

Rosemary Clarke, PhD, LPCC, Albuquerque, New Mexico
www.relationshipcoinc.com License# LPCC 94
Page(s) 138

Charles K. Schrier, LMHC, CVE, LMAO, Albuquerque, New Mexico
www.ckstherapy.com License# 0119401
Page(s) 94

Amanda S. Davison, LMFT, Albuquerque, New Mexico
nmfamilyconnection.com License# NM 0099731
Page(s) 33, 60

Dr. Suzanne Lopez, MFCC Licensed, Albuquerque, New Mexico
Dr. Suzanne lopez.com License# 0094281
Page(s) 119

Dr. Joan R. Saks Berman, Clinical Psychologist, Albuquerque, NM
www.joanberman.com www.momentumandmemento.blogspot.com
Page(s) 113

Making Marriage a Success in New York

Julie Dubovoy, LCSW-R, Babylon, New York
http://www.juliedubovoy.com/ License# R073412-1
Page(s) 7, 138, 164

Patti Geier, LCSW, Psychotherapist, Brooklyn, New York
www.pattigeier.com License# R031706-1
Page(s) 127

Katherine Clausen, LCSW, Brooklyn, New York
katherineclausenlcsw.com License# 076379
Page(s) 65

Igor Davidson, Ph.D., Clinical Psychologist, Brooklyn, New York
www.boutiquepsychology.com License# nys 016113
Page(s) 115

Valerie Chu, MA, ATR-BC, LCAT, Brooklyn, New York
www.artspringnyc.com License# 001304
Page(s) 88

Risha London Nathan, LMSW, Wellness Counselor, Brooklyn, NY
www.rishalondonnathan.com
Page(s) 121

Etan Ben-Ami, LCSW, Brooklyn, New York
http://www.effective-therapy-ny.com/
Page(s) 34, 91

John Gerson, Ph.D., Katonah, New York
Relationship-repair.com License# 013534
Page(s) 94, 112

Olubukonla (Bukky) Kolawole, PsyD, Manhattan, New York
www.drbukkyk.com
Page(s) 132

Shari Siegel, MA, CFT, LMFT, Merrick, New York
www.interpersonalsolutions.org
Page(s) 158, 178

Rachel Moheban, LCSW, New York, New York
www.TheRelationshipSuite.com License# R053394-1
Page(s) 69

Suzanne Mallouk, M.D., Physician Surgeon, New York, New York
www.drsuzannemallouk.com
Page(s) 54, 104

Rachel A. Sussman, LCSW., New York, New York
www.rachelasussman.com License# 070997-1
Page(s) 123

Hillary Glick, Ph.D., Clinical Psychology, New York, New York
hillaryglickphd.com License# 011217-1
Page(s) 26, 198

Carole Gauthier, NYS Licensed Psychoanalyst, New York, New York
www.carole-gauthier.com email: cg@carole-gauthier.com
Page(s) 132

Laurel Steinberg, LMHC, Licensed Psychotherapist, New York, NY
www.LaurelSteinberg.com
Page(s) 24, 48, 108

David Behar, MA, LMFT, Pelham New York, New York
http://www.westchester-therapist.com/
Page(s) 20

Gary R. McClain, PhD, LMHC, New York, New York
www.JustGotDiagnosed.com License# 18-000355
Page(s) 192

Leide Porcu, PhD, LP, Psychotherapist, Anthropologist, New York
www.leideporcu.com License# 000210
Page(s) 121

Kaerensa Craft, LCSW, New York, New York
www.kcraft.info
Page(s) 79

Ruth Wyatt, LMSW, MA, New York, New York
Www.ruthwyatt.com License# NYS 057890-1
Page(s) 199

Lee Crespi, LCSW, New York, New York
www.LeeCrespiLCSW.com License# 020649
Page(s) 69

Ari E. Fox, LCSW, New York, New York
www.copewithschool.com License# NYS 076234-1
Page(s) 129

Michael DeMarco, PhD, LMFT, New York, New York
www.mytherapist.info License# 136
Page(s) 170

Amy Meyers, PhD, LCSW, New York, New York
http://www.psychotherapynyc-healing.com/
Page(s) 18, 186

Diana Kirschner, Ph.D., New York, New York
www.lovein90days.com
Page(s) 125

Cheryl Gerson, LCSW, BCD, New York, New York
www.cherylgerson.com
Page(s) 40, 108, 170

Louise Mastromarino, Certified Counselor, Staten Island, New York
www.distantholistic.com
Page(s) 12, 60, 172

Karen Schwarz, LMHC, CASAC, Syracuse, New York
Page(s) 47

Michelle L. Delevante, LCSW, West Babylon, New York
www.babyloncounseling.com
Page(s) 11

Kalila Borghini, LCSW, Yoruba Priest, New York
www.childofthestones.com License# 069524-R
Page(s) 187

Making Marriage a Success in North Carolina

Rudy Rodriguez, LCSW; ADHD Coach, Asheville, North Carolina
http://adhdcenterforsuccess.com/blog License# C000238
Page(s) 132

Deborah Klinger, M.A., LMFT, Chapel Hill, North Carolina
www.pizzadreams.com/dk License# 637
Page(s) 167

Annie Fongheiser, MA, MS, LCAS Charlotte, North Carolina
Page(s) 199

Rick Deitchman, Ph.D., Charlotte, North Carolina
www.charlottepsychotherapy.com License# 892
Page(s) 37

Katrina Kuzyszyn-Jones, Psy.D. Durham, North Carolina
www.lepageassociates.com License# NC 3728
Page(s) 77

Nicole Imbraguglio, Psy.D., Psychologist, Durham, North Carolina
www.lepageassociates.com
Page(s) 84

Tina Lepage, Psy.D., Psychologist, CEO/CFO, Durham, NC

www.lepageassociates.com License# NC 2865
Page(s) 66

Dr. Gary Chapman, Winston-Salem, North Carolina
fivelovelanguages.com
Page(s) 52

Making Marriage a Success in North Dakota

Renae M. Reinardy, Psy.D., LP, Fargo, North Dakota
www.lakesidecenter.org License# 434
Page(s) 135

Making Marriage a Success in Ohio

Lora Hanna, LISW, Columbus, Ohio
www.lorahanna.com License# I 0007749
Page(s) 128

Karen S. Waugh, Psychotherapist, LICDC, Columbus, Ohio
www.waughcounseling.com
Page(s) 197

Brock A. Bauer, LISW-S, Columbus, Ohio
www.bauercounseling.com License# I.0700102-supv
Page(s) 39, 53

Michelle Risser, LISW, Columbus, Ohio
www.michellerissercounseling.com License# I 0700128
Page(s) 58

Harry Warner, MA LPC, Columbus, Ohio
www.ahlcounseling.com/Harry License# c.0800151
Page(s) 197

Making Marriage a Success in Oklahoma

Leah Danley, LPC, Edmond, Oklahoma
danleycounseling.com License# 2982
Page(s) 92

Philip C. Hyde, Ph.D., Oklahoma City, Oklahoma
http://philipchydephd.com/
Page(s) 128, 141

Angie Ridings, MHR, M.Ed., LPC, LADC, Oklahoma City, Oklahoma
http://www.angelaridingscounseling.com/ LPC #4177 & LADC #736
Page(s) 53

Toppie Lincicome, Licensed Professional Counselor, Shawnee, OK
www.counselingoklahoma.com
Page(s) 120

Robyn Undieme, MA, LMFT, Tulsa, Oklahoma
License# 947
Page(s) 206

Making Marriage a Success in Oregon

Jesse Johnson, M.A., Portland, Oregon
www.vitalcollective.com
Page(s) 166

Leah Schoen, LPC Intern, Portland, Oregon
www.schoencounsel.com
Page(s) 32, 152

Mark Saindon, LMFT, Portland, Oregon
www.MarkSaindon.com License# T0376
Page(s) 98

Risa Hobson, MA, LPC, Portland, Oregon
www.wtlcounseling.com License# C2656
Page(s) 28, 204

Julie Nelligan, PhD, Licensed Psychologist, Portland, Oregon
www.julienelligan.com License# 1663
Page(s) 85

Guy D. Burstein, LCSW, Portland, Oregon
www.guyburstein.com License# 2931
Page(s) 24, 169

Making Marriage a Success in Pennsylvania

Dr. Cynthia Chestnut, Couple, Family & Sex Therapist, Bala Cynwyd
www.drcynthiachestnut.com
Page(s) 58, 176

Dr. Jeffrey Bernstein, Exton, Pennsylvania
www.drjeffonline.com
Page(s)

Mindy Jacobson-Levy, MCAT, ATR-BC, LPC, Jenkintown, PA
www.artb4words.com and www.thecenteraptt.com
Page(s) 165

Tonya Ladipo, LCSW, Philadelphia, Pennsylvania
www.TheLadipoGroup.com License# CW015409
Page(s) 99, 111

Colleen Quinn, PhD, Philadelphia, Pennsylvania
www.NorfordPsychology.com
Page(s) 195

Keren Sofer, Psy.D., Philadelphia, Pennsylvania
drkerensofer.com License# PS016818
Page(s) 165

Perri Shaw Borish, MSS, LCSW, BCD, Philadelphia, Pennsylvania
www.perrishawborish.com License# CW016052
Page(s) 8

Susan Rua, CAC, LPC, Pittsburgh, Pennsylvania
positive-pathways.net
Page(s) 169

Making Marriage a Success in Rhode Island

Kim Leandre, CAGS, LMHC, NCC, East Greenwich, Rhode Island
www.kimleandrecounseling.com License# RI-MHC00412
Page(s) 206

Jody Eyre, MS LMFT, North Kingstown, Rhode Island
www.mfcounseling.com License# RI MFT000126
Page(s) 65

Phillip Lowry, CAGS, LMHC, RYT, Providence, Rhode Island
www.philliplowry.com License# MHC 00137
Page(s) 122

Kate Siner Francis, Ph.D., LMHC, Providence, Rhode Island
www.lifefulfillmentformula.com License# RI# MHC00438
Page(s) 168

Scott Haltzman, MD., Woonsocket, Rhode Island
www.DrScott.com License# RI7592 & MA77864
Page(s) 183

Making Marriage a Success South Carolina

Marilyn Earle, MSN, APRN-BC, Bluffton, South Carolina
scminddeva.com
Page(s) 100, 193

Daniel Cowley, PsyD, Charleston, South Carolina
www.INGing.org License# 438
Page(s) 67, 159

Barbara Radin Fox, Licensed Clinical Social Worker, Charleston, SC
www.bodyandsoultherapy.com
Page(s) 179

Dr. Jennifer A. Bennice, Licensed Clinical Psychologist, Charleston
www.wecharleston.com
Page(s) 42, 85

Dianne Greyerbiehl, Ph.D., LPC, PCC, Greenville, South Carolina
www.lifecoachinginstitute.net License# 4805
Page(s) 39, 99

Jay White, LPC, Mount Pleasant, South Carolina
www.charlestontherapy.com License# 4619
Page(s) 75

Tracy Gillette, Ph.D., LPC, NCC, Warrenville, South Carolina
www.gillettepsychotherapy-retreats.com License# 5050
Page(s) 112

Making Marriage a Success in South Dakota

Shanna Moke, Certified Family Life Educator, Sioux Falls, SD
www.knappcounseling.com
Page(s) 166

Making Marriage a Success in Tennessee

Marcel Schwantes, Life Design Coach, Chattanooga, Tennessee
www.marcelcoaching.com
Page(s) 25, 63, 131, 167

Tabi R.Upton, MA, LPC, Chattanooga, Tennessee
www.tabiupton.com and www.chattanoogacounselor.com
Page(s) 32, 89

Tom Edwards, Licensed Clinical Social Worker, Germantown, TN
tomedwardslcsw.com License# 1042
Page(s) 160

TL Holt, MA, Knoxville, Tennessee
tlholt.com
Page(s) 80

Jane A. Barton, Ph.D., Licensed Psychologist, Knoxville, Tennessee
www.drjanebarton.com License# 2456
Page(s) 158

Rhonda Hidaji, Licensed Clinical Social Worker, Memphis, Tennessee
lifevibration.com
Page(s) 159

Demarcus C. Davis, LPC/MHSP, Memphis, Tennessee
www.couples-n-families.com License# 2127
Page(s) 111

Eric Cassius LPC, MHSP, CHt, Memphis, Tennessee
Cassiusandassociates.com
Page(s) 162

Marcus Ambrester, M.A., Nashville, Tennessee
www.marcusambrester.com and www.newvisionworkshop.com
Page(s) 89

Making Marriage a Success in Texas

Bob Brewster, LPC, Addison Dallas, Texas
www.brewstercounseling.com License# 19305
Page(s) 100

Nate Havlick, LCSW, Austin, Texas
www.AustinTherapist.com License# 29883
Page(s) 194

Elaine St. Marie, M.Ed., LPC, Austin, Texas
www.hiketointegrity.com License# 64391
Page(s) 8

Brittany Neece, LMFT-A, Austin, Texas
www.brittanyneece.com License# 201534
Page(s) 59, 85, 207

Chasee Chappell Hudgins, Psy.D., Austin, Texas
ChaseeHudgins.com License# TX #33978
Page(s) 178

Keri Cooper, LPC, Austin, Texas
www.coopercounselingpractice.com License# 17351
Page(s) 155

M. Dorsey Cartwright, LMFT, LPC, CCMHC, Austin, Texas
VoiceDialogueTrainings.com License# LMFT 4437, LPC 9934
Page(s) 183

Stacy Watkins, LPC, Austin, Texas
www.therapyinsession.net License# TX 62220
Page(s) 72

Betsy Fredrickson, LCSW, Austin, Texas
www.wheatfieldtherapy.com License# 36895
Page(s) 189

Ruth D. Timmons, LCSW, Austin, Texas
ruthtimmons.com License# 53791
Page(s) 157

Susanne Slay-Westbrook, LPC-S, LMFT-S, Austin, Texas
www.aworldofrespect.com License# LPC-S #1175 & LMFT-S #1013
Page(s) 43

Shannon Sprung, MA, LPC-Intern, Austin, Texas
www.shannonsprungcounseling.com
Page(s) 196

Mary B. Mattis, LCSW, Austin, Texas
http://www.marymattis.com License # 53118
Page(s) 17

Jaleh Donaldson

Ginna Beal, LCSW, Austin, Texas
www.ginnabeallcsw.com License# 32880
Page(s) 23, 138

Rev. Daniel Gowan, LCDC, LPC-S, Dallas, Texas
www.DanielGowan.com License# TX LPC-S 20319
Page(s) 6

Denise Humphrey, Ph.D., Clinical Psychology, Dallas, Texas
www.denisehumphrey.com License# 32345
Page(s) 16

Dr. Carol Doss, LPC, Fort Worth, Texas
www.family-counseling.org License# 08962
Page(s) 14

Kimberly Gist Miller, LMFT, Frisco, Texas
www.harmony-counseling.com License# LMFT 5212
Page(s) 135

Margaret Jordan, PhD, Houston, Texas
www.drmargaretjordan.com License# 31855
Page(s) 86

Rachel Eddins, M.Ed., LPC-S, CGP, Houston, Texas
http://www.eddinscounseling.com License# 19371
Page(s) 195

Matt Zamzow, Behavioral Specialist, Houston, Texas
www.apolloleadershipsolutions.com and www.eddinscounseling.com
Page(s) 152

Robinson Arteaga, MA, LPC, Houston, Texas
www.InnovationsCounseling.com License# 66207
Page(s) 19

Susan L. Pocasangre, MA, LPC, LSOTP, Houston, Texas
www.pocasangrescounseling.com License# 17855
Page(s) 24

Ken Waldman, Ph.D., Houston, Texas
counselinghouston.com License# Psychologist # 2-1460 TX
Page(s) 73

Jayne Raquepaw, PhD., Licensed Clinical Psychologist, Houston, TX
www.myhoustonpsychologist.com
Page(s) 64

Peter C. Cousins, Ph.D., ABPP, Houston, Texas
www.changebringshappiness.com License# 23052
Page(s) 124

Santhi Periasamy, Ph.D., Licensed Psychologist, Houston, Texas
www.drsanthi.com License# TX-33429
Page(s) 5

Madeleine G. Boskovitz, Ph.D., Licensed Psychologist, Houston, TX
www.mgboskovitz.com
Page(s) 183

Lind Butler, LPC, LMFT, Houston, Texas
www.lindbutler.com License # LPC 11187 & License# LMFT 2856
Page(s) 68, 200

Peggy Halyard, BBA, MA, LPC (License# 14706), Houston Texas
http://www.couples-help.com and http://www.imagorelationships.org
Page(s) 40, 90

Ella Hutchinson, MA, LPC, Houston, Texas
www.comfortchristiancounseling.com License# 63012
Page(s) 13

Jeff Hutchinson, CPSAS, Houston, Texas
www.caribouministries.com
Page(s) 98

Daisy S. Vergara, LPC, Round Rock, Texas
www.daisyvergara.com
Page(s) 28

Brent O'Bannon, LPC, Certified Life Coach, Sherman, Texas
www.brentobannon.com License# 13223
Page(s) 9, 180

April Lok, Ph.D., Licensed Psychologist, Southlake, Texas
Doc-Lok.com
Page(s) 64

Making Marriage a Success in Utah

Haylee Heyn, AMFT, Salt Lake City, Utah
wasatchfamilytherapy.com License# 7976237-3904
Page(s) 17, 59, 203

Jonathan Swinton, LMFT, Salt Lake City, Utah
www.swintoncounseling.com
Page(s) 71

Making Marriage a Success in Vermont

Michael DeMarco, PhD, LMFT, Bellows Falls, Vermont
www.mytherapist.info License# 0073062
Page(s) 170

Christine D Moriarty, CFP, MBA, Bristol Vermont
www.MoneyPeace.com
Page(s) 185

Genevieve Jacobs, M.A., Burlington, Vermont
http://wateranddreams.com License# 097 0000640
Page(s) 88

Israel Helfand MS, Ph.D., CST, LMFT, Cabot, Vermont
www.sexploration.org and www.marriagequest.com
Page(s) 33

Cathie Helfand, MS, Cabot, Vermont
www.sexploration.org and www.marriagequest.com
Page(s) 33

Making Marriage a Success in Virginia

Elizabeth Sloan, L.P.C., L.C.P.C., McLean, Virginia
www.CaringCouples.com
Page(s) 68

Samantha Madhosingh, Psy.D., McLean, Virginia
www.kidsfirstdoc.com License# 0810003364
Page(s) 125

Melissa Swartz, LGPC, Shepherdstown, West Virginia
www.melissaswartz.com
Page(s) 152, 191

Jaleh Donaldson

Making Marriage a Success in Washington

Melodie Anderson, MA, LMFT, Bellevue, Washington
www.MelodieAnderson.com License# ML24320
Page(s) 171

Jennifer Lehr, LMFT, Orcas Island, Washington
www.WeConcile.com License# MFC 41726
Page(s) 190

Sharon Sanborn, MA, LMHC, CHT, ATR-BC, Seattle, Washington
www.SeattleArtTherapy.com License# LH00009318
Page(s) 20

Kim Illig, Certified Intuitive Counselor, Snoqualmie, Washington
www.kimillig.com
Page(s) 18

Making Marriage a Success in Washington D.C.

Anita Gadhia-Smith, PsyD, Washington, D.C.
practicaltherapy.net License# 11151
Page(s) 41, 71

Leyla Mahbod Kenny, PhD, LICSW, Washington, D.C.
www.washingtondcpsychotherapy.com License# LC3000857
Page(s) 13, 40, 177

Keith A. Kaufman, Ph.D., Washington, D.C.
www.KeithKaufmanPhD.com License# PSY1000626
Page(s) 5

Deborah Hecker, Ph.D, Washington, D.C.
www.drdeborahhecker.com
Page(s) 158

Alison Howard, Psy.D., Washington, D.C.
www.AlisonHoward.com License# PSY1000439
Page(s) 45, 47, 122

Alisa Lewis, PhD, LICSW, Washington D.C.
www.alisamlewis.com License# LC303495
Page(s) 14,

Nicholas Kirsch, Ph.D., Washington, D.C.
Bethesdapsychotherapist.com License# 1000137
Page(s) 123

Jennifer Kogan, LICSW, Washington, D.C.
www.JenniferKogan.com License# LC 302938
Page(s) 75

Kara Veigas, MSW, LICSW, Washington, DC
www.karaveigas.com License# LC50078142
Page(s) 103, 154

Michael Giordano, MSW, LICSW, Washington, D.C.
www.WhatIHearYouSaying.com License# LC3000893
Page(s) 61

Ashley Seeger, LICSW, Washington, DC
www.DCCouplesCounseling.com License# LC303583
Page(s) 168

Olivia Mellan, MS, Therapist, Money Coach, Author, Washington, DC
Www.moneyharmony.com
Page(s) 202

Jaleh Donaldson

Making Marriage a Success in West Virginia

James Williams, LPC, Princeton, West Virginia
http://home.earthlink.net/~jameswilliams2/index.html License# 691
Page(s) 201

Making Marriage a Success in Wisconsin

Dr. Jill Zimmerman, LMFT, Hudson, Wisconsin
www.integracounselingservices.com License# LMFT 189-124
Page(s) 67, 148

Making Marriage a Success in Wyoming

Andrea Berry, MHR, ATR-BC, LPC, NCC, Laramie, Wyoming
www.wyomingarttherapy.com License# LPC 1049, NBCC 216654
Page(s) 87

About The Author

JALEH DONALDSON holds a Bachelor of Arts degree in Psychology, a Master of Science in Marriage and Family Counseling, a supervisory permit in early child development, and a writing certificate from the Institute of Children's Literature. Some of her previous writing credits include Style Magazine, Sacramento's Parent Magazine, Orange County Bride Magazine, Teacher Parent Magazine, Orlando Metro Woman, and Growing Up Chico Magazine. She also published a book called, "Life's Little How To Book." She had the wonderful opportunity to share her tips from her book by making appearances on television programs such as Fox40 News, Good Day Sacramento, Sacramento & Company and Livewire.

Jaleh has traveled around the world but has lived in California for most of her life. She currently works as a public school teacher and enjoys spending time with her husband and two young boys. For more information about Jaleh Donaldson or her work you can check out her website at jalehdonaldson.webs.com

CPSIA information can be obtained at www.ICGtesting.com
Printed in the USA
BVOW040301241011

274287BV00008B/2/P